The Happiness Project

The Happiness Project

Transforming the Three Poisons That Cause the Suffering We Inflict on Ourselves and Others

by Ron Leifer, M.D.

Snow Lion Publications
Ithaca, New York, USA

Snow Lion Publications
P.O. Box 6483
Ithaca, New York 14850 USA
607-273-8519

Printed in Canada on recycled paper.

ISBN 1-55939-079-4

Library of Congress Cataloging-in-Publication Data

Leifer, Ron, 1932-
The happiness project: transforming the three poisons that cause the suffering we inflict on ourselves and others / by Ron Leifer.
p. cm.
Includes bibliographical references.
ISBN 1-55939-079-4
1. Four Noble Truths. 2. Suffering—Religious aspects—Buddhism. 3. Religious life—Buddhism. I. Title.
BQ4240.L45 1997
294.3'422—dc21 97-11067
CIP

Table of Contents

This book is dedicated to the liberation
of human beings from the pain
we inflict on ourselves and others.

If we view the world's religions from the widest possible viewpoint, and examine their ultimate goal, we find that all of the major world religions, whether Christianity or Islam, Hinduism or Buddhism, are directed to the achievement of permanent human happiness.

H.H. The Fourteenth Dalai Lama

Only our searching for happiness prevents us from seeing it.

Ven. Gendun Rinpoche

If a way to the better there be,
It lies in taking a full look at the worst.

Thomas Hardy

Introduction

CHAPTER ONE

The Secrets of Happiness

> An essential feature of 'being in the world' is therefore the danger of forgetfulness or ignorance. This forgetfulness turns the revealing of the awakened mind into a secret....
>
> —Lodro Zangpo, *Vajradhatu Sun*

Everyone in the world wants to be happy. The desire for happiness is the universal wish of humankind. On this, everyone would agree. Yet everyone suffers and dies. The basic fact and the basic tragedy of life is that every human being longs for peace and happiness, yet everyone is haunted by the specter of suffering, unhappiness, and death.

This fact of life corresponds to the two basic motivations of life, which are the desire for happiness and the desire to avoid suffering and death. These are the standards by which we measure our days and our lives. The world is right with us if we are happy today and feel optimistic about the possibilities of future happiness. The world is bleak if we are unhappy today or have lost the hope of being happy tomorrow. We like, approve of, and defend that which we think will bring us happiness, and we dislike, condemn, and attack that which we think will bring us unhappiness, suffering, or death.

Although we all want lasting happiness, it is not easily found. Although we all fear suffering and death, they are not easily avoided. The secrets of happiness, therefore, are eagerly sought and highly treasured. Our search for knowledge is driven by the desire for happiness. We search for knowledge not out of some value-neutral curiosity, but because we believe it will help us to gain some control over our lives and thereby to find happiness. We are interested in scientific knowledge not primarily because it gives us a true picture of the universe, but because it gives us the practical means to fulfill our desires. If science gave us a true picture of the world but magic gave us the means to achieve happiness, people would believe in magic, not in science.

The Search for Happiness Through Religion

Historically, people have looked to religion for the secrets of happiness. There are many ways to view the search for happiness through religion. One way is to look at the two traditional religious paths: the exoteric and the esoteric. The exoteric path relies primarily upon a superior external agency—a god or a divine representative. People who rely upon God for happiness tend to believe that the secret is to please God by faithfully following divinely prescribed precepts. Intrinsic to this view is a principle of divine justice according to which God rewards the virtuous with happiness and punishes the sinner with suffering and death. This implies that the secret of happiness is virtue. As Mohandas Gandhi wrote, "The essence of religion is morality."[1]

The idea that virtue is a precondition of happiness is a basic teaching of every religion in the world, although each may define virtue differently. For one religion virtue may be the avoidance of killing. For another it may be death in courageous battle. In each case, the believer is following the ethical precepts of his or her religion. The relationship between virtue and happiness is not always obvious or conscious, however. It is partially hidden. Many otherwise religious people seem to be unaware of it, or minimize its importance, which may be why they are so often caught in acts of corruption and hypocrisy. The relationship between virtue and happiness has been largely forgotten or deeply repressed in modern society. Recently, however, the insight is being rediscovered and revived in seminaries and amongst religious fundamentalists.

While exoteric believers search for happiness through faith and virtuous obedience to religious laws, others search for the keys to happiness through esoteric knowledge. Every religion has an esoteric tradition. In the West, under the impact of science, technology, and secularism, the appeal of traditional exoteric religions has diminished and the esoteric has become glamorous and popular. Many Western Jews and Christians have become disillusioned, dissatisfied, or disinterested in the religion of their birth and instead look to esoteric traditions of the Orient for the secrets of happiness. Until very recently, these traditions have been inaccessible to Westerners. Today, many Eastern religions are available to Western seekers, particularly Buddhism. Many people read Buddhist literature, visit monasteries, and study with spiritual teachers, searching for the treasury of secrets to inner peace and bliss. If they are unfamiliar with Buddhism, it may seem mysterious and exotic, and this exoticism may easily be misinterpreted as esoteric.

There is an irony in this situation of which it is necessary to be aware, especially for the beginner. Many seekers of esoteric spiritual knowledge mistakenly believe that the source of this secret knowledge is outside themselves. They believe it is to be found in the words, books, and teachings which are possessed and closely guarded by an elite priesthood of knowing insiders. Or they regard it as a body of potent knowledge which is inaccessible or too difficult for ordinary mortals to understand. They tend, then, to worship the word, the texts, the teachers, and the images of God, looking to these for salvation, much as the exoteric believer does.

The irony is that, from the Buddhist point of view, esoteric, or secret, knowledge is not to be found in an outside power or agency. On the contrary. Buddha kept no secrets. He taught that "secrecy is the hallmark of false doctrine."[2] From the Buddhist point of view, esoteric wisdom means "self-secret." It consists of knowledge we hide from ourselves. No one is keeping secrets from us. Nor is esoteric wisdom too complex for us to understand. Esoteric wisdom consists of truths about ourselves and the nature of reality that we hide from ourselves. We also hide the fact that we hide them from ourselves, thus converting them into "secrets."

The core of the esoteric knowledge we seek consists of secrets we hide from ourselves. We hide from them because they are not what we want them to be. The world is not what we want it to be. Life is not what we want it to be. Others are not what we want them to be. We are not what we want ourselves to be. We hide from these truths because they mystify and terrify us. The terror of reality is expressed in the Old Testament story of God refusing to show his face to Moses because it would drive him mad.[3] This story is a metaphor for the fact that, actually, it is reality that drives us mad. We cannot face it and so we struggle to put it out of mind, to repress and forget it. But reality is more powerful than we are. It bursts and leaks through our defenses and returns to haunt us in our nightmares, our neuroses, and our everyday worries.

After the Fall, Adam and Eve became ashamed of their nakedness and covered their genitals with fig leaves. This is a metaphor for one way that we hide from ourselves. We cover our bodies so we will not see that we are mortal animals. We hide ourselves from ourselves because we do not want to see our flaws, faults, weaknesses, and excesses. It would make us feel vulnerable and anxious. We will not confess our lies. We are ashamed to admit to ourselves that some of the things we want are forbidden, illegal, unethical, or fattening. We are taught to be considerate of others and so we are ashamed of and hide our selfishness. We do not want to admit to ourselves our unrelenting, selfish demandingness. At various times, we want more food, more sex, more pleasure of all kinds, more money, more equipment, more security, more power. We all want things to be as we want them to be—forever.

We are equally afraid to face our fears. We may appear to others to be self-confident, but nevertheless, we are all vulnerable to, and afraid of, failure, defeat, humiliation, loss, pain, and death. It is often difficult for us to clearly see our fear of death, and, therefore, our fears of life. We do not want to appear weak or neurotic. We do not want to admit our vulnerability or our confusion.

From the Buddhist point of view, the unwillingness or failure to see the facts of life as they are, to see ourselves as we are, and to conduct ourselves in harmony with these realities, is the chief cause of our self-inflicted suffering and, therefore, the chief obstacle to our happiness. This state of denial, or lack of realization of the facts of existence, is called *avidya* in Sanskrit—literally, "the failure to see, or know"—translated as "ignorance." One of the great contributions of Gautama Buddha was the realization that ignorance is the primary cause of the sufferings we impose on ourselves and others.

If ignorance is the underlying cause of our self-inflicted suffering, then it follows that knowledge, or wisdom, is the remedy. The keys to the kingdom of happiness lie in wisdom. On this, most reasonable people would agree. The same insight can be phrased the other way around: What makes wisdom wise is that it helps us to find a greater degree of happiness and to reduce the load of sufferings we impose on ourselves and others.

Wisdom does not mean mere intellectual understanding, however. Intellectual understanding alone is not sufficient to enlighten the darkness of avidya. A mere intellectual understanding of the facts of existence will not change our habitual negative patterns of thought, speech, and action. The reason for this is that the intellect serves the ego, and the ego is a trickster who is continually the victim of its own trickery.

Ego literally means "I." Ego refers to "I," "me," "myself." Psychoanalysts, who first used the word to refer to self, typically defined ego as the psychological executive. The executive function of the ego is to mediate and moderate between the *id*'s desires for pleasure and urges towards aggression and the super-ego's inhibitions and prohibitions. Thus, the ego is the product of, and would-be conciliator of, a split in the inner being of the human organism. This split is created by complex factors intrinsic to human nature, particularly the development of moral consciousness, the function of which is to differentiate good desires and fears from those that cause pain and suffering, and to promote choosing the good over the evil. The ego presides over this inner conflict as the mediator between our forbidden—illegal, immoral, or selfish—desires, and the prohibitions, inhibitions, and aversions to pursuing and satisfying them.

In such a dilemma, it is a difficult task to gracefully balance these competing psychic forces. Most of us cannot do it well. It requires a degree of maturity that most of us cannot achieve. Most people tend to be out of balance in one direction or the other: towards grasping for happiness through the desperate, compulsive, instant satisfaction of our desires, or towards rejecting, denying, and repressing desire and pleasure as if they are the doings of the devil.

The ego is a trickster in the sense that, as the discursive thinker and speaker in the name of the person, it is also the locus of the lies we tell ourselves. Ego can rationalize and justify both selfish desires and self-denial. We are all clever enough to be selfish and deny it, or hide it, or disguise it as love or generosity. We can repress and isolate our feelings of fear while justifying the accompanying inhibitions as prudence or caution. People often say that "life is tricky." True, but not because life is trying to trick us. No one, or nothing, is trying to trick us. We trick ourselves. In the words of Chogyam Trungpa Rinpoche, "Things are very tricky. They are very tricky, and they play tricks on you spontaneously. There's nobody who is the game-maker, who conceives of the game. Nobody's playing tricks on you. But things as they are are full of trickery."[4]

We cannot achieve wisdom without seeing through the trickery of the ego which denies truths it does not wish to see. This requires changing our habitual patterns of thought and action. These habitual patterns, which have been developed unconsciously, out of the ignorance of pure selfishness, so to speak, create the rebounding karmic ripples which cause our sufferings. To be truly wise, our understanding of the facts of existence must penetrate to the "heart which fully realizes."

This means that in order to *realize*—as opposed to merely understanding—the truths about ourselves and the facts of existence, we must undergo a personal transformation. The time it takes for any particular person to do this varies widely. Some people are transformed by one radical experience. For others, the process may take a lifetime or, as some Buddhists like to say, *lifetimes*.

The price of avidya, or ignorance, is high. The price is pain and suffering, depending upon the degree of ignorance. The habitual denial and repression of the facts of existence results in the suffering of negative emotions such as anxiety, stress, anger, depression, guilt, shame, and so on. These negative emotions, in turn, motivate negative actions, which create negative situations, which stimulate more negative thoughts and emotions. Denial creates these negativities because it requires us to struggle futilely to evade realities we cannot escape. Inevitably and continuously, the facts break through our defenses and force their reality upon us.

Thus, realizing the "secret" truths that yield the harvest of inner peace and equanimity requires a journey within. This means a journey into our own minds in order to understand and transform our negative thinking, negative emotions, and negative actions. This, in turn, requires an inquiry into the nature of mind and of phenomena. This inner quest is the essence of the spiritual journey. I once asked Khenpo Karthar Rinpoche, abbot of Karma Triyana Dharmachakra Monastery in Woodstock, New York, to define "spiritual." His answer was, "Anything having to do with mind."

Like every mission into the unknown, the spiritual journey requires courage. We must be brave enough to look at what we do not want to see. We must have the courage to admit what we want and what we fear. The spiritual journey requires honesty, an honesty that can detach enough from desire and fear to acknowledge observable facts and reasonable analysis. It also requires taking responsibility for our thoughts, feelings, and, especially, our actions. Responsibility is "response-ability"—the ability to respond appropriately to what we see and experience. Our responses to our perceptions of the world—our "response-ability"—thus shapes the conditions of our own suffering and happiness.

From an overarching perspective, the spiritual journey involves the transformation of our ordinary state of denial, repression, defensiveness, armoring, self-constriction, tension, anxiety, and negativity into a state of courageous openness, honest awareness, guileless spontaneity, trusting vulnerability, and joyous equanimity. It requires accepting and relaxing into existence as it is, rather than anxiously rejecting and fighting it because it is not what we want it to be. Easy to say, difficult to do.

Many people are unwilling to make progress on the spiritual journey because they do not want to face their desires or their fears. This is understandable. Nevertheless, if we could see how our demanding desires and blind fears, especially our fears of fear, are often the source of our sufferings, might we not take pause and reflect? This is the ironic nature of spiritual realization. As we progress spiritually, we begin to see how we, ourselves, are the primary and ultimate cause of our own sorrows. Paradoxically, this is good news! It means that we can also be the cause of our relief, our release, and our happiness.

Our denial of the facts of existence creates the esoteric knowledge we so eagerly seek. In our ignorance, we think that something has been hidden from us. So we search for it outside of ourselves. In reality, however, what is "hidden" is what we do not want to see and, therefore, have hidden from ourselves. Ironically, our spiritual search is impeded by our own fearful reluctance to accept what is plain to see but we hide from ourselves.

We are like the religious seeker who all his life has been looking for God. One day, a holy man gives him God's address. He walks up to God's door with his fist raised ready to knock, eager to experience the fulfillment of his life goals, when suddenly the thought occurs, "All my life I have been a seeker of God. After I find Him, what will I do?" He feels the panic of this prospective meaninglessness, and so he turns and walks away from the House of God, muttering to himself over and over again, "I will continue to seek God, only now I know where not to look."

We seekers of esoteric truth are often like this man. We seek the truth, but are afraid of it, and so we know where not to look. Instead of looking within ourselves, we look to exotic religions, apocalyptic cults, ancient sorcery, witchcraft, fortune telling, astrologers, and phony gurus of all sorts who claim to have access to special, hidden wisdom. In my work as a therapist, I have been surprised to see how truth is the first thing people ask for, and the last thing they want to hear.

If esoteric knowledge consists of secrets we keep from ourselves, then access to the esoteric depends upon our own effort to inquire into ourselves, openly and without defensiveness. We can realize the so-called esoteric truths which lead to inner peace only by helping ourselves to see for ourselves. Buddha encouraged this kind of self-reliance. "You are your own refuge," he said, "who else could refuge be?"[5]

From this point of view, this is an esoteric self-help book. Its purpose is to face squarely what we are hiding from ourselves. This is a delicate undertaking for both the writer and the reader. The attempt to reveal or interpret what is hidden, no matter how well motivated, will make people angry. We all tend to become defensive and aggressive when we are told something we don't want to hear. This is why therapists must be careful with their interpretations. A "wild" or premature interpretation may frighten and anger a patient who is not ready to accept it into fleeing therapy. At the other extreme, one can politely avoid the unspeakable and rely instead on palatable platitudes and cliches, thus creating and perpetuating illusions, rationalizations and diversions. We shall attempt to find the middle ground, probing and exploring with a slow and light touch. The process of diligently and honestly probing oneself is a worthy undertaking. For the revelation of something hidden has the potential to radically change our view of ourselves, and therefore, the potential to change our lives.

The Search for Happiness Through Psychotherapy

With the decline of religion and the rise of science, jurisdiction over the problems of happiness and suffering were transferred from the former to the latter. Scientific medicine took responsibility for the sufferings of the body and scientific psychology and psychiatry—and their common issue, psychotherapy—assumed authority over problems of the mind, emotions, and behavior.

There is an intriguing symmetry (not an identity) between the twenty-five hundred year old search for happiness through Buddhism and the hundred year old search for happiness through psychotherapy. Having practiced psychotherapy for thirty-five years and Buddhism for fifteen years, I have noticed striking similarities as well as differences between the two. Others have also noticed the resemblance. Alan Watts observed that Oriental religions, particularly Buddhism, are more similar to psychotherapy than to Western religions. At the same time, he noted, Western psychotherapy resembles religion with its own charismatic leaders, dogma, and rituals.

> If we look deeply into such ways of life as Buddhism and Taoism, Vedanta and Yoga, we do not find either philosophy or religion as these are understood in the West. We find something more nearly resembling psychotherapy....The main resemblance between these Eastern ways of life and Western psychotherapy is in the concern of both with bringing about changes of consciousness, changes in our ways of feeling our own existence and our relation to human society and the natural world. The psychotherapist has, for the most part, been interested in changing the consciousness of peculiarly disturbed individuals. The disciplines of Buddhism and Taoism are, however, concerned with changing the consciousness of normal, socially adjusted people. But it is increasingly apparent to psychotherapists that the normal state of consciousness in our culture is both the context and the breeding ground of mental disease.[6]

Buddhism and psychotherapy share significant common ground.[7] Comparing them will help illuminate hidden features of each. By comparing the two, however, I do not mean to equate them. Buddhism is a twenty-five hundred year old exquisitely developed tradition with a core of profound truth. By comparison, psychotherapy is immature, fragmented, and superficial. Nevertheless, Western psychotherapy may contribute something to our understanding of ourselves and the truths we hide from ourselves, even if it may only be to rediscover and confirm traditional Buddhist insights.

Buddhism and psychotherapy share a common ground of concern with suffering and the means of relief and release from suffering. This is the foundation and *raison d'etre* of both. That they share this common ground is neither a coincidence, nor a minor consideration. It has profound implications. The experience of suffering is the foundation of Buddhism and, arguably, of all religions. Gautama Buddha began his spiritual quest when he became aware of suffering and dedicated his life to finding the cause and cure for it. From the Buddhist point of view, the spiritual journey begins with awareness of suffering and it is fueled and motivated by the desire to escape suffering and find happiness.

The problem of suffering is also the central concern of psychotherapy. Indeed, it is the common boundary of psychotherapy, medicine, and religion.[8] Each of them deals with a different form of suffering. Medicine deals with the sufferings of the body, psychotherapy deals with the sufferings of the mind, and religion deals with the sufferings of the soul. Because of this common ground, some people think of psychotherapy as a medical technique while others, with equally good justification, think of it as a form of spiritual healing.

People seek psychotherapists because they are suffering—from painful emotions, painful thoughts, painful relationships, painful experiences. The negative emotions—anxiety, stress, depression, anger, guilt, shame, frustration, boredom, and so forth, are all forms of suffering. What psychiatric patients want from their therapists is not a technical treatment or cure for illness, but, like Buddhists, they want relief and release from their suffering, and a chance for some peace and happiness in life.

Buddhism and psychotherapy also share a second significant common ground of an abiding interest in mind. From the Buddhist point of view, suffering is not caused by external, traumatic events, but by qualities of mind which shape our perceptions and responses to events. Accordingly, happiness is not to be found in the outer, social world, but in a transformation of mind which generates wisdom, tranquility, and compassion.

Many psychotherapists hold similar views. Many therapists believe, as Buddhists do, that suffering is caused not so much by external traumas *per se*, but by our responses to these traumas. These responses are conditioned by mental factors such as desires and fears which may be denied and repressed. This is one of the basic tenets of Freudian psychoanalysis. Psychoanalysis is based on the axiom that neurotic suffering is caused by an individual's active response to life, rather than passively and mechanically by the life events themselves. If neurotic suffering is caused by an individual's *reactions* to life events rather than by the events themselves, then that suffering potentially can be relieved through a personal transformation in which life events are experienced from a different frame of reference.

Given the significant common ground of Buddhism and psychotherapy, it is not surprising that a stream of thought has developed in psychotherapy similar to the Buddhist view on esoteric self-secrets. This stream of thought shares with Buddhism the notion that we suffer from ignorance, from secrets we keep from ourselves. Two of the fundamental, classical concepts of psychotherapy are repression and the unconscious. The concept of repression is similar to, although more narrow and more shallow than, the Buddhist concept of ignorance. Like avidya, repression is the failure or unwillingness to see important facts or aspects of experience. As Norman O. Brown observed, "the essence of repression lies in the refusal of the human being to recognize the realities of his human nature."[9] The difference between avidya and repression is that the former is the failure to face basic facts about *the nature of self and phenomena,* while the latter is the more narrow failure to face certain *facts about one's self,* particularly one's responsibility for one's responses to the painful experiences of life.

The generally accepted view of repression is that it is a defense against anxiety. Anxiety, especially high anxiety, is one of the most common and intense forms of suffering. People will do almost anything to relieve their anxiety, especially to palliate it with alcohol and drugs. The anti-anxiety drug business, both legal and illegal, is a multi-billion dollar industry. We are afraid of our anxieties and we react to the memory or prospect of anxious experiences by repressing them. Repression, like avidya, is only partially successful, however. The repressed returns to haunt us. Neurotic symptoms are painful because they are manifestations of the suffering which has been repressed—the so called "return of the repressed." In the psychoanalytic view, the mental and emotional content of painful experiences are repressed, modified, attenuated, and re-experienced as the neurosis.

The psychotherapy of mental and emotional suffering is similar in many vital ways to the Buddhist approach. Both involve developing a relationship with a teacher or guide, sometimes called a guru or a psychotherapist. The function of the guru/psychotherapist is to guide the sufferer on a journey of self-discovery and self-transformation which, in Buddhism, is at the same time, a discovery of the facts of existence. The teacher helps the patient—the sufferer—to develop increased awareness, acceptance, and realization ("emotional working through") of painful emotions and the facts of life. In both Buddhism and psychotherapy, the individual's growing awareness of the origins and dynamics of his or her neurotic suffering is facilitated by the guru's *teachings* and the therapist's *interpretations.* Both potentially convey *insights.* The realization and integration of these insights leads to relief from the painful symptoms of denial and repression. This involves a courageous willingness to examine one's self honestly, to face and take responsibility for one's desires and fears.

The truth about ourselves and our lives that we do not wish to see, which is the inverse of our neurotic symptoms and our character defenses, forms part of the content of the unconscious. The unconscious contains our denials and repressions—the lies we tell ourselves. Our neurotic symptoms and character defenses are products of the lies we tell ourselves. In this sense, the unconscious can be construed as containing the esoteric psychological knowledge we seek. Carl Jung was the first to make this connection when he discovered the correspondences between dreams and myths. Dreams reveal the personal unconscious and myths reveal the "collective unconscious." He called this sphere of denial and repression "the shadow." Jungian therapy consists in large part of confronting the shadow, facing what one has rejected about one's self and the fundamental qualities of experience, which he called "archetypes."[10]

Freud, too, explicitly described the aim of psychoanalysis as making the unconscious conscious. In the psychoanalytic view, neurotic sufferings are caused by the denial and repression of painful experiences. Relief from suffering comes from bringing the repressed experiences into awareness and working through the painful emotions. Thus, in both Freudian and Jungian therapy as well as in Buddhist practice, the expansion of consciousness requires an inner transformation—a realignment of character with the facts of life which leads to a corresponding softening of neurotic tendencies.

In the Buddhist view, avidya is not only the denial of facts about oneself and the world, it is also a projection onto the world of something not originally there. This state of ignorance is also called "illusion" or "delusion." From the Buddhist point of view, illusion consists of the projection of permanence and/or substantial existence onto phenomena. We can see that rainbows and clouds are ethereal, but we project the quality of enduring permanence and substantiality onto solid objects and onto ourselves. The highest wisdom in Buddhism, the wisdom which realizes emptiness, sees through these projections and understands that all phenomena, including self, are impermanent and insubstantial.

Ernest Becker (1925-1974), my dear old friend and colleague who won the Pulitzer Prize in non-fiction in 1974 (two months after he died) for *The Denial of Death,* reinterpreted some of Freud's central ideas in a way that brings them into harmony with Buddhist views on ignorance and emptiness. Becker proposed that both character and neurosis are shaped by ignorance, specifically, the denial of death.[11]

In his early work, Becker reinterpreted the Oedipus Complex as a stage of psychological development rather than as a neurotic complex. The classical psychoanalytic myth of the Oedipus Complex is a caricature of lust and aggression in the form of a boy-child who loves and wants to have sex with his mother and who hates and wants to kill his father. Becker reinterpreted this caricature as a period of transition, the Oedipal Transition, which represents a crucial period of development of the human personality.[12] In this transitional stage, the child's attachment to the mother and fear of the father represent the resistance to growing up—the resistance to losing the narcissistic, self indulgent, paradise of childhood. During the Oedipal Transition sexual and aggressive drives are controlled and repressed. The child grows beyond a physical dependence on and attachment to the mother into a relatively independent adult who relates to his or her parents and others through a more mature, distanced, social relationship mediated by language and symbols.

The Oedipal Transition, which is the process of human socialization, signifies the evolution of the human individual beyond the purely animal. This process involves a denial of the body as the ground of self and its replacement by the social self. Since the body dies, the denial of the body implies a denial of death. During the Oedipal Transition, primitive, animal, and childish desires are repressed and sublimated. Many desires which demand instant gratification are denied, delayed, and projected into the future through the creation of an "Oedipal Project." The Oedipal Project is a project for the creation of self in a world of social time and meanings. It involves not only the development of the capacity to think and act in a world of conventional symbols, but also the contrivance of a system of desires, goals, and ambitions which embody the hope for future happiness. In this project of self-creation, the child's present-centered search for pleasure is transformed into a search for future happiness—the Happiness Project.

The pursuit of happiness, thus, is a universal means for the construction and maintenance of self. Self is constructed through the denial of the body and the development of a social self-consciousness predicated on language. This state of mind, which Buddhists call "dualistic mind," conceives of itself as a social-historical entity whose existence and well being are dependent upon the achievement of future happiness. When the happiness project fails, the individual experiences a negation of self which often leads to frustration, aggression, depression, and even to suicide—the murder of the negated self. The title of this book, "The Happiness Project," reflects the fact that the pursuit of happiness is, at the same time, the project for the construction and maintenance of self. Tragically, it is also the major source of the unhappiness and suffering we inflict on ourselves and others.

In the Buddhist view, the primary cause of suffering is attachment to self, an inborn state of ignorance which develops into ego. However, fully developed ignorance, as we have already indicated, is not merely the infantile lack of awareness of the nature of self and phenomena. It is also the projection on to existence of something which is not there. Ignorance is ego mistaking itself as real by falsely attributing substantial existence to itself. The capacity for this attribution is dependent upon language and develops during the Oedipal Transition. Language makes possible the creation of the illusion of an inner soul or a person which is then projected on to others and on to existence.

This does not mean that self does not exist. From the Middle Way Buddhist view, called Madhyamika, it is false to say either that self exists or that it does not exist. Self exists but only as a self-created fiction, a self deception. It is, indeed, a necessary deception. Becker called it a "vital lie." It is vital because interpersonal relationships and social life depend upon it. We need an ego to relate to each other, to make a living and pay our bills. It is a lie because it denies the facts of existence and attributes false substantiality to itself. This clinging to the illusion of self is, in the Buddhist view, the source of suffering we cause ourselves and others.

In a Buddhist practice known as "analytic meditation," self is unmasked to itself. The guru asks the practitioner to look within for this self. Where is it? In the body? In the head or the heart? In the mind? What part of the mind? What color is self? The reader can try this exercise. No self can be found. This self which cannot find itself anxiously fears its insubstantiality and the loss of itself to itself. Through the psychological mechanism of reaction formation, self denies its insubstantiality by asserting itself, by striving, through its various Happiness Projects, to protect, preserve, and expand itself—here and now on earth and forever after in heaven, or through serial reincarnations.

This self-created, self-deluded, self-asserting self mistakenly believes that happiness is to be found by pursuing its desires and avoiding its aversions. Buddhists know these three factors, ignorance (the creation of a substantial self), desire, and aversion, as "The Three Poisons." Taken together, they are regarded as the complex of causes of the suffering we humans inflict on ourselves and others. Desire and aversion are also known as passion and aggression, attachment and anger, and other synonymous antithetical pairs. For simplicity's sake, we shall use desire and aversion as the most general representation of these dichotomous pairs. It is important to recognize, however, that not all desires and aversions are evil. Those that cause suffering to oneself or others are regarded as vices, while those that cause happiness to oneself and others are regarded as virtues.

This should not be unfamiliar to Westerners. The antithetical pair of desire and aversion are the twin foundations of modern behavioral psychology. The basic principle of behavioral psychology is that organisms are polarized around pain and pleasure. The desire for pleasure and the aversion to pain are regarded as the basic bipolarity of mind and the basic motivations of behavior. In this respect, behavioral psychology echoes Buddhism. Add self, or ego, to the pair and one has the nexus of our negativities.

In the Buddhist view, the basic secret of happiness that we hide from ourselves is that the three poisons are the root causes of the pain and suffering we cause ourselves and each other. The three poisons are the basis of our neurosis, our negative emotions, and our unhappiness. The shocking central insight that Buddhism gives us, therefore, the secret of happiness we hide from ourselves, is that our selfish strivings for happiness are, paradoxically, the greatest cause of the suffering and pain we inflict on ourselves and others. From this point of view, the secrets of genuine happiness involve a self-transformation, including a reconfiguration of our idea of happiness itself, based on a deeper awareness of the nature of reality and a sense of values derived from this realization.

A Westerner's Meditation on the Three Poisons

This book is a meditation on the three poisons. It is an inquiry into how they generate and also obstruct our Happiness Projects. Our hope is to increase the general awareness of the principle that, in order to understand and resolve our personal and collective problems, we must understand ourselves. This means being willing to examine our desires and our fears, our hopes and our expectations, our aversions and hatreds, and our profound and stubborn selfishness.

The book is divided into four parts. Part one presents my formulation of the Buddhist paradigm of suffering and the causes of suffering. Part two examines the theme of suffering as it is woven through Western science, religion, psychology, and politics. Part three analyzes the role of desire (and aversion) in Western religion, ethics, law, and psychology, including the development of the Happiness Project. Part four offers a view of ignorance, or ego, from the perspective of evolutionary biology. To the degree that they accurately convey the wisdom of the Dharma, these reflections, hopefully, may add a dimension of self-knowledge and compassion for ourselves. This, in turn, may give us some desperately needed insights into some of our most vexing personal, social, and political problems.

Over the past twenty years or so, Westerners have become increasingly interested in Buddhism. This is especially true of Western psychotherapists and their patients, many of whom attend Buddhist teachings and even take the vows of refuge.[13] I have heard Tibetan lamas speculate that Buddhism may come to America through psychotherapy. If Buddhism is to succeed in the West, it must be compatible with Western science. The reader should be cautioned, therefore, that the interpretation of the Buddhist paradigm presented here is designed to convey the orthodox Buddhist view in a form which is acceptable to scientifically minded Westerners.

One of the problems educated Westerners have with the "wisdom traditions" is that many of us believe and trust in science for our valid knowledge about the world and the technology for manipulating it. We mistrust religion out of which the wisdom traditions have descended. It is necessary, therefore, first to attempt some reconciliation of this breach between religion and science so we can more freely and intelligently use the best of both to help us to see the truths we hide from ourselves.

CHAPTER TWO

The Reconciliation of Science and Religion

> In the last analysis, it is the ultimate picture which an age forms of the nature of its world that is its most fundamental possession.
>
> —E.A. Burtt, *The Metaphysical Foundations of Physical Science*

> Science without religion is lame.
> Religion without science is blind.
>
> —Albert Einstein, *Out of My Later Years*

If the business of life is the pursuit of happiness and the escape from suffering and death, and if the main obstacle to happiness is that we get in our own way by hiding from ourselves and from the nature of reality, then the question naturally follows: How can we induce ourselves to open our eyes? How can we help ourselves to see clearly that which we prefer to see "as through a glass darkly?"

Our dilemma is complicated by the fact that the two great historical traditions on which we have relied for answers to these questions are each both powerful and deeply flawed, and each is suspicious of the authority and validity of the other. Traditionally, religion has had jurisdiction over the problems of suffering and happiness. Until very recently in human history, religion has had the exclusive authority for explaining suffering and death and prescribing the means to avoid and evade them.

All the religions of the world explain suffering in the same basic way and prescribe the same basic means for relief. The traditional religious view of human suffering and happiness is that they are *moral problems*. And the traditional religious means for achieving happiness is to live a moral life. This view is expressed in such phrases as, "human suffering and unhappiness are subject to the will of God," i.e., must conform to the moral law. This means that we humans are granted by God some responsibility and, therefore, some influence over our fate through our thoughts, intentions, and actions. The righteous, who obey the divine will as it is expressed in nature or in scripture, can expect to be rewarded with happiness and eternal life. By the same principle of cosmic justice, the sinner, who defies the sacred law, is doomed to suffer and die.

From the traditional religious point of view, the sufferer bears some responsibility for his or her pain and unhappiness, if not by causing it then by the manner of experiencing, enduring, and relieving it. From our limited human perspective, the particular reason for our sufferings may not be apparent. Theists say that God's motives are inscrutable. It sometimes seems that good people suffer and bad people prosper. Buddhists say that the workings of the laws of karma are inscrutable. In the long run and in the big picture, the traditional religious view is that happiness and suffering are moral states which are experienced according to the formula taught by the Old Testament prophet Isaiah:

> Say ye of the righteous, that it shall be well with him;
> for they shall eat the fruit of their doings.
> Woe unto the wicked! It shall be ill with him;
> for the reward of his hands shall be given him.[1]

Over the past four centuries of Western history, the power and influence of religion has declined and been replaced by science. The scientific revolution, of which we are all the beneficiaries, and the much lamented decline of religion are reciprocally related events. The new scientific world-view of the European Enlightenment undermined the traditional Catholic cosmology, and the technological changes brought by science have undermined the power and influence of religious authority and order. Modern people now rely on science for the knowledge to pave the way towards happiness and to avoid and evade suffering and death.

The Power and Limitations of Science

The momentous historical transformation stimulated by the rise of science has bequeathed to the modern mind a legacy of profound conflict. We have come to think of science and religion as incompatible, but we need them both. On the one hand, we respect, even worship science as the valid source of knowledge because science has tangibly improved the quality of our lives. On the other hand, we long for lost religious meanings and guidance.

Auguste Comte (1798-1857), a French philosopher of the Enlightenment, expressed a view of the relationship between science and religion which is widely held today by many educated people. He viewed religion as the oldest and lowest form of human thought because it is riddled with superstition and false belief. He regarded science as the culmination of mature human thought. Comte believed that human consciousness evolved through three stages: from religion to philosophy to science.[2] In Comte's view, primitive humans perceived the world in the animated myths, metaphors, and superstitions of religion. Classical peoples perceived the world philosophically, in abstract concepts such as substance and essence, truth and justice. We modern people, by contrast, in what we think is the most advanced wisdom, perceive the world as a collection of positive scientific facts and laws.

Today, science is generally accepted as the highest authority on knowledge about ourselves and our world. Indeed, the belief that all genuine knowledge is based on scientific fact is a hallmark of the modern world. Any claim to knowledge which has not been authenticated by science is viewed with skepticism or rejected. Such a radical-empirical manifesto on the "epistemological correctness" of science was articulated succinctly by Bertrand Russell in the early years of this century: "Whatever knowledge is attainable, must be attained by scientific methods; and what science cannot discover, mankind cannot know."[3]

As the influence of religion has declined, science has assumed jurisdiction over the knowledge and means to achieve happiness and avoid suffering and death. As we have noted, medical science has inherited from religion authority over physical suffering and health. Psychiatry and psychology have assumed responsibility for mental and emotional suffering and personal happiness. To religion has been left the quest for immortality.

The world has benefitted enormously from the fruits of science and technology. But we pay a high price for granting to science the exclusive franchise on knowledge about ourselves and assigning to science the exclusive responsibility for the search for happiness. The problem is that while science is reliable and powerful, it is also limited. Indeed, the power of science is also its vital flaw. The power of science and the basis of its demarcation from other modes of thought is that it limits itself to facts and the mathematical relationship between facts. Statements which are not, at least in principle, falsifiable through empirical observation and measurement are meaningless from the point of view of science.[4] This restriction is not a fatal flaw, but a vital boundary, a strategic self-denial. Science thrives on this snobbish principle of exclusion, and humanity has benefitted enormously from its technological fruits. But as a result of this self-imposed limitation, which is the essence of its power, science cannot address the subjective, moral questions about the meaning, value, and purpose of human existence. Nor can it prescribe the path to happiness. Science is prevented by its own methods from giving us the wisdom to distinguish between good and evil.

Science can help us to predict and control the material world. It can provide us with a factual understanding of human beings as sociobiological machines. It can even give us information and techniques that may help control people and maintain an orderly society. But science cannot give us the full view of life required to avoid suffering and achieve inner peace. Science cannot formulate the goals, ideals, and values by which to live. As a result, science cannot guide us through life. It cannot help us to understand or control the interior dimensions of our minds—our contradictory desires for freedom and security, for purpose and inner peace, for power and happiness. Science cannot explain the mystery of life, nor can it save us from the bewilderment and confusion of our personal existence.

By the self-imposed limitations of its own method, science must strive for moral neutrality. It must avoid moral evaluations and partisanship in the study of the human being. As a result, science cannot view personal suffering as a moral problem. It must view suffering as the effect of non-moral causes. Modern, medical psychiatry has come to view specific forms of personal suffering and unhappiness, such as anxiety, depression, anger, and addictions as the result of non-moral causes such as genetic defects, biochemical imbalances, childhood traumas, or pathological social conditions. Cognitive neuroscience, which is the most advanced scientific study of mind and brain, by its own admission can only formulate theories at the "sub-personal level," not about the whole person as a moral agent.[5] By thus ignoring and negating the moral dimensions of suffering and happiness, science has unintentionally and unwittingly contributed to the increasing failure of individuals to take responsibility for their experience and conduct of life.[6]

The rise of science has thus, ironically, contributed to the confusion and suffering of the thinking, feeling subject. Sophisticated scientists, like Albert Einstein, understood this. Einstein realized that without the thinking subject—what Einstein called "the free creations of the human mind"—scientific facts would be incomprehensible, incommunicable, and useless. The paradox of science is that to be objective, scientific facts must exclude subjective thought, but by themselves they are dead. Without the human interpretive imagination, scientific facts are, in the words of William Barrett, "utterly disconnected, and lie external to each other in a logical space [with] no internal, necessary, or organic bond between them."[7]

Einstein's scientific genius was the fruit of his creative imagination: he solved the problem of special relativity by imagining himself traveling through the universe astride a beam of light! Einstein understood that science and religion are complementary. Science gives us a superior understanding of the physical world. Religion provides us with guidance for life. "Science without religion is blind," Einstein wrote, "and religion without science is lame."[8] They are like a man who cannot walk sitting astride the shoulders of a man with no eyes: together they can both see and walk.

The Power and Limitations of Religion

Like science, religion is also powerful but limited. The power of religion is that it offers what science cannot: a moral perspective on life. While science views the material world objectively by excluding the subjective perspective, religion views the world from the point of view of the subject and its journey through life. The word "religion" comes from the Latin *legere* meaning "to bind." The words "ligate" and "law" come from the same root; *re-legere* means "to bind back," to go back to the origin and ground of human existence in order to orient oneself properly in the world and guide oneself intelligently through life.

Although the objective view must exclude (or at least specify) the subjective perspective, it does not follow that the subjective view must exclude the objective perspective. The ideal function of religion is to provide a sound, fundamental world-view which correctly orients the individual to the cosmos, and thus can serve as the basis of an intelligent guide to living. Science can provide such a sound view, and the subject is free to accept all scientific facts as true. Science views the world logically and rationally, and expresses its knowledge in mathematical equations and parsimonious, descriptive language. Religion views life in the context of universal human experiences, like birth and death, initiations and transformations, yearnings and disappointments, trials and transcendence. Religions represent these universal human experiences not as factual propositions or theories, but as metaphors embedded in myths and tales, song and art, sermons and sayings.

The concept of balance, for example, which is vital to the happy conduct of life, is more easily communicated with a story or a tale than with objective, scientific language. The idea of balance can be illustrated in scientific language, with an equation or a set of scales, but it is dry and intellectual and no moral lessons can be drawn from it. A story, on the other hand, gives the subjective point of view which enables the hearer to understand the concept of balance from the point of view of life as a whole.

A famous Hasidic story illustrates the point. In the olden days, it was customary in the Jewish culture of eastern Europe for rabbis to travel through the countryside giving teachings in return for food and lodging. At the end of the meal, the head of the household was invited to pose questions to the Reb. On one occasion, after dinner, the man of the house asked, "Reb, how can I best please God?" This is an important question, for in the tradition of the Old Testament contract with Yahweh, the Hebrews were promised the reward of prosperity and long life in return for obedience to God's commandments.

The Reb answered, "I cannot tell you directly how to please God, but I can tell you by means of a story. In the olden days, people accused of a crime were tried by ordeal. If they survived the ordeal it meant that God had judged them innocent. If they were guilty, they did not survive. Judgment and punishment were issued on the spot.

"One time," the Reb continued, "two men were accused of theft. The King's soldiers took them to a deep ravine which was bridged by a narrow tree trunk. They were ordered to walk the plank. If they survived, they were judged innocent and released. If they did not survive, justice was done. The first man spread his arms like wings and, flapping them gracefully, traversed the tree trunk.

"The second man yelled across the chasm at the first man, 'How did you do it?'

"The first man shouted back, 'All I can tell you is that when you lean too far to the left lean back to the right, and when you lean too far to the right lean back to the left.'"

The story is a metaphor. The meaning of this simple but profound metaphor is to be found in the nature of mind. Ordinary mind is dualistic, that is, it operates in terms of antithetical meanings such as right/left, up/down, in/out, past/future, good/bad, and so on.[9] The traditional wisdom of the Middle Way, or the Golden Mean, teaches that the path to happiness is through centering, or the balancing of the extremes. Interpreted in this light, the rabbi taught that to please god, meaning to achieve happiness in life, one must avoid the extremes and find the Middle Way. This is done subjectively through the awareness of opposites, through the awareness of leaning too far towards one extreme or the other, and taking corrective action. The rabbi was giving a very Buddhist sermon on balance as the hidden key to the Middle Way which, in the rabbi's language, is the path which best pleases God.

If unskillful, this balancing act may actually increase the extremes of oscillation between opposites. We can see this in the oppositional behavior of adolescents who swing between compliance and rebellion. Out of the desire for independence they rebel and do the opposite of what their parents or other authority figures want, thinking that doing the opposite is freedom. Psychologists call this "pseudo-independence." By doing the opposite they are still dependent on their parents for the reference points of their thoughts and actions (as well as for room, board, and money.)

Gradually, as one matures, one hopefully learns that happiness is not found at the extremes, particularly not at the extremes of either the uninhibited indulgence in one's desires or the ascetical renunciation of them. The practice of mindfulness helps to clarify the subtle and complex drama of opposites which characterizes dualistic mind. With clarity, one can become more skillful and graceful at balancing the extremes on the journey through life. This profound and vital lesson of moderation can be conveyed through a simple story, but is difficult or impossible to communicate with scientific language.

Myths convey the same kinds of truths. We have come to view myths as fairy tales, as charming, antique stories which have properly become obsolete because they contradict known scientific facts. How could ideas that contradict scientific facts be useful guides for life? Myths, however, are metaphors, not literal statements of fact. The philosopher Gilbert Ryle has phrased this in the language of logic: "A myth is, of course, not a fairy story. It is the presentation of facts belonging to one [logical] category in the idioms appropriate to another."[10]

Myths are metaphorical representations of the world. They crystallize around a nucleus of natural, social, and historical facts, but they are not statements of fact. They are metaphors of reality, exemplary models of the world, of history, and of eternity. They represent to us in acceptable, indirect form, truths we do not wish to see or cannot articulate directly. Mircea Eliade holds the view that myths reveal the structure of reality:

> Every primordial image is the bearer of a message of direct relevance to the condition of humanity, for the image unveils aspects of ultimate reality that are otherwise inaccessible.[11]

Myths are metaphors which enable us to integrate or deny unacceptable elements of experience. An immortality myth may help us to transcend our fear of death or to deny it. A myth is a metaphorical representation of subtle aspects of our mental life, of our relationships, of our frantic search for happiness and our hopes for salvation from suffering, or of our sense of ourselves and of the ground of being which is our origin and destiny.

The word "subtle" is related to "subliminal," which means "below the limits of sense perception." What is denied and repressed becomes subliminal. The minds of other people, the character of human relationships, our orientation to life as a whole—none of these can be directly observed. They are also, in a sense, subliminal. To communicate with each other about the ineffable, about private thoughts and feelings, we must use familiar external events as metaphorical representations.

In the language of myth and metaphor, anger is "hot and fiery." A self-controlled person is "cool as ice." When we are inhibited, we are "frozen" or "paralyzed." When we are depressed, we are "down," and when we are excited we are "up." The thinking mind is full of "objects." The empty mind is "spacious" and "radiant." Thinking about ourselves is "self-reflection," as if we are looking into a mirror. Life is a journey, as if we are pilgrims on a perilous journey to the promised land.

Religious myths, stories, and epigrams are metaphors which enable us to understand our minds, our selves, and our journey through life.

To create a picture of reality through myth is not sufficient for the guidance of life, however. Myths must be integrated into life. The integration of myth into the practical activities of everyday life is accomplished through ritual and ethics. Ritual is the incarnation of myth through its symbolic enactment. Ethics provides the rules for everyday living according to the mythic picture of reality. Myth is related to ritual and ethics as scientific theory is related to technology:

MYTH : RITUAL + ETHICS = SCIENCE : TECHNOLOGY

Ritual and ethics, like technology, are praxis. They are the means to the sacred end of avoiding suffering and achieving happiness. Without myths that are relevant and cogent, and without rituals and ethics which are alive and meaningful, the human person becomes disoriented, fragmented, and tortured by bewilderment and anxiety.

Many of the psychological and social problems of modern life can be traced to the rise of science and the decline of religion. The historical fact is that the development of science has demythologized and depersonalized the cosmos and thus contributed to our sense of alienation from nature. Technology has made us more dangerous to each other and to our planet. It has fostered a growing inequity in the distribution of resources and catalyzed the conflict between nations. The crime, violence, and neurosis which are pandemic in our society are aggravated by the loss of working myths and rituals and by the decay of moral consciousness. Most educated people take the myths of their religion with a grain of salt. Most of the rituals that accompanied traditional myths have become meaningless, even to their practitioners. Ironically, this loss of meaning is expressed in our language in the word "ritualistic," which means compulsive, repetitive actions with no inner logic or relevance.

As a consequence of the decline of the mythic image, generations of people have suffered from a fragmented and ineffective view of life. This is one of the basic reasons for the profound alienation, disorientation, and moral deterioration which generate the restlessness, anxiety, and aggression which, in turn, are at the root of our most vexing social and personal problems.

While religion illuminates the mind's journey through life, it also has a dark side which, over the centuries, has proven to be extremely hazardous to human life and well being. Every major religious tradition is riddled with superstitions and false beliefs, wish-fulfilling fantasies, ideals shaped by desires and fears, obsolete dogmas, and lifeless rituals. Far worse, organized religions tend to be authoritarian, repressive, tyrannical, and violent.

Religious power is potent. Prayer and ritual can serve the motives of changing oneself, changing others, or influencing nature and the conditions of life. The belief that one's religion has the power to bring rain, or famine, or war, is potentially ego-enhancing. Religion can be used to enhance one's sense of personal power. Indeed, aggressive, egotistical men acting in the name of their religions are today, without a doubt, the greatest source of violence in the world, as is evident from the bloody conflicts between religious groups in the Middle East, Southeast Asia, Northern Ireland, the Balkans, and elsewhere. The ego-enhancing aura of religious power makes religion a fertile ground for self-clingers. And these self-clinging egos have caused great suffering and destruction in the name of religion.

Most modern religions are organized hierarchically, with an elite clergy at the top who articulate and administer the "true (official) faith" to the subordinate masses. Historically, this has fostered tyranny and injustice. In Western civilization, political revolution began with the overthrow of religious tyrants—"Royal Highnesses"—who claimed to rule by "divine right" and justified their oppression and cruelties in the name of their god. The founding fathers of the American Revolution were well aware of the danger of mixing religion and politics. The First Amendment to the Constitution was written with the underlying motive of protecting Americans from the tyranny and repressiveness of religion by separating church and state.

Western civilization is founded in the assertion, if not the achievement, of the separation not merely of church and state, but also of religion and science. The one is an historical expression of the other.

Toward a Balance of the Objective and the Subjective

How are we to solve this dilemma? Science and religion each have their strengths and weaknesses and, historically, each has been distrustful of the other. Science provides us with reliable, objective knowledge of the material world which gives us the power to tangibly improve the quality and length of our lives. But by the rules of its own methodology, science must eschew the subject and maintain neutrality about the subject's yearnings for happiness. Religion provides us with the language of myth and morals which the subject needs as guidance for life, but it falls into authoritarianism, repression, coercion, and corruption, and often champions baseless beliefs, silly superstitions, rigid dogmas, obsolete rituals, and wish-driven illusions.

Our challenge is to draw the best from science and religion while avoiding their defects and flaws. This means finding a balance between the principle of objectivity in science and the principle of subjectivity in religion.

The principle of objectivity is the fundamental rule of science, namely, that valid, objective knowledge is value free; that is, it is independent of the perceptions or values of any particular individual subject or group of subjects. Valid knowledge is obtained through careful, accurate and controlled observation and logical deduction rather than through the dictates of an authority, divine revelation, social convention, or personal opinion.

Paradoxically, the principle of objectivity *embodies certain values.* The objectivity of science is dependent upon the subject's valuation of valid knowledge. This implies that the human context is larger than the scientific context. Indeed, the pursuit of knowledge is embedded in the human context, that is, in the context of values. The desire to know arises out of the desire to quiet the anxiety which is the companion of confusion.

One way to describe a proper balance between the objective and the subjective is that the objective view must exclude, or bracket, the subjective while not losing the awareness of being embedded in it. Indeed, the embeddedness of science in the subjective is sufficient reason for it to exclude the subjective in order to neutralize the distorting influence of the subject's desires and fears on its perception of the facts and the construction of theories. At the same time, science must not lose sight of its relationship to (and debt to) the subject.

Historically, the objective point of view has also depended for its existence upon the valuation and respect for the freedoms of inquiry and expression. Science embodies these values of freedom even though it purports to be value free. To be sure, these values cannot be certified as factually true since they are not facts but ideals. Nevertheless, freedom is a precondition for the validity of the corpus of scientific knowledge. For if inquiry is coerced or influenced by subjective or social interests, then the results of that inquiry are not certifiably objective. The valuation of freedom is thus a precondition for the very existence of science itself.

Freedom is also a precondition for the existence of the unique human subject. The Fall represents an evolution from the choiceless, instinct- and reflex-driven behavior of the beast, into the freedom of thought and choice that shapes historical time. Without freedom, individuals are like animals, homogenized into a group and motivated by instinct and learned reflexes. The religious despot may be more subtle than the political despot, but all despots coerce and constrain the individual to conform to a norm which, to varying degrees, negates individuality. The rise of science, and the resulting freedom of inquiry and expression, coincides with the historical emergence of the human individual. The objective and the subjective principles, thus, are equally dependent upon the valuation of freedom for their existence. A supreme irony of history is that the unique human subject, who yearns for moral guidance, is the product of the rise of science which necessarily required expunging moral thought from the library of valid knowledge.

The principle of subjectivity represents the standpoint of the thinking subject who is compelled by the instinct for survival to create a picture of the world on the basis of which to formulate a guide for life. The life interests of the individual require a guide for life which will maximize the possibilities of happiness while minimizing the prospects of suffering and annihilation. A good guidance system helps to distinguish attitudes and actions which are likely to bring peace of mind from those which are likely to cause suffering to ourselves and others. The principle of subjectivity is, therefore, fundamentally moral. Those thoughts, words, and deeds that bring happiness are morally righteous. Those that bring suffering are evil.

A guide for life is, basically, a system of ethics. The Talmud Torah, for example, is a holy book of the Jewish tradition. *Talmud* means "guide for life." The Talmud is filled with exhaustive ethical prescriptions on how to live, what to eat, when, how, and with whom to have sex, how to relate to the body, how to conduct social life, and how to praise God. The same is true of the Koran and, indeed, of all other religious teachings.

To be in balance, the objective and subjective principles must share another common ground. An effective, workable guide for life must be based on a factual picture of the world. If we follow a map which does not accurately reflect the territory we are traveling, we will become lost, confused, and imperilled. An effective guide for life must accurately represent the world in which we live. It cannot deny what is true or affirm what is false.

This implies that the subject, to be in balance with the objective, must accept all scientifically demonstrated facts as true. The subject's view of the world must be compatible with science or it will be out of tune with the reality that science describes.

A number of conditions are required for this to be possible. First, there must be some understanding of the difference between fact and metaphor. Religious myths, while the carriers of higher wisdom, are not facts. They are metaphors. Mistaking them as facts may bring them into conflict with actual scientific facts. If myth is understood as metaphor, it cannot contradict scientific fact. The myth that God created the world in seven days contradicts the theory of the Big Bang only if taken literally. As a metaphor it is an anthropomorphic depiction of the origins of the universe.

Secondly, for a subject to be compatible with science, he or she must accept all scientifically established facts as true, and must not assert as true any proposition which is contrary to scientific fact. This does not require rejecting myths or other religious metaphors as having high truth value, superior to science for the purposes of guiding the subject through life. It means not rejecting scientific facts which may seem to contradict religious metaphors. A balance of the objective and the subjective principles thus requires the synthesis of a science which stipulates the moral values of freedom and autonomy with a religion which accepts all empirical facts as true.

CHAPTER THREE
The Case History of a Typical Sufferer

> The intention that man should be 'happy' is not included in the scheme of creation.
>
> —Sigmund Freud, *Civilization and Its Discontents*

To see how a balance of the subjective and the objective principles can help us to better understand ourselves and more skillfully navigate the treacherous waves of *samsara*,[1] it will be helpful to reflect on the life of a typical sufferer. Michael D. is a fictional, composite character. In his early forties he lapsed into a clinical depression. His psychiatric case history will help us to understand a common imbalance of the subjective and the objective principles and, by contrast, show how they can be brought into balance.

The imbalance is the currently prevailing tendency to attempt to understand and help people who suffer from mental and emotional distress by scientific means alone. This trend began with the rise of the "new science" and manifests in the present era as the preference to examine all phenomena with quantified scientific method and to explain all phenomena in scientific language—in terms of causes. It represents a historical over-swing from the religious-subjective to the scientific-objective point of view.

Over the past fifty years, psychiatry and psychology have become increasingly scientific, and scientistic. They have not only adopted scientific method and language but they have also assumed the social identity and posture of scientists, and sometimes disguise their moral values and social actions in medical-scientific jargon.[2] Increasingly, mental and emotional problems are explained causally, in terms of genetic inheritance, biochemical imbalance, or personal-social trauma. This has tended to blind us to the spiritual problems of suffering subjects and the relationship of these problems to their mental and emotional distress.

A more balanced view of the human being can be achieved by accepting valid scientific facts as true, being mindful of the psychological and spiritual dimensions of the subjective human experience, and integrating the two. This is not an easy task. In the current sway of opinion only scientific facts constitute valid knowledge. Spiritual or moral statements, no matter how wise, are viewed as value laden, individual, or culturally relative, therefore not factual, therefore not valid. In addition, moral sentiments often masquerade as facts; for example, in the current controversies about the relationship between race and intelligence. One side argues that the scientific facts indicate a genetic basis for intelligence and that certain races are inherently more intelligent than others. The other side argues that intelligence is more significantly correlated with social circumstances and that the theory of genetically inherited racial intelligence is racism masquerading as science.

A particularly thorny problem is posed by developmental psychology, which presents a causal theory of human suffering, but in a social-interpersonal rather than a neurochemical context. This makes it seem fundamentally different than neurochemical theories of mental suffering. It is different in that it focuses on social-interpersonal variables rather than biochemical ones. But it is similar in that both explain suffering causally, one on the basis of errant neurotransmitters and the other based on the psychological-emotional traumas of childhood.

This form of psychological determinism began with Freud and the early psychoanalysts and psychologists. Striving to be accepted by the prestigious scientific community, they explained suffering causally and couched their ideas in the language of science.[3] The thorniness of the problem is that there is some valuable truth to this view, but it is limited and incomplete without some understanding of the spiritual and moral dimensions of psychological problems.

Early psychological-emotional traumas no doubt cause future suffering. The child who is abused—physically, sexually, or emotionally—

suffers enormously and usually develops into an anxious, depressed, and angry adult. There is no question but that the traumas of childhood are the historical-developmental cause of the emotional pain of many adults. On the other hand, individuals differ in their responses to these traumas. Some hold on to the memory of the trauma and form their identity as a survivor out of it. Others let go and move on. Some feel guilty and ashamed. Some can forgive themselves and reconcile with their abuser, while others remain angry and vengeful.

Obviously, there is a moral quality in one's response to trauma. Jesus preached turning the other cheek. Others call for justice. Although the child's response to trauma has a moral quality, the child is not a moral agent. Every society recognizes that children are not morally responsible until they make the transition into adulthood. The age of this demarcation varies from culture to culture, but it is usually marked by a rite of passage, such as a confirmation ceremony, at which point the neophyte acquires moral (and sometimes legal) responsibility, not only for the harm they do to others, but also for the harm and suffering they bring on themselves through their responses to the traumatic experiences of their lives.

For some adults, the harm done by the emotional traumas of their childhood are irremediable. Their neuro-psychological development has been irreversibly retarded. Others have the potential to develop insight into their problems and to learn new ways of coping with their neurotic patterns and pain. One problem is that the opportunities to examine themselves, to develop insights and learn new ways of thinking and acting, vary from culture to culture and from time to time.

In primitive and traditional societies, sufferers usually consulted the priest or shaman who diagnosed the malady and prescribed some medicinal, ritual, or moral remedy. The basis and value of these medical, religious, and moral instructions were usually accepted without much dissent by the local community. Today, the family, church, and community, which used to be the vehicles for raising morally responsible individuals, have broken down. In many technologically advanced societies moral teaching and training have been diluted and are ineffective or vestigial. There is virtually nowhere to go to learn how to accept responsibility for one's own suffering and to deal with it constructively. An increasing number of families are dysfunctional for raising children. Traditional wisdom is not taught systematically in the schools. Where can one find a course on "How to work with your painful emotions?" These subjects are not taught in church, except perhaps during a brief Sunday sermon. The one place in modern societies where people can learn how to take responsibility for their suffering and their lives is in psychotherapy.

People go into psychotherapy for relief of their suffering: their anxiety, depression, and other painful emotions. They go into therapy to learn what they cannot learn anywhere else. This is why psychotherapy is so popular. As we have already noted, successful psychotherapy requires the active participation of the patient in talking, listening, reflecting, and acting on newly gained insights. By reflecting on the past, people can gain some understanding of the historical origins and dynamics of the habitual patterns of thinking and behavior associated with their suffering. Therapy consists of both gaining insight and developing certain skills. Having been shaped by their past experiences, they must now seek to reshape themselves. To take responsibility for oneself, one must understand oneself and one's motivations to some degree. And one must develop the discipline and skill to conduct oneself and one's life in a way less likely to perpetuate the suffering which was conditioned by the past traumas.

The Case of Michael D.

Michael D. is a forty-five year old lawyer who consulted me because of depression. He opened the interview by saying that he was referred to me by his primary physician who told him that he was suffering from a biochemical imbalance and needed an antidepressant, such as Prozac. His primary physician was operating under the prevailing assumption that depression is caused by a biochemical imbalance.

Since he was viewing himself from an extremely objective-medical point of view, as he had been led to do by the first medical doctor from whom he sought help, I tried to bring some balance to the situation at the very start by focussing on his subjective experience. I advised him that in order to evaluate him for an antidepressant, I needed to know something about him. I could not assume that he suffered only from a biochemical imbalance. I had to know about his life history, his relationships, his patterns of behavior, his thoughts, and his innermost feelings.

He began with the complaint that he had been depressed for several years, over which time he was gradually losing interest in his law practice, his marriage, and his life. He had been led to believe that his depression was causing the loss of interest. He had a successful law practice with which he was very happy for the first few years, but he gradually became more unhappy over the past decade. He thought that his depression had become worse in the past six months because he now felt that work was unbearably tedious, boring, and unrewarding.

As he talked he became caught up in his story. He was the son of an Irish-Catholic banker and his Jewish wife. He had two younger brothers born three years apart. He was his mother's favorite. She often whispered in his ear that she thought he was special and would accomplish great things in life.

He was an excellent student, a talented writer, and a dabbler in painting. He chose to study law during the sixties because he wanted to be well positioned to do something meaningful with his life. He was a serious member of the sixties generation, leaning towards what were then called radical views. He protested racism, he marched against the war in Vietnam, he was a champion of human rights, and he had a passionate interest in the environment. He wanted to help change the world for the better. He saw that lawyers were a powerful group, politically and socially. He thought that law would give him the opportunity to work for peaceful social change. He had a strong sentiment for oppressed people, for the underdog and the disadvantaged. He decided to practice general law, helping the innocent to find justice; trying to counsel a divorcing couple and save a marriage rather than trying to get the best settlement and the highest fee; helping to establish fair, environmentally considerate business practices by writing enlightened contracts. He took pride in his work. He met a beautiful girl in college whom he courted and married. He loved her very much. They had three children, ages fourteen, twelve, and nine.

Paradoxically, as he talked about his professional success, his beloved wife and children, and his comfortable, middle class life, Michael spoke with audible increments of sadness in his voice, as if the story of his life was taking a downward turn, becoming progressively more tragic. He interjected comments which blamed his depression for his downward spiral. He complained that his depression had robbed him of the energy and interest to pursue his youthful ideals. He now finds them unreachable and irrelevant. His expectations of the practice of law did not include the routine and ruthless adversarial proceedings of everyday legal practice. He loved to write but he detested writing tedious legal briefs and letters. He had always wanted to write fiction and was frustrated by the stereotypical, formal language of the legal document. While he used to enjoy philosophical discussions of law with his classmates, the opportunities for such dialogue seemed to have disappeared, and he was losing patience with the insincere negotiations and cynical bantering of his colleagues, some of whose politics and values he loathed.

He felt that his depression was also affecting his marriage and family life. He was often irritable towards his wife and children, or uninterested in them. His only complaints about his wife were that she had gained a little weight and had lost interest in sex. He felt that their relationship had become routine, uninspiring, and boring. Because of his insomnia he no longer slept in the same bed with his wife. In the past week he had had thoughts of suicide, which scared him enough to seek psychiatric help.

Balancing the Objective and the Subjective

How are we to interpret this story of Michael's suffering? How are we to help him, or help him help himself? Let us compare the objective and subjective points of view and see whether there is a middle ground where they can coexist.

The objective view is represented by the modern medical model of psychiatry. From this point of view, painful thoughts and emotions, such as depression, are regarded as symptoms of a disease. From this perspective, Michael D. suffers from clinical depression. Most contemporary psychiatrists view depression as a medical disease which is caused by a disruption of neurochemical transmitters in the brain. It is believed that genetic factors increase the biological vulnerability to this "chemical imbalance," which may be triggered by a traumatic life experience. The proper treatment, accordingly, is an antidepressant like the famous Prozac, which corrects the underlying chemical imbalance.[4] Psychotherapy is viewed primarily as an adjunct which helps the individual to deal with the illness and the traumatic situation which may have triggered it.

The objective point of view characteristically explains depression and other forms of human suffering in terms of antecedent, non-moral causes. According to this view, the primary causes of Michael D.'s depression do not have their primary roots in his character, his view of life, his values, his choices, his courage, or his selfishness. They lie in brain biochemistry and traumatic social circumstances, of which he is the victim. The objective point of view excludes any concept of the individual's moral responsibility for his or her suffering.

The objective position may contain valid facts. Depression does seem to be correlated with low levels of serotonin in certain parts of the brain. Further research is needed to confirm this. Michael D. may, indeed, have a deficiency of serotonin in his cerebral synapses, although there is, at present, no clinical method for routinely measuring brain serotonin levels in the living person. Prozac, or some such drug, might be helpful. Only a clinical trial would tell.

In my view, if a particular drug helps people to overcome their suffering without imposing unacceptable side effects, it should be made available, as long as its administration is voluntary and the patient makes an informed choice. But even if a correlation is proven between low serotonin levels and depression, it does not explain depression completely. It describes one physical component of depression, but it does not explain depression as a human experience.

The significant question remains whether this deficiency is the cause or the effect of the depressed mental state. In my opinion this question has not yet been either adequately debated nor conclusively decided.[5] There is a great deal of evidence that experiences can physically change the brain. The experience of danger, for example, stimulates the adrenergic nervous system into the fight-flight reaction which involves a cascade of physiological events, including changes in the activity and functions of the brain. Classical experiments on anaclitically[6] depressed and normal children suggests that the lack of mothering and social stimulation can inhibit the development of the brain. Conversely, sufficient stimuli actually stimulate brain growth in children. Our perceptions, interpretations, and reactions to external events can strongly affect brain and body chemistry.

As an analogy, think of football fans witnessing a close Super Bowl game. At an exciting moment, after a brilliant run in the final seconds of a close game, the fans will become excited and agitated—shouting, jumping, cheering, and jeering. They are likely have elevated levels of catecholamines and other neurochemicals in their brain corresponding to their level of excitement. If biochemical assays showed that the catecholamine level of these fans were elevated, no one would claim the elevation alone causes the excitement. The excitement is in the game. The elevated levels are the *result* of the excitement of the game, a *part* of the excitement of the game, but they are not the primary cause of it. They form the material basis of the excitement, but not its mental or emotional aspect.[7]

After making a diagnosis of clinical depression and prescribing and monitoring the antidepressive medication, the psychiatric psychopharmacologist has little to offer. But lowered serotonin levels are not the only possible explanation for Michael's depression. Human behavior cannot be viewed exclusively from the point of view of brain physiology, as is currently the trend in psychiatry, psychology, and philosophy. The dominance and official use of the medical model of psychiatry has the unwitting effect of leaving the subjective aspects of depression unexamined, thus helping people to ignore, deny, and repress a subjective understanding of themselves and their own contribution to their suffering.

The objective and subjective points of view can be balanced by accepting valid scientific facts about Michael D. as true, then examining the meaning of his life *to him*. A balanced treatment of his depression would include both pharmacotherapy and psychotherapy. Combining the objective and subjective points of view is the balanced approach to any understanding of the human situation. Science can provide us with valid knowledge of the biology of the human body, as well as some aspects of social behavior. Biology and society certainly shape and influence human experience and behavior. Biological and sociological facts and theories may be valid, but they are incomplete. They are only two thirds of the necessary triad. To fully understand human emotions and behavior it is vital that we also understand the dynamics of the subjective mind.[8]

If Michael D.'s serotonin level is, indeed, depressed, the prolonged stress of feeling helpless and hopeless due to his existential struggle with the meaning of his life and his work might have caused it. Even if low serotonin is a result rather than the sole cause of depression, it may contribute to the listlessness and lack of energy which makes recovery more difficult. Even if the cause of depression is primarily psychological, it has a physiological momentum which is difficult to reverse. Antidepressants can reverse this inertia. I tell my patients that Prozac is like a hand crank on an old car. You have to turn it to get the engine going, but once it is running you can stop cranking. The same is true for antidepressants, provided that the patient also engages in self-reflection. If not, relapse is more probable. I strongly advise my patients on antidepressants to also diligently examine themselves, preferably together with a mature, experienced psychotherapist.

Psychological Aspects of the Subjective

To understand Michael D. from the subjective point of view we must know something about his view of life, his hopes and expectations, his desires and his fears, his denials and defenses. He had always been an idealist. It was a derivative of his mother's ideals and vicarious ambitions, her love and high expectations of him. To be a good son who made his mother happy, he assumed the complementary role of wanting to be the person his mother wanted him to be and striving to do something worthwhile in life so she would be pleased. In themselves, these are worthy motives, but they were not Michael D.'s spontaneous motives. They were implants from his mother, attached with the glue of guilt and, hence, were unauthentic.

An idealist is one who thinks that life can be what he or she thinks it should be or wants it to be. Michael D.'s Happiness Projects were based on unrealistic expectations. As a young man he thought he could save the world or, at least, leave it significantly better than he entered it. His ego demanded it. If he could not feel his self-importance through his work, he would be faced with a crisis of self-worth and meaninglessness. He idealized life, his profession, and the woman he married. He thought that if he worked hard and tried to do the right thing he would be successful, rewarded, and satisfied. He thought that teaching and writing, marriage and family, and middle class living would fulfill him. The irony and tragedy of Michael D., to which we are all vulnerable, is that life was not what he thought and wished it to be. When he had what he thought would make him happy, he didn't want it anymore.

The practice of law was not as altruistic or glamorous as he hoped and imagined. Every day he faced demanding clients. Some were guilty. Some lied. Others were innocent but he, nevertheless, billed them heavily in order to support his family and his lifestyle. He dreaded the drudgery of office details. He detested the hypocrisy of drinking and lunching with boring colleagues whom he neither liked nor respected, simply to get referrals from them. He was stressed by the tensions of billing and paying bills, by the tender trap of obligations and responsibilities to career and family which prevented him from exploring his talent as a writer and artist. Marriage to the woman he loved was not the paradise he thought it would be. They had endured a number of conflicts and quarrels that left a thin but potent barrier of resentment between them. Their sexual relationship had become unimaginative, routine, and dull. Michael was attracted to other women, but did not dare act out his desires. He felt that life was passing him by. His quest for happiness had become a hopeless and meaningless cause. Unable to imagine how he could be happy in the future, he considered ending it all.

If the objective point of view, through the prescription of an antidepressant, could help Michael D., how could the subjective point of view help him? First, it would encourage him to look at himself, at his views of life, at the choices he had made, and at his responses to life situations. Given the opportunity for self-examination and reflection, Michael might see that he bears some responsibility for his depression and, therefore, for his recovery. This is very difficult for many people to accept. It smacks of blaming the victim. They ask, "How can depression be an illness for which the victim is responsible? And would insurance companies pay for therapy if the patient is considered responsible for the illness?"

Recall, however, that psychotherapy cannot work unless the patient takes responsibility for his or her states of mind and actions. Success in psychotherapy requires the subject to understand and take responsibility for his or her own suffering.[9] Not everyone responds to therapy because not everyone takes responsibility for themselves. Some people work at it and others don't. Some people are courageous enough to openly look at painful aspects of their past, their character, and their life. Others are not. The effectiveness of psychotherapy is based on the patient's openness and flexibility. It depends upon the ability and willingness to express oneself openly, to be mindful, to reflect on life from different perspectives, and to respond to what has been learned and apply it in actual life situations. To think that people are responsible for working their way out of depression but not responsible for working their way into it seems skewed.

If he looked and reflected, Michael D. might realize that his depression is the result of his own views and attitudes towards life, particularly his unrealistic desires, hopes, expectations, and ideals. His self-esteem was based on pleasing his mother, although he had incorporated her values as his own. All his life he strived to be successful and special. He wanted to be widely known as a brilliant lawyer who helped people. He wanted to be married to a beautiful wife whom he loved and who loved him and with whom he could have an exciting life. He wanted to enjoy a high standard of living. He believed these things would make him happy. He achieved them all, but they did not make him happy. An inner confusion and dissatisfaction remained.

From the subjective point of view, Michael is depressed because he counted on the realization of his ideals for his future happiness. Rather than relate to life as it is, as it develops, he related to his ideals, dreams, wishes, and desires as his guides. As a result, he wanted more out of life than it was possible for him to get. He experienced this as a devastating loss. He wanted his profession to be pure and exciting but it was dull and routine. He wanted his wife to be continuously warm and glamorous but she is older now and sometimes grows weary. Michael believed that if he lived what is conventionally considered to be "the good life" he would be happy. His failed Happiness Project was the source of his suffering.

As he engaged in therapy, Michael D. became more confused. Actually, it would be more accurate to say that he became more aware of his confusion which he had tried to evade and deny with his wishful beliefs and assumptions about life. He didn't know what to make of the suggestion that his depression involved more than a biochemical imbalance, that it also involved imbalances in his thoughts, feelings, and actions. At first, Michael explained his problem in terms of the medical model. The reason he was not happy was because he was depressed. He was not ready to consider the possibility that his depression was a symptom of his unhappiness rather than a cause of it. His belief that he suffered from a biochemical imbalance became a defensive maneuver which permitted him to stubbornly cling to his immature fantasies of life, continuing to hope for the hopeless.

As we talked and he recalled and reviewed the story of his life, he began to think more subjectively and to experience feelings he had previously stuffed away. He began to realize that his depression had developed in the context of his ideas, feelings, interpretations, and responses to situations and people. As he began to think more subjectively, he began to see how his depression was related to his idea of how life should be and the correlated feeling that his life was not what he wanted it to be. This, his one and only life, has not turned out as he wished. He had hoped for a fulfilling career and marriage. He found them boring and uninspiring. He felt like a worthless failure and loser.

Gradually, he began to accept the idea that he was depressed because of the gap between his desires and expectations and his actual experiences. To overcome his depression he had to face this fact. As he struggled with his disappointments he began to realize that the problem was not what life had not given to him, but that he wanted more from life than it was possible for him to get. This turned everything sour. He wanted his profession and his wife to be different than they were. As a result, he could not enjoy aspects of them as they actually were. He wanted everything to be wonderful—he wanted his work to be exciting and socially significant, his wife to be glamorous and interesting, his children to be obedient achievers. He dreaded disappointment, dullness, and dreariness. He wanted to be happy forever, without suffering—a project which is bound to fail.

As he talked and reflected, he began to see how it could be possible that all careers, no matter how glamorous they may seem, are in some way routine and repetitive. When he thought about it, he realized that few people can influence the course of social and historical events as he had egotistically hoped he could. Reluctantly, he conceded that his wife was an ordinary person, not a perpetually glamorous nurturer of his needs. In a flash of insight, he could see that he was jealous of his children and had been angry with his wife for not paying more attention to him, as he was angry with his mother for the attention she gave to his younger siblings. He was also angry with his wife for not being more interested in sex.

As he saw things differently, he began to act differently. He lowered his expectations to a more reasonable level. Instead of expecting his work to be automatically rewarding, he trained himself to look for the positive in situations, to do what he could to make his days more interesting and rewarding, and to accept what he could not change. Instead of expecting his wife to minister to him and satisfy his needs, he began to listen to her, see her point of view, and to address her needs. Gradually, they became friends—and lovers—again.

Spiritual Aspects of the Subjective

Sigmund Freud distinguished between the extraordinary suffering of neurotics and the ordinary suffering of everyday life. He conceded that all psychoanalysis could do was to reduce neurotic suffering to ordinary suffering. Many people today agree with Freud that psychotherapy can help to relieve extraordinary suffering such as severe anxiety, deep depression, explosive anger, intense feelings of guilt or shame, and so forth, but it does not address the ordinary sufferings which are an intrinsic part of being human and are experienced by everyone. This form of suffering, they believe, is the province of religion.

Each school of psychotherapy addresses suffering from its own unique but limited view. Cognitive psychotherapists affirm, with good basis, that neurotic suffering stems from wrong views and that cognitive therapy can help a person to examine and correct views of life which are idealistic, unrealistic, distorted, or self-defeating. Behavioral psychotherapy can help decondition habitual patterns of behavior which are negative and self-destructive. Gestalt and other forms of therapy can help people to work through and integrate the traumas and disappointments of the past and to develop more positive thoughts and feelings, particularly feelings of self-esteem. Analytic therapy can help people to better understand their past and its relationship to their motives, fears, and defense mechanisms. But psychotherapy, because of its excessive reliance on science, cannot easily incorporate the wisdom of the ages, which has traditionally been the jurisdiction of religion. Psychotherapists think of themselves as relying on scientific knowledge and, therefore, must avoid seeming to be influenced by religious ideas. Religious wisdom is officially excluded from psychotherapy because it cannot be measured, quantified, and evaluated by managed care companies.

A spiritual approach to suffering does not require a belief in god or any particular religious dogma or teaching. It requires developing a more mature approach to life. It means opening one's eyes to the facts of life and to the role of the mind in causing suffering and achieving happiness. And it involves putting into practice the wisdom which comes from deeper awareness and reflection.

One of the basic teachings of all religions, and one of the basic facts of existence, is that life is difficult and suffering is an intrinsic part of life. Moments of happiness are possible, but they are difficult to achieve and impermanent. In the Judeo-Christian tradition, this fact is metaphorically represented in Genesis where God punishes Adam and Eve for their original sin in the Garden of Eden. He punishes Eve with painful childbirth and obedience to her husband. And he punishes Adam with working by the sweat of his brow to survive in a nature indifferent to his needs. In the Old Testament tradition, life is a "vale of tears." The same realization brought Sigmund Freud to lament, "The intention that man should be 'happy' is not included in the scheme of creation."[10]

This insight is expressed in the Buddhist tradition as the first noble truth—the truth of suffering. Becoming aware of the truth of suffering, the nature and causes of suffering, is the first step towards enlightenment. One of the teachings of the "four ordinary foundations" of the *ngondro*[11] or preliminary practices is that "secular life is inherently unsatisfactory." In other words, lasting happiness is difficult to find in this vale of tears which is the vicious state of samsara. The basic fact is that pain is a part of living in this world—not only physical pain, but the psycho-emotional pain of disappointment, loss, anxiety, depression, guilt, shame, boredom, and so on. The point to be reflected on is the choice between trying to avoid the unavoidable, which only causes greater suffering, and experiencing the unavoidable fully, with awareness and skill.

The awareness and investigation of suffering is an important part of psychotherapy, although it is not recognized as a spiritual teaching. When Michael examined his feelings of disappointment, he realized that it was unrealistic to expect life to yield to his desires, wishes, and demands. He also realized that pinning his hopes for future happiness on the realization of his dreams was a setup for a letdown. It would be living in a dream-world. The idea that our Happiness Projects will always be realized, and that it is possible to be happy forever, is one of the main causes of human unhappiness, pain, and suffering. Michael had to face his unrealistic desires and the negative thinking which they it generate. He had to face and experience his suffering, his disappointments, his boredom, his low self-esteem, his anger—the whole internal mess—and work to transform it into something positive. He had to alchemically transform himself, from the lead of suffering to the gold of inner tranquility. As the Tibetans say, he had to make vinegar into honey. The same sentiment is expressed in the aphorism, "If all you have is lemons, make lemonade."

A second spiritual truth, which is relevant to psychotherapy, is that the proximate cause and quality of our suffering lies in our minds rather than in the external world. The external world is neutral. It contains both life and death. The idea of a cosmos indifferent to our desires and demands, if not to our needs, is compatible with the Buddhist view which holds that the source and origin of our suffering lies within ourselves. Christian's identify this inner source of suffering as original sin. In every tradition the spiritual journey is a journey within. A Christian's silent prayer is a form of meditation, an opportunity to examine and become familiar with one's own mind.

As Michael examined his mind and his feelings, he began to see how his mental and emotional life were fueled and motivated by his selfish desires and fears. He began to see how his depression was the suffering of his dashed hopes. This is a very fundamental insight which is relevant to both psychotherapy and spiritual life.

In the Judeo-Christian tradition, this truth is expressed in the Lutheran prayer, "Thy will be done Lord, not mine." This axiom expresses the view that happiness is to be found through acceptance of what is "god's will" rather than through the futile pursuit of the satisfaction of our endless selfish desires. This latter state is the position of the narcissist, whose contrary motto is, "My will be done, not thine." The narcissist thinks, "Life should be what I want it to be, not what it is." As one matures, the axiom becomes reversed. Michael learned that one of the secrets of happiness is the mature realization, "Life is as it is, not as I wish it to be."

In Buddhist teachings, the three poisons, desire, aversion, and ignorance, are the source of the suffering we cause to ourselves and others. Michael's desires, the satisfaction of which he thought would make him happy, were the source of his suffering. The tragic realization, which we hide from ourselves, is that whatever we think will make us happy is the source of our problems and our pain.

The Buddhist View

CHAPTER FOUR

View, Path, Fruition: The Empirical Approach to Wisdom and Self-Transformation

> Meditating without listening and reflecting is blind. But listening and reflecting without meditating is like having eyesight and no legs.
>
> —Khenpo Tsultrim Gyamtso, *Progressive Stages of Meditation on Emptiness*

The search for a common ground of science and religion, the objective and subjective points of view, is a daunting task. The contradictions between them seem fundamental and pervasive. Science, champion of the objective, owes its power to purging itself of empirically unfounded beliefs and values, while religion, champion of the subject, seems to cherish scientifically unprovable beliefs, such as the existence of supernatural beings, and to champion moral imperatives, sometimes fanatically and tyrannically. Yet we must undertake the quest if we are to integrate knowledge and value, overcome our ignorance, see through the secrets we hide from ourselves, and approach the problems of life more sanely and intelligently.

Our problem is simplified if we remember that we are not seeking to unify science and religion, but only to find their common ground. Science and religion are different enterprises and we must not pretend to ignore their differences. On the other hand, the fact that they are different does not mean they do not have a common ground. As men and women are opposites, yet both are human, science and religion may differ and yet share a common ground.

For a religion to share a common ground with science it must, at a minimum, accept established scientific facts as true. In the Western world, some religions, particularly the fundamentalist variety, reject the authority of science and certain scientific claims. The famous Tennessee Scopes trial, which pitted Protestant fundamentalists against Darwinists, has come to symbolize the conflict between religion and science. Fundamentalists, who interpret the Bible literally, believe that humans are the special creation of God, and they reject the scientific view that humans evolved from the animals. Darwinists, on the other hand, reject creationism as scientifically unprovable. From this point of view, religion and science seem fundamentally contradictory and irreconcilable.

There is no intrinsic or necessary conflict between religion and science, however. On the contrary, the more a religion is willing to accept scientific facts as true, the more believable and reliable it is. In principle, a religion could accept all scientific facts as true. Buddhism is such a religion. Buddhists are free to accept all established scientific facts as true. The Dalai Lama, the spiritual leader of Tibetan Buddhists, has explicitly encouraged his followers to accept all scientific facts and theories.[1] If a point of doctrine is contradicted by scientific fact, he advises that it should be re-examined and reconsidered. In Buddhism, there is no intrinsic incompatibility between religion and science.

Unlike religions which reject scientific findings that conflict with their dogma, Buddhists may openly accept the findings of science as "relative truth." Relative truth is knowledge acquired by the subject about the object world. It includes all factual scientific knowledge and concepts. Modern scientists are familiar with the concept of relative truth since, by the postulates of Einstein's Theory of Relativity and of quantum physics, our knowledge of the physical world is a product of the relationship between the observer and the observed.[2] By accepting scientific facts as relative truth, Buddhism shares a common ground with science.

Even if a religion meets this minimum standard, however, it would not share *significant* common ground with science if it also held beliefs which are contradicted or not confirmable by scientific method.

For example, the belief in a supernatural, omnipotent creator of the universe is not compatible with science, because such an invisible being cannot be observed by empirical methods and seems beyond such verification and inaccessible to it.

The belief in an omnipotent creator is not shared by all religions, however. Buddhism is an atheistic religion in the sense that it does not believe in an omnipotent creator. Oriental Buddhists usually do believe in supernatural gods. Some Oriental Buddhists believe in the literal existence of such beings. Others view them as projections of mind. However, it is not necessary to believe in the literal existence of these gods to be a good Buddhist. One can be a good Buddhist and still be skeptical of or reject any belief which conflicts with scientific fact. Buddhism is unique amongst religions in that the practitioner is free to reject or suspend belief in any idea, including belief in gods, supernatural powers, and reincarnation, which is contradicted by established scientific facts, or which cannot be known and checked through one's own experience and observation.

Buddhism as a Science of the Mind

If modern, scientific-minded individuals are to have full access to the esoteric wisdom which helps us to see the truths we hide from ourselves, it is necessary to have access to a religion which is compatible with science, which accepts all scientific facts as true and does not hold beliefs that are contradicted by scientific facts. The fact that Buddhism is such a religion partially explains why it is attractive to many Westerners. Indeed, most Westerners do not appreciate the degree to which Buddhism is compatible with science.

Buddhism is compatible with Western science not only because it can accept all scientific evidence as valid, but also because its approach to knowledge is fundamentally empirical. The idea that a religion may attain its truths by empirical methods is alien to the West. The Western religions of the Old Testament—Judaism, Christianity, and Islam—all rely primarily upon faith and the authoritative word of scripture for knowledge about God and God's will.

In Tibetan Buddhist epistemology, called *lo-rig* (literally: consciousness-knowing), the two primary forms of incontrovertible and non-mistaken knowing are direct perception and inferential cognition.[3] The former is akin to empirical observation; the latter is equivalent to logical inference. In this sense, the Buddhist view of mind and the world is based upon experience, observation, and logic, rather than upon the appeal to authority, traditional doctrine, superstition, or common belief.[4] For this reason, Buddhism has been aptly described as a "science of the mind."

Buddhists also study scripture, called *sutras*. And Lamas often appeal to the authority of sutra for their teachings. Buddhists also often rely on the word of revered *yogis*. Certain yogis are supposed to have the power to directly perceive the truth—so called "direct yogic perception." Nevertheless, the empirical approach to knowing is fundamental to the Buddhist path. It is not necessary to accept the non-empirical teachings of Buddhism in order to accept its empirical insights. It is not necessary to accept the word of scripture or of an honored yogi if they contradict known scientific fact. It is written in the sutras that, at the end of his life, Buddha pleaded with his disciples not to accept his teachings as valid on blind faith or because of respect or deference to him as an authority. "Be a lamp unto yourselves," he advised, a legacy with which the modern scientifically minded individual can comfortably agree.

Buddha asked his disciples to rely upon their intelligence to discover the fundamental truths of life and mind. He asked them to use the "jewelers test"—an empirical test for gold used at the time. A jeweler would not take a seller's word that a stone was gold; it could be fool's gold, brass, or copper. The jeweler tested the stone by rubbing it, cutting it, heating it, weighing it—using every known method to determine whether it is gold or not. In the same way, Buddhists are encouraged to test the teachings by observing, analyzing, and reflecting to determine for themselves what is true and what is false.

The Buddhist reliance on evidence and logic rather than on authority and faith is illustrated by a story about Mullah Nasrudin, an infamous Sufi mystic who taught through foolishness and madness. One day a friend came to borrow Mullah's donkey. "The donkey is not here," Mullah said. At that moment, the donkey brayed audibly outside an open window. "I thought you said the donkey's not here," complained the visitor indignantly. "Who are you going to believe," Mullah replied equally indignant, "me or the donkey?"

Buddhists are free to believe the donkey. Like scientists, Buddhists need trust only in their own observations and logical analysis. True, many Buddhists, including Westerners, regard faith as a valid basis of spiritual knowledge and accept as true many beliefs which are not verified or verifiable by science.[5] But this is not required to be a Buddhist. As a Buddhist, one is not obliged to believe anything on faith or authority. Buddhists are free to reject any proposition which has not been or cannot be directly verifiable or logically deduced.

As a Westerner trained in science, I do not believe in many ideas which are mistakenly stereotyped as Buddhist, such as the belief in "paranormal" psychic powers or psychic phenomena, including literal personal reincarnation, clairvoyance, tele-transportation, sortilege, disembodied minds, or other forms of soft-minded spiritualism. As a student at Namgyal Monastery Institute of Buddhist Studies I have often engaged in friendly debate with my fellow students, Western teachers, and even some lamas who seem to believe in literal personal rebirth, clairvoyance, and other special, supernatural powers allegedly possessed by advanced yogic practitioners. I express my reservations about these phenomena because I have no direct knowledge of them, nor can I logically deduce their existence. On such matters I must, therefore, remain agnostic and silent. The Namgyal lamas graciously accept my skepticism (even if some of them may privately believe that I lack the skill needed to observe these subtle truths) and note approvingly that the Buddha taught us to base our views on observation and logic.

The Basic Principles of Science

We have seen how Buddhism shares a common ground with science because Buddhists are free to accept scientific facts as true and to reject ideas which cannot be falsified by direct observation or logical deduction. Moreover, we have seen how the Buddhist view of life is fundamentally empirical. Let us now examine what constitutes the empirical approach.

The hallmark of the empirical approach is that valid knowledge is based on an appeal to observation, experience, and reasoning rather than on an appeal to authority, tradition, or superstition. Experience is the foundation of the scientific method. We tend to think of scientific method in the stereotypical images of experts conducting experiments with sophisticated measuring devices and deducing empirical facts and predictions through complicated mathematical analysis. This is a caricature, however. Scientific method is broader than this. Scientific method is, basically, intelligent problem solving.[6] It is a precise, systematic, disciplined and *critical* inquiry into the nature of phenomena, in order to understand, manipulate, and control them in the service of human needs, desires, and interests—even if only in the interests of curiosity.

The standard scientific approach to solving problems involves a number of basic steps: (1) The first step is to define the problem. From the Buddhist point of view, the problem is suffering. (2) The second step is to become familiar with the problem, observe it, and collect data about it. (3) The third step is to interpret the data by drawing reasonable and logical inferences about it. (4) The fourth step is to test those inferences or hypotheses, by conducting further systematic observations, including manipulating independent variables, if possible. (5) The final step is to formulate a plan of action, based on the knowledge gained through observation and reasoning, which, if skillfully followed through, is most likely to satisfactorily resolve the problem.

The knowledge gained from such empirical investigations often leads to the development of more useful and interesting tools and techniques. John Dewey believed that science is based on a continuous process of action and reflection, action and reflection. The knowledge gained from empirical investigations often leads to the development of interesting and useful tools and techniques. This reciprocal relationship is characteristic of science and technology, and of theory and praxis. Science discovers knowledge which, when properly applied to human problems, produces effects which lead to new knowledge and, hopefully, to an increase in human happiness. In Buddhism, this same principle is known as *view, path,* and *fruition*.

The Science of Transforming the Mind

The Buddhist approach to the problem of suffering is orderly and methodical, like science. Buddhists deal with the problem of suffering in three stages called view, path, and fruition. The logic is the same as the logic of scientific problem solving. When confronted by a problem, whether a mechanical problem with our cars, a medical problem with our bodies, an emotional problem, or a spiritual crisis in our lives, the rational approach is, first to try to understand the nature of the problem and then, in the light of that understanding, to devise the best means to solve it. View is the understanding. Path is the means. Fruition is the solution.

Only someone who understands how a car works can fix it when it stalls. Only by understanding anatomy, physiology, and pathology can the physician apply the proper methods and techniques of treatment and restore health and well being. Similarly, only by understanding the nature of mind can the path to happiness be found. In Western terms, View and Path = Science and Technology = Theory and Praxis = Wisdom and Method. Fruition is the positive result of using *right view* and *right path.*

Right view is vital to the intelligent pursuit of happiness. We are not talking about right view in terms of one person's or one group's views being superior to another's. Right view refers to the harmony of the knowing mind with the nature of phenomena as they actually are. How we view the world shapes how we act and feel in it. If we view the cosmos as personally hostile towards us, or disappointing, or meaningless, we are bound to be haunted by an anxiety which lurks in the dark recesses of our minds and periodically erupts into consciousness with disabling intensity. If we view existence as benevolent or at least benign, it is easier for us to relax into it; we might be more tolerant, more grateful, more gracious, and less inclined to be thrown off balance into the pain of negative emotions.

How we view the world shapes how we feel and act in it. If our view of the world corresponds to reality—to the actual facts of life—we will be better prepared to roll gracefully with life's incessant changes. We might—in the words of the Serenity Prayer—muster the courage to change the things we can, cultivate the serenity to accept the things we cannot, and strive for the wisdom to know the difference. On the other hand, if our view of the world contradicts the nature of things, if we fight against reality, we will lose. Reality is stronger than we are. If we fight reality we are sure to fail, bound to suffer and likely to go mad.

The Buddhist concept of *view* uses the metaphors of vision to represent wisdom. The words "vision" and "wisdom" come from the same root as the Latin "video"—*videre*—meaning "to see." The sacred Hindu texts, the Vedas, are so named because they "see" the truth. Vision is associated with cognition. Seeing connotes knowing. A visionary is one who can see or know what others cannot see. Wisdom is seeing clearly the nature of existence and the human situation in it. The opposite of seeing is ignorance. The Sanskrit word for ignorance is *avidya*—literally, "without seeing," i.e. blind. The Tibetan word for ignorance is *ma-rig-pa*—literally, "unintelligence." In these metaphors, vision is equated with knowledge and blindness with ignorance.

View is also called *ground* because our perception of ourselves and our world is the foundation of our actions in the world. When Buddha was asked on what authority he based his views, he pointed to the ground, indicating with this gesture that existence is the authority for his views. Many statues of Buddha show him sitting in meditation with his finger pointing towards the earth.

View is our ultimate picture of ourselves and our world. Right view means "clear seeing," that is, seeing without the obscuration of our wishful and fearful thinking. If we see our world clearly and understand how we fit into it, then we can move through life more gracefully. Wrong view means seeing the world through the obscurations of our wishes, fears, false beliefs, and illusions. A wrong view of existence and our place in it is ignorance or avidya. Ignorance produces foolish and futile actions which are out of harmony with the facts and flow of life and create great consternation, commotion, and suffering for ourselves and others.[7]

Path is praxis, practice—what we actually do, how we actually live our everyday lives. *Path* is the "Way To Go."[8] The word *tao* is depicted in Chinese by a combination of two ideograms which mean "head" and "going"—the correct path of the head, or mind, through life, "the soul's journey towards god."[9] Seeing the tao means having right view and taking right path or action. Together they lead to *fruition*. Together, view and path are the science and technology of the mind, the method for finding relief from suffering and achieving some degree of clarity, equanimity, and enjoyment of life.

In Buddhism, the method for the observation of experience is meditation. Jamgon Kongtrul Rinpoche defined meditation as "becoming familiar with."[10] Meditation is a method for becoming familiar with the nature of mind and of phenomena. There are two basic types of Buddhist meditation. The first is called *shamatha*—a Sanskrit word which means "dwelling in peace." Shamatha meditation is also called "tranquility" or "stabilizing" meditation. Its function is to focus, stabilize, and quiet the mind. Normal mind suffers from hyper-mentation: the continuous buzzing confusion of the stream of consciousness which is energized by the biology of desire and fear. This hyper-mentation obscures the natural potential of the mind for clarity. Traditional shamatha practice helps quiet and focus the mind. Once the mind is quiet and able to concentrate, it is possible for it to examine itself to discover the truths of existence.

The second type of meditation is called *vipashyana*, which literally means "superior knowledge" or "special insight." This is an analytical form of meditation which enables us to see more clearly the workings of our mind and the way in which we cause our own sufferings and interfere with our potential for happiness. Although the core of Buddhist truth is accessible through study, reflection, observation, and reasoning, the full realization and personal integration of this knowledge requires extensive and rigorous training and discipline. When properly applied, the wisdom gained from the path of meditation leads to the development of compassion, virtue, and skillful means. The fruit of right view and right path is an increased measure of happiness for oneself and others.

CHAPTER FIVE

Who Is Buddha and What Did He Teach?

> And what, Malunkyaputta, have I explained? Misery, Malunkyaputta, have I explained; the origin of misery have I explained; the cessation of misery have I explained; and the path leading to the cessation of misery have I explained.
>
> —The Buddha, *The Teachings of the Compassionate Buddha*

We have noted that if the Buddhist or any other religious view is to be compatible with science, it must meet three requirements. First, it must accept all established scientific facts as true. Second, it must reject any view which is contradicted by science or is, in principle, not verifiable by empirical methods.[1] Third, it must use the methods of experience, observation, and logic to derive its view, rather than the appeal to authority, revelation, scripture, superstition, or arbitrary belief.

At the same time, such a religious view must satisfy the longings of the subject for a realistic, workable picture of the cosmos, and the subject's identity within it, which provides a meaningful and competent guide to life.

Can Buddhism meet these criteria? A good way to begin this inquiry is to reflect upon the life and character of the founder of Buddhism: Siddhartha Gautama, Shakyamuni Buddha. What kind of man was the historical Buddha? How is his life relevant to ours? What can we learn from him that might help us to address our own suffering and unhappiness?

We may well wonder about a man whom some regard as "the greatest human being who ever lived." In the West, only Jesus of Nazareth competes for this exalted reputation. Siddhartha Gautama lived twenty-five hundred years ago. He was born around 563 B.C. and died around 483 B.C. Few facts are known for certain about his life, and these have been embellished with miraculous legends and myths, as has been done with Jesus and other culture heroes. The culture hero symbolizes the aspirations of a people. He or she transcends the standard and the norm to solve a fundamental problem, realize a common dream, or represent a universal truth. Buddha and Jesus are both culture heroes who represent the truth and the transcendence of suffering, and whose lives are enshrined in myth and legend.

According to legend, Buddha, like Christ, was born miraculously. When Siddhartha's mother, Queen Mahamaya, was sixteen, she was overcome with a great sense of peace and dreamed that an elephant with six tusks entered her womb. When she was nine months and ten days pregnant, she stopped to rest in a vast forest and gave birth, while standing, to the baby Buddha, who emerged painlessly from her abdomen without the stain of blood or mucous.[2] The infant took seven steps in each of the four directions and then, pointing to the sky said, "In this universe, I have come to purify the confused mind of all living beings."[3] Many people believe that the Buddha could perform miracles at will, levitate, fly, and read minds. His disciples also believed that he was omniscient, that everything past, present, and future simultaneously was within the scope of his knowledge. When he died, it is said, streams of water came from the sky to extinguish his funeral pyre.[4]

Buddha never boasted or made a show of possessing superhuman powers. He would neither confirm nor deny that he had them. He taught that to use spiritual power for the sake of displaying power is destructive and bolsters the ego. He continuously insisted that he was a mortal being, not a god. Nevertheless, people want deities with magical powers. Many contemporary Buddhists attribute magical powers to Buddha and his successors. I have met several otherwise intelligent Americans who believe that lamas can fly! This seems to me to be childish hero worship. In my view, great spiritual leaders are mortal human beings, extraordinary human beings, but, nevertheless human, mortal, and fallible.

Freud thought that the idea of god is a projection of a frightened humanity's wish for a protective, benevolent parent.[5] The projection of divine power on to a human image creates a fictional personage at whose feet one can pray for help, for guidance, redemption, and salvation. People want to believe in magical beings because they believe that friendly magical powers can overcome the obstacles to their desires and make happiness possible; thus, the genie in the bottle who grants three wishes, the Excalibur sword which defeats all enemies, and the omnipotent god who answers prayers.

The worship of a divine human personage no doubt offers spiritual consolation to a suffering humanity, but it carries the disadvantage that the exalted person is thrown out of reach. How can one understand a god, or emulate one? It is therefore vital to see our gods in human terms, to see Buddha as what he claimed to be, an ordinary mortal, so we can identify with him, so we can understand his achievements from our own perspective, so we can visualize his accomplishments as possibilities in our own lives.

Stripped of miraculous legend and myth, Buddha was a mortal human with extraordinary qualities of intelligence and compassion, who was so saddened by human suffering that he devoted his life to learning its causes and cures and teaching what he learned for the benefit of others.

The historical Buddha was born Siddhartha Gautama near Kapilavastu, in North India, just south of Nepal. His father, Suddhodana, was a prince. The story is told that when Siddhartha was an infant his father consulted a seer who predicted that if the boy chose a secular life he would become a great king, and if he chose a spiritual life he would become a Buddha.

His father wanted his son to perpetuate the royal line. Worried that his son would leave home and become an itinerant monk, Suddhodana indulged Siddhartha in great luxuries and comforts, tempting him to a sensuous, secular life with all the diversions that only great wealth and power can obtain.

As an extra precaution, Suddhodana ordered that his heir should be shielded from the sight or knowledge of sickness, suffering, and death. Siddhartha was a beautiful boy, intelligent, athletic, and talented. He grew to manhood enjoying all the benefits and luxury that wealth and power can buy. As was customary, he married young, at the age of sixteen, and settled down to raise a family.

No one can be insulated forever from suffering, however. As he grew older, Siddhartha became restless and dissatisfied with the easy life, as inevitably happens to the idle rich. He longed to see the world beyond the gilded fences of his family compound. One day, when he was twenty-nine years old, Siddhartha asked a servant to take him around the town and its environs. What Siddhartha saw on these trips catalyzed his transformation into a Buddha. He saw "the four sights" that turned his mind inward. He saw a sick man lying in the street; an old man walking feebly with the aid of a cane; a dead man being cremated by the banks of the river; and a monk, meditating serenely.

Siddhartha was profoundly affected by the sight of sickness, sorrow, suffering, and death. He thought deeply about their meaning and longed to know their causes. He became intrigued by the wandering monks and yogis who talked about the meaning of life and sought understanding through meditation and yogic concentration. Yashodhara, Siddhartha's wife, had given birth to a beautiful baby boy, Rahula, but Siddhartha was not happy. He longed to fulfill his destiny and find the cause of suffering. At the age of twenty-nine, Siddhartha committed himself to "the great renunciation." Clandestinely, in the middle of the night, he abandoned his society, his family, his beautiful wife, and infant son to become a homeless, wandering ascetic.

For six years Siddhartha lived with the forest monks, studying yogic systems with various teachers, but he became disappointed with them one after the other. He encountered a group of monks in a forest practicing ascetic penance. Impressed by their sincerity and strenuous exertion, he joined them and practiced severe self-denial and self-mortification. Siddhartha became progressively weaker until, one day, when he was thirty-five years old, he could hardly pull himself out of the river in which he was bathing. Near death and no closer to enlightenment, he accepted food from a maiden. He had learned the limits of asceticism and self-denial, just as he had learned the limits of self-indulgence from his previous life.

Siddhartha sat in that place, under the *bodhi* tree (*ficus religiosa*), determined not to leave until he discovered the truth within himself. Through what Christians call "the dark night of the soul," challenged by confusion and the possibility of failure, humiliation, and death, he faced and defeated the temptations to return to a life of worldly success and pleasure. Gradually, his mind cleared. He was overcome by a feeling of inner peace and light. He gained insight into the causes and cures of human suffering. He had become enlightened. He had become a Buddha: "one who has awakened."

Buddha sat silently under the Bodhi tree for seven weeks, reluctant to reveal what he had learned for fear that people who had not earnestly and arduously sought the truth would not understand him, or would mock and reject him. A few of his old friends from his days of asceticism wandered by and marveled at his beauty and grace. Buddha glowed with the clear light of lovingkindness. He spoke to them simply, but with poetic elegance. The ascetics were so impressed by Buddha's teaching that they became his disciples. They urged Buddha to go to the Deer Park near Benares to give public discourses. In his first discourse, known as "The Turning of the Wheel of the Dharma," Buddha taught "the four noble truths."

Buddha taught his insights on the causes and cures of suffering for forty-five years in North India. Many people heard his teachings, and many became his disciples. After his death his disciples transmitted his teachings by word of mouth from generation to generation. Within just a few decades disputes about the teachings developed and divisions formed amongst his followers. Over the centuries, Buddhism spread from India, throughout Southeast Asia, China, Tibet, Korea, and Japan.

In 1950, the Chinese invaded Tibet, and in 1959 they violently suppressed a popular revolt. They repressed and nearly destroyed the monastery system, and did destroy the theocratic culture of Tibet. This led to the massive emigration of Tibetan lamas who spread across the globe like dandelion seeds carried by the spring breezes. Over the past thirty years Buddhist teachers in the West have grown in numbers and many Westerners have been guided by the Buddha's views. Let us now consider the basic Buddhist paradigm as it is taught in the four noble truths.

The Four Noble Truths

The Buddha repeated over and over again that the four noble truths are the foundation and nucleus of his teachings. All Buddhist wisdom is contained within them like the layers of an onion, each layer more subtle and more profound than the previous, leading to a central core of insight. "Monks," Buddha said, "by the fact of understanding as they really are, these four noble truths, a *Tathagata* is called an *Arhat,* a fully enlightened one."[6]

What are the four noble truths? When students and critics asked him exotic questions about the nature of the universe, the history of creation, the fate of the soul after death, and so on, Buddha declined to answer on the grounds that his answer would not be helpful to people seeking relief from their suffering. "I teach only this," he said,

"I teach the fact of suffering, the arising of suffering, the cessation of suffering, and the path to the cessation of suffering." These are the four noble truths.

Because of his compassion for sufferers, Buddha became known as the Great Physician, a physician of the spirit. Using the medical model as a metaphor for the four noble truths, the first noble truth describes the disease; the second noble truth tells of the cause of the disease; the third noble truth reveals the cure of the disease; and the fourth noble truth teaches the means of curing the disease.

One of the great metaphors of Buddhism is "The Three Jewels." The Three Jewels are the Buddha, the dharma, or teachings, and the *sangha*, or assembly of the followers of the dharma path. In the medical model of Buddhism, Buddha is the physician; the dharma, or teachings is the medicine; and the sangha, or community of Buddhist practitioners, is the nurse who administers the medicine.

The First Noble Truth

The first noble truth is the fact of suffering. At first, this may not seem to be a profound or esoteric truth. Sir M. Monier-Williams, a renowned British Indologist and Sanskrit scholar, once remarked that he marveled at how such a popular religion could be based on such a trivial fact.[7] It seems obvious to anyone with open eyes. Suffering is at the top of the news, the topic of our gossip, and the constant theme of our private thoughts. The fact is that suffering is an integral part of our lives. We are fascinated by suffering because we have suffered in the past and know we will suffer again, but we don't know how or when. We are curious to know whether others bear their suffering bravely or poorly. At the same time, we dread suffering, and make strenuous efforts to avoid, deny, and repress it.

But to think, as Monier-Williams did, that the fact of suffering is trivial is to convert its central importance into a secret. We fail to see our suffering clearly because we try to put it out of mind. The repression of suffering renders us incapable of working intelligently with it. If we are not willing to experience our suffering with awareness, we will not be able to understand it and will not learn how to reduce it where we can, and to live with it where we must. The first noble truth brings the fact of suffering to the center of awareness so we can look at it with open eyes and learn about the vital role it plays in our mental life. This "eye-opener" is the beginning of wisdom.[8]

The Second Noble Truth

The second noble truth teaches about the causes of suffering. The Sanskrit word for the cause of suffering is *tanha*—which literally means "thirst." Tanha refers to our selfish cravings, desires, and attachments. The key word is *selfish*. The essence of tanha is selfishness. From the Buddhist point of view, tanha is the culprit behind human tragedy and evil. Selfish desires are the source of the suffering we humans impose on ourselves and others. This is an empirical fact which is accessible to each of us to confirm or falsify for ourselves. But to do so, we must have eyes that see.

Tanha has three aspects, the previously mentioned three poisons: desire, aversion, and ignorance. Of the three, desire and aversion are an antithetical pair. Our selfish cravings are bipolar. In one aspect, we want to have something, to bring it closer, possess it, control it, use it, enjoy it. We want good health, loving friends, a supportive family, security, self-esteem, power, money, and the many goods that money can buy.

In its opposite aspect tanha is aversion. We want to get rid of something, push it away, out of sight and out of mind. We fear that our loved ones may fall ill and die. We abhor poverty, dislike our bills, hate our enemies and more. Tanha is the sum of both our cravings, ambitions, and attachments; and of our aversions, hatreds, and avoidances.

Ignorance is our refusal or failure to see the truth about ourselves, our lives, and our situation and, instead, to project our wishes and fears onto our perceptions of other people and our world. It is a state of mind born of the futile wish for permanence and immortality. It is the hopeful attribution to oneself of an eternal and substantial soul. Ignorance is the root cause of suffering because it promotes or fails to adequately temper our passions and our aggressions.

The Third Noble Truth

The third noble truth teaches that our suffering can be relieved or transcended. What is required is letting go of our selfish cravings and hatreds. This insight is at the heart of esoteric wisdom. It is esoteric, to repeat, not because it is inaccessible or complex, but because we refuse to accept it and, hence, hide it from ourselves. In this sense, esoteric means self-secret, a secret we keep from ourselves because it is counterintuitive. It requires us to confront one of the most painful paradoxes of our existence: that our selfish strivings for personal happiness through our Happiness Projects are the causes of our suffering. Whatever we think will make us happy is what we will suffer from. If we think money will make us happy, our worst problems will be money problems. If we think relationships will make us happy, we will suffer from relationship problems. If we think a career will make us happy, our most worrisome problems will center on our jobs.

The tragic paradox of our lives is that we suffer from the wrong-headed ways in which we pursue happiness. We are like addicts who suffer because we cannot stand being deprived of what we want and can never get enough of it. Much of the pain we inflict on ourselves and others comes from the obstinate, relentless, self-centered pursuit of what we think will make us happy—sensuous pleasure, success, power, fame, money, relationships, and so on. What a dirty trick! No wonder the Greeks thought the gods were laughing at them.

The third noble truth teaches that true happiness is the product not of the satisfaction of desire but of an inner transformation, a transfiguration of consciousness. This does not mean that we must give up all our desires. It means that happiness is the fruit of the awareness and acceptance of the nature of mind, self, and phenomena. True happiness comes from understanding and relaxing into existence. This requires calming our selves down and disciplining our thoughts, words, and deeds. Easy to say and difficult to do; but necessary to say and understand before it can be done.

The Fourth Noble Truth

The fourth noble truth is a practical guide for living. It delineates the thoughts, words, and actions—what Buddhists call the path—which minimizes suffering and maximizes happiness. The path is a system of ethics; more than that, it is a program for moral living.

From this point of view, ethics are not a fixed list of rights and wrongs, arbitrarily handed down by a high authority which enforces its laws with the punishment of pain and the reward of heavenly bliss. Ethics are an intelligent, practical guideline for avoiding suffering and achieving happiness here and now on earth.

The fourth noble truth consists of the "eightfold path," *marga* in Sanskrit, which divides into three branches: wisdom, virtue, and mental discipline. Wisdom is view, virtue and mental discipline are path.

WISDOM GROUP
1. Right Understanding
2. Right Thought

VIRTUE GROUP
3. Right Speech
4. Right Conduct
5. Right Livelihood

MENTAL DISCIPLINE GROUP
6. Right Effort
7. Right Concentration
8. Right Meditation

The four noble truths can also be divided into two groups. The first two truths deal with the negativities of mind. Christians call them "sins"; Buddhists call them *kleshas*—impurities, defilements, or obscurations. The first noble truth deals with the various kinds of sufferings to which we humans are vulnerable. The second noble truth deals with the causes of suffering. Together, these two are the disease and the cause of the disease—the infection and the bacteria.

The second pair of truths deals with cleansing, healing, and purifying—with pulling ourselves out of the dark pit of our self-imposed pain and negativity. The third noble truth describes spiritual well-being: inner peace, clarity, and kindness. The fourth noble truth teaches the methods for achieving spiritual well-being: the eightfold path. Woven together, these two truths are the formula for transforming vinegar into honey.

Let us now take a closer look at the first and second noble truths, in order to shed light on the hidden causes of the suffering and negativities we impose on ourselves and others.

CHAPTER SIX

The First Noble Truth: Suffering and the Three Facts of Existence

> And what, friends, is the noble truth of suffering? Birth is suffering; ageing is suffering; death is suffering; sorrow, lamentation, pain, grief, and despair are suffering; not to obtain what one wants is suffering; in short, the five aggregates affected by clinging are suffering.
>
> —The Buddha

The Buddhist view of suffering is dramatically different from the official Western view. The generally accepted wisdom of modern psychology and psychiatry is that psychological suffering is caused by specific, external, traumatic factors such as loss, abuse, neglect, unjust or inhumane social conditions, failure, misfortune, or by biochemical imbalances, such as neurotransmitter deficiencies.

This view, forged on the template of value-free science, holds that individuals are not responsible for their mental suffering. Possible exceptions are cases where there are obvious connections between an individual's actions and his or her subsequent suffering, such as a smoker who develops lung cancer or someone who is caught and legally punished for a crime. Otherwise, the politically correct assumption today is that persistent, painful, or disabling emotions, including depression, anxiety, and anger, are symptoms of mental illness for which the individual is not to blame and, therefore, is not responsible.

The Buddhist point of view, by contrast, holds that the causes of suffering are rooted in the mind. Suffering is experienced through the mind and processed by the mind. The quality of suffering depends upon the way the individual responds to the events of life. Our response to the events of our lives, our *response-ability*, depends upon mental factors, for example, upon our sense of entitlement and expectations, as well as upon our perception of the nature of existence and our relationship to existence. It also depends upon our self-discipline, patience, perseverance, and other virtues or, contrarily, upon our selfishness, demandingness, undisciplined reactivity, laziness, and tendency to blame others.

While Buddhists are free and willing to accept all scientific facts as true, most psychiatrists are not willing to accept or in some cases even consider the Buddhist view that the causes of suffering lie in the mind. A well-known psychiatrist recently wrote that any member of his profession who believes that negative emotions such as anxiety, depression, and anger are caused by the mind, should be an outcast, and would not be welcome at the same table with most modern psychiatrists![1]

At the bottom of this conflict is the dialectic between the objective and subjective points of view. Modern scientific psychiatry and psychology are the champions of the objective position: that the human individual should be studied and understood basically the same way as a physical object, in the sense that behavior is not explained by moral-purposive considerations, but rather by external causal factors. They do not recognize the traditional religious view that intentions and purposes are also causes of our actions, that they have a moral quality, and that they have the consequences of increased happiness or suffering.

Buddhists are free to accept the scientific facts of the objective view, but we also regard subjects as moral agents whose views, perceptions, desires, aversions, lapses, intentions, choices, and actions create the conditions for their happiness and suffering. This is the "law of karma" which seems hidden from the scientists and objectivists.

From the Buddhist point of view, the critical cause of suffering, unhappiness, and the various painful and disabling emotions, is the individual's view of him- or herself and of the facts of existence. Generally speaking, the individual who is aware of and has accepted and integrated these facts will respond more gracefully to misfortune than one who ignores or represses them. To the degree that an individual ignores or rejects the facts of life, he or she will suffer more intensely.

To such an individual the facts of existence are the esoteric knowledge which they lack, and in many cases, which they seek. From the Buddhist point of view, therefore, to understand and heal our suffering requires that we first consider the basic facts of existence.

The Three Marks of Existence

In the Buddhist view, existence has three fundamental qualities which are known as "the three marks of existence." They are marks in the sense of being characteristics, but also in the sense of being stains or blemishes. They are considered stains because the failure to understand them and work realistically with them are the chief obstacles to inner peace and happiness. Hence, they are also called "the three stains of existence." They are suffering (*duhkha*), impermanence or change (*anitya*), and emptiness or selflessness (*anatman*).

Suffering—Duhkha

Suffering is a fact of life because all conscious beings suffer. All conscious beings suffer because they are all born and are subject to changes such as aging, sickness, and death. This is an empirical fact which can be falsified by finding conscious creatures who have not suffered at birth, during the changes of life, or at death. Lacking any significant falsifying examples we must accept the fact that suffering is an intrinsic, albeit inconstant, fact of life.

If we accept suffering as a universal fact, then we must look into the meaning of it. The significance and implications of suffering are neither as obvious nor as simple as they may at first appear. Suffering is an ominous and haunting presence in all our lives. Each of us has suffered in the past, many of us are suffering now, and all of us know in our hearts that we will suffer again in the future. Suffering is inevitable, but we do not know when or how it will be inflicted on us. We are frightened by the prospect of it, yet we instinctively try to forget it, avoid it, and cover it up; and we are uncomfortable with the suffering of others. We will entertain suffering only when it is entertaining—in myths, stories, plays, soap operas, and films, where we can experience it vicariously and safely, as if we are inoculating ourselves against the inevitable future pain.

The fact of suffering is a truth we hide from ourselves. But the awareness of suffering can be only half repressed. We cannot repress it well enough so it ceases to nag us, for it is the essence of our worries. Yet we repress it enough so we cannot see it clearly. As a result we often fail to appreciate how much effort and ingenuity we devote to the avoidance of it, and how it towers as a commanding presence at the center of our lives.

One of Freud's fundamental discoveries was that vast mental energy is devoted to the repression of suffering.[2] The psychological mechanisms of defense, which are the essence of our neuroses, are defenses against anxiety, which is an excruciating form of suffering.[3] Ernest Becker maintained that the denial of the painful fact of death is the chief mechanism through which the personality is formed.[4] Personality and character are organized around what Becker calls "immortality vehicles," patterns of belief and habit which fortify the individual's illusory sense of security and hope for eternal happiness. Although he did not live long enough to become aware of it, Becker's ideas are consistent with the Buddhist view.[5] The denial of death is one of the most vital mechanisms through which we humans attempt to avoid and evade suffering.

In the Buddhist view, the basic cause of suffering is ignorance, *avidya*, literally, "the failure to see." The ego is the locus of our ignorance. We think of the ego as the locus of our knowledge, and indeed it is regarded as the locus of our logical faculties, but the ego itself is formed out of ignorance, in the sense that it is built upon a view of itself and the world which denies, represses, or distorts the facts of existence, especially the facts of suffering and death. The denial and distortion of reality is embodied in the psychological mechanisms of defense, which are universally found in human beings in varying degrees. The mechanisms of defense are all falsifications of reality. They are lies we tell ourselves. Denial, for example, is the rejection of unpleasant or unacceptable facts. Repression puts these facts out of consciousness. Rationalization gives acceptable justifications for otherwise unacceptable motivations or actions. Projection is the attribution to someone else of one's own perceptions, wishes, or fears. Reaction formation is acting the opposite of how we feel.

The falsification of reality is also manifest in our pride, in our overestimation of our importance and power, which is sometimes mistaken for high self-esteem. The denial of death is manifested in our preoccupations with the distant future, with how we will "end up," and in wishful religious beliefs such as personal salvation or reincarnation, immortality, and heaven.

The denial of the facts of existence, including the fact of death, is motivated by the instinct for survival which is inherent in all life. In humans, the instinct for survival is sublimated into the selfish desires for security, power, and immortality. We want to live forever, so we think we can. The instinct for survival, in all its forms, is frustrated by the two other facts of existence, particularly the fact of change or impermanence. The fact of change creates a tension between the perceived stability of the present and the uncertainty of the future. This tension motivates the individual to undertake often futile, and therefore painful efforts to resist change. Ultimately, however, and tragically, the fact of impermanence frustrates the individual's future happiness projects, as well as the wish and struggle to survive and transcend death.

The Pain of Pain—Duhkha Duhkhata

Each of the three marks of existence is associated with its own form of suffering. The suffering associated with suffering is called *duhkha duhkhata*. It reflects the fact that there are two primary forms of suffering which we all can observe for ourselves: the suffering intrinsic to conscious life, and the suffering caused by the attempts to avoid and evade it. The suffering which we cause with our attempts to avoid and evade pain is the "pain of pain" (*duhkha duhkhata*).

In this interpretation, *duhkha duhkhata* is the pain that comes from trying to avoid pain. It is the continuous struggle to deny, repress, and avoid suffering. The undisciplined mind is constantly chewing the cud of past pleasures and regretting and wishing to undo past sufferings. And it is constantly anticipating future happiness and dreading future suffering. The fear of future suffering is the essence of our worries and the root of our anxieties.

A great deal of confusion exists about the difference between fear and anxiety. Many people claim that fears are realistic and anxieties are unrealistic or imagined. This is only a half truth which hides the full truth. The difference is that fear is oriented towards the present. We feel fear in the presence of a definite threat, such as fire, a predator, or a mugger. *Fear* is a response to present danger. *Anxiety* is the fear of future danger. Our minds are constantly scanning the future for problems, and we can find them in abundance. There are a thousand ways for things to go wrong and only a few ways for them to go right. Sometimes we are aware of the future danger we are afraid of. We may be thinking of taking an initiative and be afraid of failure or rejection. At other times, we may be anxious but cannot identify the reason for it. So-called "free floating anxiety" is the fear of future danger which intuition correctly assumes is inevitable, without our being aware of specifically what future danger we are afraid of.

The similarity between fear and anxiety is in their physiology. The body cannot tell the difference between the fear of a present danger and the fear of a future danger. The body responds the same way, with the "fight-flight" reaction. So the physiology is the same. The best way to understand the difference between fear and anxiety is to observe and reflect upon our fears of perceived present danger and our anxieties about imagined or possible future dangers.

Suffering often takes the subtle form of attempting to resist change. For example, we know we are destined to grow old and die. We all know that no one stays young and beautiful forever. We know for certain that our health inevitably will be consumed by time. As a result, we engage in desperate searches for the fountain of youth, for the elixir of health, for the secret of eternal life, beauty, and happiness. The search for eternal life is an effort to escape the suffering of aging, illness, and death.

The reality of our inevitable aging, illness, and death is especially painful to winners, to people who have it all, the rich and famous, the young and the beautiful. They must struggle to hold on to their power, wealth, beauty, and fame. Fame, as we know, is fleeting. And power is the most fragile possession of all, for it must be guarded against everyone—not only our enemies, but also our friends and family. Youthful beauty fades, and wealth cannot be taken beyond the grave.

The pain of pain, *duhkha duhkhata*, is the pain of maintaining, preserving, and defending our good fortune. If we are successful we must continuously struggle to hold on to our gains. The Tibetans have a saying: "If you have a camel, your troubles are as big as a camel." A poor man has to worry only about himself and his family. A rich man has these worries but also worries about his wealth, about how to hold on to it and multiply it. We all struggle to defend what we have. We defend our things, our family, our friends, our reputations, and our very identities, as in so-called nationalistic wars which are actually wars for the preservation and expansion of ethnic identity.

The successful businessman must keep the customers coming, order new merchandise without overstocking, and pay the bills on time. We must all change the oil in our cars, repair our leaking roof before it rots, and faithfully go for our annual physicals. No one ever "makes it" forever. No one lives happily ever after. Life is a struggle to the death for everyone.

We create our own pain by trying to avoid future pain by maintaining, preserving, and defending all that we have, all that we have achieved, all that we are attached to. We search for permanence, stability, and security in our relationships, in our possessions, in our social traditions, in our national identities, and in our religions. All of these are brick and mortar of our identity—our sense of who we think we are. Indeed, identity itself is a fictional construct of permanence which we build in the futile hope of resisting and containing the relentless river of change.

The fact of suffering is the first noble truth because it is a basic fact of life. It is first also because the awareness of and acceptance of the fact of suffering is the first step on the spiritual path, as it was for Shakyamuni Buddha. Without suffering, wisdom would be neither necessary nor likely to be achieved. This is why there are few wise young people. Without suffering there is no reason to seek the truth or search for salvation. In the Judeo-Christian tradition suffering is the fire that purifies. It is the experience which is necessary to turn the mind inward towards the understanding of self and its relationship to the world.

For this reason Buddhists honor suffering. Suffering is viewed as the manure which fertilizes the fruit of wisdom, just as the farmer spreads manure to fertilize his crop. The manure stinks. It is ugly, smelly stuff. But it brings the precious nutrients to the soil from which the crop of wisdom can be harvested.

Impermanence and Change—Anitya

The fact that everything is impermanent is a painful fact of existence. Impermanence is painful because we want the good things of life to last. We long for stability and safety. We want to survive, prosper, and live on. We don't want to lose people or things that are important to us. Swimming in a river of change we desperately yearn for something enduring to hang on to. Our egos, our sense of self, depend upon fixed reference points which locate us in relation to others, in relation to nature, and in relation to eternity.

Yet, all is flux. The Greek philosopher Heraclitus (c. 500 B.C.), roughly a contemporary of the Buddha, compared existence to a river with his famous aphorism, "It is not possible to step twice into the same river."[6] A river may seem to us to be an enduring structure. It may run the same course for a thousand years. It may seem so stable that we use it for boundary lines between neighbors, states, and nations. The flowing river seems eternal: "Ol' man river, he jus' keeps rollin' along." But the permanence of the river is an illusion. Rivers are constantly changing, as dwellers along the Mississippi well know. A river is not the same from one moment to the next. Step into a river once, step into a river twice. The second step is not into the same river. The water that wets us the first time has flowed on to merge with the ocean. The second step is into different water, a different river. A river is pure movement, pure change, pure dance. When the water stops flowing, the river ceases to exist.

The experience of life is like a river, constantly changing. Life is a continuous flow of phenomena—sensations, perceptions, feelings, and thoughts. The flow of life's events is like the current of a river: peaceful and engaging at times, dizzyingly rapid at spots, boringly slow in other places, but flowing on and on.

We cannot experience the same historical moment twice. One can discern patterns in history, of course. But historical patterns are not objective facts. They are the projections of minds which ignore differences for the sake of highlighting similarities. The sun comes up every day, but every day is a new day. Patterns of history depend upon our desire to locate fixed reference points, even if they are only periodic. The human mind thirsts for patterns, for general principles, universal laws, historical cycles. Patterns are fictions, however, analogous to the Big Dipper. The stars of the Big Dipper have no special relation to each other except the one made by the observer who draws the line which connects them.

It may seem that history repeats itself, but this is *déjà vu*. Déjà vu is the illusion of experiencing the same moment twice. It is an illusion because there is a vital difference between the two moments if only by virtue of their succession. The first moment was not a déjà vu. The second moment is. So the second moment is quite different from the first, although they seem identical. Indeed, the unique strangeness of the déjà vu lies precisely in the impression of having stepped twice into the same river of time. Every moment of existence, however, every moment of life, is unique. As the Buddhist inspired poet Rilke wrote:

> Once for each thing.
> Just once; no more.
> And we too, just once.[7]

The Pain of Change—Viparinama Duhkhata

After winning a championship football game, the coach was depressed. As he watched the winning field goal split the uprights he raised his hands in the joy of victory. "It was the greatest feeling in the world," he said later in the locker room, "because it was such a great feeling and you wish it could last forever...but it's gone so fast. The next thing, you're in the dressing room...you're up there accepting the trophy, and it's all over. All of that is over."[8]

A moment of triumph lasts only a moment. Soon it is history, swept up in the historical tide of ceaselessly changing phenomena. Change is the constant factor in life. The changes of life never cease. Growing up is constant metamorphosis and discovery. The religious ritual of confirmation, a girl's first menstrual period, and the fraternity drinking marathon are all rites of initiation which mark the transition from child to adult. Marriage is a drastic change! Sickness is a change from health and vigor to pain and weakness. Growing old is a traumatic change, enough to cause mid-life crises from age forty on. Death is the most dramatic and frightening change of all, painful to the dying who must let go of life and all that is dear, and painful to the bereaved who have lost someone they love.

Life begins with change—from the fertilization of the ovum to the rapid growth of the embryo to the expulsion of the fetus from the womb. The crisis of middle age is nothing special. There is a crisis at every age and every change of life. Buddha taught that life is change and that change is stressful and painful. "Where there is change, there is suffering," he said.

The pain of birth is the archetype of the pain of life. This is the basic premise of the psychology of Otto Rank.[9] In the Judeo-Christian tradition the pain of "the Fall" is a metaphor of the pain of life. In the myth of Genesis God punishes Adam and Eve for their "original sin" by expelling them from paradise and cursing the woman with the pain of birth and the man with the pain of toil. The expulsion from Eden is the primordial change, the change which begins history. It is the change from innocence to sin, from permanence to impermanence, from the eternal rock of changeless paradise to the flowing river of historical time.

Change is stressful and painful because every change is a death and a rebirth. Change means the end of something old and familiar and the beginning of something new and strange. The pain of change does not come from the change itself, however. It comes from resisting change. Change is painful because we cling to what is familiar but gone, and we resist accepting what is new and unknown.

Change is disorienting because we orient ourselves in relation to fixed reference points—durable objects, regular patterns, repetitions, habits, laws, and eternal truths. We cling to these reference points like a child clinging to a security blanket. We cloak ourselves in them like king's robes. We identify with them and derive our identity from them.

When we are threatened by the loss of our reference points we become confused, bewildered, and anxious. Anxiety is regarded by modern psychiatry as a primary symptom of mental illness. As we have noted, anxiety is the fear of dangerous change. The tons of Valium and other tranquilizers that are dispensed for anxiety are the official medical remedy for the pain of change. When it is mild it is the pain of our nagging worries. When it is more severe it is our tension and neurotic anxiety. At its most intense it is like a bad LSD trip: a dizzying nightmare of groundlessness, of nothing to cling to, of falling through space into a black hole. Panic!

We are terrified of change, and so we try to step into the same river again and again, to repeat the same experience, to go back to the same moment in time. Sigmund Freud often wondered about the motivation behind the repetition compulsion—the tendency to perseverate, or repeat, the same mannerism, gesture, habit, word, or game, like a child who wants to play hide and seek over and over again. Or like the outfielder who compulsively touches second base on his way in to bat. Or like each of us repeating our daily routines and habitual patterns.

Freud viewed the repetition compulsion, which is the essence of obsessive-compulsive neurosis, as an effort to master anxiety. Some obsessive people tend to play out painful life situations over and over again with the hope of finding a new way of mastering the pain. The repetition compulsion can also be a psychological defense against the anxiety of change, impermanence, and loss. The obsessive compulsive may be trying to resist change by repeating the same patterns of thought, speech, and behavior over and over again.

The child playing hide and seek is trying to master the anxiety that the parent will go away and not return. The outfielder who touched second base and got a hit at his next at-bat wants to repeat the circumstances hoping to get a hit again. Each of us wants to preserve and protect the stable reference points of our lives because they create the illusion of a solid, continuous, unchanging island of permanence in the midst of the ceaseless river of changes. But clinging to our fictional walls of permanence, our illusory reference points, inevitably leads to frustration and suffering because everyone and everything ultimately disappears in the relentless tide of change.[10]

The fact of change may at first seem very gloomy and pessimistic. But it too has a bright side. It is both bad news and good news. The bad news is that change makes everything impermanent, unstable, and uncertain. My patients often complain of feeling insecure. Sometimes their anxiety has been conditioned by severely traumatic events, such as an inconstant or abusive parent. On the other hand, people try to make life more secure than is possible. I tell people that it is not possible for anyone to feel totally secure because life is uncertain. They often feel reassured when I tell them that their feeling of insecurity is based on the insecurity of life itself. How can anyone feel totally secure when no one knows what the future holds except for the certainty of suffering and death? We are all insecure, to varying degrees. The problem is not our feelings of insecurity themselves, but how we accept the fact of insecurity and skillfully work with it. The secure person is one who accepts insecurity. The insecure person futilely grasps for security in life's river of impermanence.

The good news is that change is a breath of fresh air. Our fixed, stable reference points are also our chains. We are imprisoned by them. We are tied to our security blankets, bound up and suffocated by them. They are our bondage and our unfreedom. Permanence can be constricting and boring. Indeed, boredom is the pain of sameness which seeks relief through change.

By itself, change is neither negative nor positive; or, it is both negative and positive. It is both a loss and a gain, depending on whether we look at the glass as half empty or half full. If every moment of life is unique, then every moment is fresh and new, even the moment of death. Living in the flow of change means constant death and renewal, continuously being born again and again, into the midst of an awesome and magical creation.

The Dance of Emptiness—Anatman

If nothing endures unchanged, then there can be no *uhrstoff*, no fundamental world-substance. There can be no world-matter or world-mind which has existed as an independent entity from the beginning of time. A basic substance is something which does not change. It is complete, self-sufficient, enduring, and eternally true to itself. If all is change, then there can be no basic stuff or essence of which the universe is made.

In the Buddhist view, neither matter nor mind are real in the sense that neither is an irreducible, permanent substance. The Buddhist view is that the physical world is empty of true substance. This does not mean that nothing exists. Things exist, but not from their own side.

They exist as the result of our projection of *thingness* onto them. This also does not mean there is no basis for our attributions of thingness. *Samsara* consists of a flux of appearances, combinations of interdependent particles which are constantly in flux, constantly rearranging, constantly arising and decaying. This state of insubstantiality is called "emptiness," or "non-self" (*anatman*). The denial or failure to see that phenomena are empty of true substance, and the projection of substance and soul onto phenomena, is ignorance.

Emptiness refers to the fact that the world is not "solid," as it appears to our senses. This view is compatible with modern science. When examined scientifically, the material world appears as patterns of energy in movement. A piece of iron, for example, seems like a solid mass, but in scientific reality iron is a pattern of protons, neutrons, and electrons in homeostatic motion. Even the protons, neutrons, and electrons are forms of energy. Nothing is solid, enduring, or transcendent. Everything is apparent, transient, and immanent.

Emptiness is a like a dance. The "dancer" has no independent identity. The dancer's identity derives from the dance. When the dance stops, the dancer ceases to exist. At the same time, the dance also has no solid, independent existence. Yet it is not a complete illusion or fabrication. There is a basis for the perception of it. It is energy in motion which, in its continuous flux and change, defines the reality of the dancer. The dance is like a river, a constant flow of energy, of phenomenal appearances and disappearances. Buddhists call this dance of emptiness *samsara*. The word "samsara" means something like "perpetual wandering."[11]

In the Buddhist view, everything in the world—every object, entity, and person—is empty of an essential substance which makes it what it is. Everything is composed of combinations of constituents which, together, form the phenomenon. When the constituents disintegrate, when they decompose, the compound object disappears.

A table, for example, looks like a definite, independent entity. What is more solid than the oak table in the dining room around which the family gathers for dinner? In reality, however, the dining room table is not a solid object. It is a compound object, a fiction, a product of the human mind. Tables exist only because humans use tables. Tables are objects we use to eat on, write on, put things on. My dog has no concept of a table. She sits on the table but eats on the floor. For her, the table is a chair and the floor is a table. Tables are the products of human intentions and the human imagination.

A table is the name of a compound object, a combination of combinations. We think tables are solid because they have names. Actually, if we separate the legs from the top, we no longer have a table, we have a pile of wood. All the parts are there, but the table is not. If we burn the wood, the table turns into fire and smoke which could be further reduced to atoms of hydrogen, carbon, oxygen, and so forth. These atoms, in turn, are composed of protons, neutrons, and electrons which, in an atom smasher, would decompose into subatomic particles whose existence is known only to the physicist through the streaks and spots on photographic plates.

In his teachings on emptiness, the Dalai Lama likes to say that there is no flower in the flower. Take a daisy and pull its petals off, pull the stamens and pistils off, separate the stem from the leaves: where then is the daisy? All the parts are there, but there is no daisy. There is no daisy in the daisy. It is only the perceived unity of a combination of interdependent flower parts.

The same is true for self. In the Buddhist view, there is no self in the self. In his meditations Buddha looked deeply into himself, searching for the core of his being. He could not find it. He could not find any identifiable, substantial, enduring core of self. He found only a series of components which, in dynamic relation to each other, constitute the changing, impermanent, empty flow of appearances onto which the holographic image of self is projected. Like the flower, there is no self in the self. Self and phenomena are empty.

It is a mistake to think of emptiness as a vacuum. This idea is a product of ordinary mind which perceives in terms of antithetical meanings. Ordinary or dualistic mind conceptualizes through contrast, in terms of antithetical qualities such as you and I, life and death, good and evil, up and down, right and left, and so on. From this point of view emptiness is perceived as the absence of phenomena. This conception of emptiness is distorted by the very process of conceptualization.

In the illusory images of dualistic mind, emptiness and phenomena are antithetical qualities. In contrast to phenomena, emptiness is thought to have no qualities, no internal distinctions. In this sense, it is regarded as whole and pure. The word "holy" comes from this concept of an entity which is whole, i.e., undivided and pure, i.e., without negative qualities. This concept of emptiness is also called the "void" or the "one." Void and one are identical. Neither can be known. The "one" cannot distinguish itself, for then it would become two—subject and object—the knower and the known.[12] From this mistaken point of view, the phenomenal world is full and real, and voidness and emptiness are nullities.

This is a misconception of the Buddhist view of emptiness, however. Emptiness is a not an ontologically negative state. It is not a vacuum, a deprivation, or a lack. On the contrary, emptiness is a plenum, a fullness, the fertile source and container in which all phenomena arise and decay, emerge and disappear. Emptiness is an epistemologically false state, however. It refers to the falseness of the attribution of substance to phenomena and the falseness of the attribution of substance to self. Emptiness is a lack only in the sense that phenomena lack essential substance.

With some reflection, it will be evident that emptiness itself has no true qualities and no essential defilements. It is simply the lack of true substance inherent in phenomena from their own side. In the sense that it is whole, pure, permanent, and that from which all things emerge and return, emptiness is the Buddhist concept of the sacred and is comparable to the Judeo-Christian God who is also whole, pure, eternal, and the source and destiny of all things. That is what Buddha meant when he told his disciple, Sariputra, in *The Heart Sutra*, "Form is emptiness and emptiness is form."[13] The phenomenal world is emptiness masquerading as form, a dance without a dancer.

The Pain of Emptiness—Samskara Duhkhata

Most people cannot tolerate the thought that they will one day die and disappear. Death is perceived as nothingness and nothingness is experienced as the negation of self. Self strives to survive with the desperate energy of life, seeking to substantiate itself, protect itself, expand and perpetuate itself.

The constant effort of ego, dimly aware of its own ineffability, is to create a solid self out of no-self, as if something could be created out of nothing. The primary goal of ego is to create, maintain, and perpetuate the self forever. In the Buddhist view, the illusion of self-substantiality, the subsequent self-grasping, and the self's selfish striving to substantiate itself are the greatest causes of the suffering we humans inflict on ourselves and others.

Otto Rank and Ernest Becker are among the few Westerners who have realized that the desire to deny and avoid the negation of the ego by the nothingness of death, and the antithetical quest for substantiality through the pursuit of power and immortality, are the two primary motivations of the ego. These twin desires are the foundation stones of character and personality and the breeding grounds of our negative emotions and our neuroses.

The desire to assert and protect one's identity, one's property, one's flag, and one's pride, the desire to assert and perpetuate our meanings forever, is the main source of aggression, violence, and war. The enemy, the mark, the opponent is the "not me," the destruction, defeat, and domination of whom, by antithetical contrast, affirms and celebrates one's self. This is the function of the scapegoat.

The Jews were Hitler's scapegoat. Indeed, the Jews were Europe's scapegoat for centuries. As clans and tribes coalesced into ethnic groups and ethnic groups into nation states, the heterogeneous collective required a scapegoat to seal their common identity. This was achieved by means of the creation of a common enemy, a common "not-me." The Aryan was defined in terms of the Jew as a "not-Jew." Hitler himself was far from the tall, blond Aryan ideal he so admired. But he was not a Jew, or so he asserted, and through that assertion identified himself as an Aryan, indeed, the Führer of the Aryan nation.

In Yugoslavia, Tito amalgamated Christian and Muslim Serbs, Bosnians, and Croats into a single nation in the fight against Hitler. Hitler was Tito's scapegoat. As these groups lived together on the same streets, in the same neighborhoods, in the same villages, in the same regions, as they mixed together in the marketplaces, their young fell in love and intermarried and their ethnic identities became diffused. After Hitler was defeated and Tito died the union began to disintegrate. The ethnic groups of Yugoslavia turned against each other, making scapegoats of each other in order to reaffirm their ethnic identities, particularly Christians and Muslims. Through conflict with the ethnic "not-me" ethnic identity is antithetically reaffirmed. So-called "wars of ethnic nationalism" are actually wars of "ethnic identity," of insubstantial selves struggling to establish their identity through separation and conflict with other identities. One might say, cynically but truly, that the hidden psychological motivation of the ethnic wars in the former Yugoslavia is to prevent Christians and Muslims from making love.

Freud was puzzled by what he called "the narcissism of minor differences." He was amazed that people with minor differences would act so selfishly and aggressively towards each other. The reason is that self and identity, having no substantial basis, can be established only antithetically, by contrast to an other "not-me." This is the basis of the old Arab aphorism, "I will fight my brother until my cousin fights my brother, and then I will fight with my brother against my cousin until the neighbor fights with my cousin, and then I will fight with my cousin against the neighbor until foreigners attack my neighbor, and then I will fight with my neighbor against the foreign invader." Self is an algorithm of identities. Insubstantial self, with no inherent, essential identity of its own can establish its own identity only antithetically, in relation to and in opposition to others. This totem-pole pattern of identity with and differentiation from others is the basis upon which self signifies itself to itself.

Since emptiness is the absence of fundamental, enduring substances, physical or mental, it may seem to present a pessimistic and gloomy view of the world. If there is no fundamental substance or being, then there are no substantial reference points, nothing to hang on to. But emptiness, too, has a positive side. If we reflect upon emptiness, it becomes evident that if phenomena were definite, enduring, self-sufficient, and complete substances, nothing could interact with or affect anything else. Nothing could undergo fundamental change or evolution. Everything would be frozen in its own nature, forever isolated from other substances.

The fact of emptiness means that everything in the world is related to everything else. Everything in the universe is a compound object, composed of energies and elements from which everything else in the universe is made. Emptiness is the basis of the interdependence of all things. Everything in the universe is related to everything else because of emptiness. Because of emptiness, the world is one.

The Facts We Hide from Ourselves

The three facts of existence—suffering, impermanence, and emptiness—are a major part of the truth we hide from ourselves, thus creating the esoteric secrets of happiness for which we longingly search. We can glimpse the facts of existence, but they are difficult to hold onto. We need constant reminders in order to keep them in mind as we struggle with the problems of life. We have difficulty maintaining awareness of them because they are not what we want to see. Even after we have seen them and acknowledged their verity we quickly relapse and revert to our ordinary way of seeing, which is to deny and avoid suffering, impermanence, and insubstantiality and, instead, to search obsessively for happiness in fixed, stable reference points and apparently substantial material objects.[14]

Chogyam Trungpa Rinpoche was reportedly once asked what it would take for Westerners to understand the Buddhist way of seeing. He answered, "A new mind." The same is true of the facts of existence. To see them we must drop our ordinary way of seeing and our ordinary desires and fears, and practice mindfulness without motivation or projection. This is difficult to achieve. To achieve a stable awareness of suffering, impermanence, and emptiness requires years of discipline and practice.[15] It requires conquering oneself.

CHAPTER SEVEN

The Second Noble Truth: Desire

> What now is the Noble Truth of the origin of suffering? It is that craving which gives ris-e to fresh rebirth, and, bound up with pleasure and lust, now here, now there, finds ever fresh delight.
>
> —The Buddha, *A Buddhist Bible*

> The psychic conflict which produces dreams and neuroses is not generated by intellectual problems but by purposes, wishes, desires....Now if we take "desire" as the most suitably abstract of this series of terms, it is a Freudian axiom that the essence of man consists not as Descartes maintained, in thinking, but in desiring....History is shaped beyond our conscious wills, not by the cunning of reason but by the cunning of desire.
>
> —Norman O. Brown, *Life Against Death*

In the dark night of his soul under the Bodhi tree, Buddha looked everywhere in the outer, material world for the causes of suffering and unhappiness. Finally he realized that the causes of pain cannot be located in the outer world, for the appearance of the outer world and our reaction to it depend on mind. So he looked within his mind for the causes of suffering and discovered *tanha*—selfish desire. Tanha is the culprit behind our negative emotions, our dissatisfactions, our frustrations, and our neurotic suffering. This vital realization is expressed in the second noble truth, the truth of the cause of suffering.

Tanha can be roughly translated as "thirst" or "craving," but it goes by many names: attachment, grasping, clinging, wanting, wishing, longing, yearning, hoping, aspiring, desiring, and so on. We will follow Norman O. Brown and use the generic term "desire" to stand for all its synonyms. The Random House Dictionary defines desire as follows:

> DESIRE — 1. To wish or long for; crave; want. 2. To express a wish to obtain; to ask for, request... 3. A longing or craving, as for something that brings satisfaction or enjoyment: a desire for fame. 4. An expressed wish; request. 5. Something desired. 6. Sexual appetite or a sexual urge... Synonyms 1. covet, fancy. See wish. 2. solicit. 3. aspiration, hunger, appetite, thirst. Desire, Craving, Longing, Yearning suggest feelings which impel one to the attainment or possession of something which is (in reality or imagination) within reach: a desire for success....[1]

The essence of tanha is *selfish* desire: pursuing *my* needs, *my* wants, *my* preferences, *my* objectives and goals, *my* happiness projects and purposes. Desire is the family name of all the selfish longings that haunt the human heart. Instincts are desires shaped by biology. Motivations and drives are desires in the guise of causes. They seem to push us from behind. Goals and purposes are folded into our happiness projects as desires with an eye to the future. Needs are urgently pressing desires. Obsessions, compulsions, and addictions are desires out of control, desires gone wild. Choices and preferences are desires moderated by reason. Tanha is the sum of all our selfish desires, all our efforts to find pleasure, to satisfy ourselves, to meet our needs, to reach our goals, to achieve self-fulfillment and self-realization.

Desire has cosmic scope. It can take as its object anything in the universe, real or imagined, grandiose or trivial, earthly or sublime. Desire is the sensuous hunger for food, sex, comfort, and play. It is the subtle hunger for love, identity, fame, power, wealth, success and meaning. It is the divine hunger for salvation and immortality. Desire is omnivorous, but whimsical. One moment it grasps for fame or eternal life, the next moment it settles for a trinket, a piece of candy, a cigarette, or a kind word.

Buddhists say that selfish desire turns the wheel of life. This means that selfish desire is the motivating force of our thoughts, our dreams, our actions and, hence, of the drama of our lives. The problems of life are not intellectual or mental, they are problems of satisfying desires, pursuing goals, meeting needs, protecting and advancing interests. We tend to repress and deny this obvious fact. We hide our selfish desires from others because we are trained not to appear selfish, but we also hide them from ourselves, thus converting them into secrets—secrets we keep from ourselves.

This is a fundamental axiom of psychoanalysis, although one not often stated in this way. Our repressed desires, sometimes called "drives" or "impulses," are at the center of our neuroses. One of the most fundamental axioms of psychoanalysis is that desire is the driving force behind thought and behavior. This crucial idea, phrased succinctly by the neo-Freudian, Norman O. Brown, and quoted at the beginning of this chapter, is worth reflecting upon:

> The psychic conflict which produces dreams and neuroses is not generated by intellectual problems but by purposes, wishes, desires....Now if we take "desire" as the most suitably abstract of this series of terms, it is a Freudian axiom that the essence of man consists not as Descartes maintained, in thinking, but in desiring....History is shaped beyond our conscious wills, not by the cunning of reason but by the cunning of desire.

If we have the courage and the will to make an effort to look, we can each observe for ourselves how our desires cause our suffering. Desire causes suffering in two ways: first, because of its own nature; and secondly, because of the nature of existence.

Desire causes suffering by its own nature because it is inherently unsatisfactory. *Desire means deprivation*. To want something is to lack it, to be deprived of it. We do not want things we have, we only want what we don't have. Thirst is the desire for water and it occurs in the absence of water. Hunger is the feeling of lacking food. Desiring means not having, being frustrated, suffering. Craving *is* suffering. This is a most important insight, one which we drive into secrecy by our refusal to acknowledge it, thus creating the esoteric knowledge we then seek.

The nagging dissatisfactions of everyday life are the results of the frustrated desires of everyday life. We complain about our frustrations but we are unwilling to give up our desires. Plato recognized the inherent unsatisfactoriness of desire and the bliss of desirelessness in a poetic phrase that captures the Buddhist view of desire:[2]

> ...he who desires something is in want of something. And he who desires nothing lacks nothing.

Desire causes suffering not only because of its own inherent nature as deprivation, but also because it involves a struggle against the facts and conditions of existence. "If anything becomes a problem," writes Piyadassi Thera, "there is bound to be suffering, or if we like, conflict—conflict between our desires and the facts of life."[3] We want things to go our way. We want the flow of life to fit our plans and aspirations. Martin Luther humbly deferred to the will of God: "Thy will be done, Lord," he prayed, "not mine." The motto of the selfish self is the opposite: "My will be done, Lord, not thine."

Our desires cause our suffering because existence rarely cooperates with our desires. It does not care what we want; as it says in Genesis, nature is indifferent to our needs.[4] We want to be happy forever, but we are compound beings who suffer at birth, suffer in old age, and suffer at death. We desire stability and enduring reference points, but we must live insecurely, in the flowing waters of change. We believe in the solid existence of matter, mind, and God, but material things arise and decay, and God and self are ghostly mirror images—the projections of dualistic mind. Even if we achieve success our victories are temporary, as transient as life itself. The bird of perpetual happiness is an elusive mirage.

The second noble truth is profound and subtle. It is profound because it illuminates the deepest secrets of the mind. In depth psychology a mental quality is deep when it is powerful and hidden. Desire is a powerful psychic force because it motivates consciousness and behavior. Desire is hidden when we are not aware of it, when we repress it, when we remain ignorant of its powerful influence on our lives and our happiness.

Desire is subtle because it is often not easy to recognize. It travels in disguise. It is a trickster, a master of illusion. Sensuous desires are the most obvious because they work through the body: the spasms of hunger, the pressures to urinate and defecate, the dryness of thirst, the aching loins of sexual excitement.

Ego desires are more subtle. They work in the spheres of language, symbols, and meanings. They are often ambiguous, cunning, and deceptive. They cloak themselves in virtue, in righteousness, in logic, and reason, in social convention, law, tradition, and ideology. But if we look closely, we can often see through the clothes to the naked ego, craving, and clinging. We see examples of this everyday in the greedy merchant who claims to be only a law-abiding businessman working for profit, in the politician who claims to be serving the public but who is actually pursuing personal power, in the lover who professes love but is primarily interested in sex, money, or power.

The search for the secrets of happiness begins necessarily with the awareness of suffering and unhappiness, but then must continue by searching for the causes of suffering. The spiritual seeker with an inquiring, scientific mind will ponder selfish desire and its relation to pain, to tragedy, to frustration, to negative emotions, to violence, to all the agonies we humans visit upon ourselves and each other.

Suffering and selfish desire are woven together into a single fabric which covers our vision like a veil, obscuring the true nature of mind and material existence. Desire dwells in darkness, in ignorance, in the illusions of selfhood. Tanha and avidya, desire and ignorance, are mates, bonded to one another. The old saying, "love is blind," tells only half the story. Not only is romantic love blind. All selfish desires are blind if they repress or deny the truths of impermanence, emptiness, and suffering.

The Three Poisons

The interplay between desire and ignorance is expressed in Buddhist psychology as the "three poisons." The three poisons are known as greed, hatred, and illusion. There are many synonyms: Greed may be called passion, lust, craving, or attachment; hatred may be referred to as aggression, anger, or aversion; illusion is sometimes replaced by delusion or ignorance. In the Buddhist view, these three mental qualities are the root cause of human suffering, the suffering we impose on ourselves and others.

Phrased in Western terms, the three poisons are desire, aversion, and ego. We have used the word desire as a generic equivalent of the Sanskrit *tanha*. But tanha itself is bipolar, divided into greed and hatred, or passion and aggression. On the one hand is the desire to have something, to possess it, experience it, pull it in, and own it. On the other hand is the desire to avoid something, keep it away, reject it, renounce it, destroy it, and separate it from oneself. If we call these two poles desire and aversion, we can see more clearly that they represent the antithetical poles of tanha—the desire to possess and the desire to get rid of.

Tanha is bipolar because all beings are polarized, including human beings. All beings are "tropistic," that is, they move towards what will bring more life and they avoid what will bring death. The higher organisms experience this duality as the desire for pleasure and the fear of pain. We humans strive for sensuous pleasure and life, for happiness and immortality. We struggle against pain and death, unhappiness and final oblivion. This is the dialectic of tanha which shapes mind, life, and history.

The polarization of desire is the mark of the samsaric world, the world of "perpetual wanderings," of birth, decay, and death. Samsara is a projection of dualistic mind which, as we have already noted, perceives the world in terms of polarities, antithetical pairs, each member of which is defined in terms of the other, like up/down, right/left, hot/cold, male/female. Each pole depends upon its opposite for meaning. Without up, down would have no meaning. Without the female, the male would disappear. Self depends upon other. Happiness loses meaning without unhappiness. Good cannot exist without evil. Death is the necessary correlate of birth.

The primary antithetical qualities of dualistic mind, and hence of the samsaric world, are pleasure/pain, life/death, self/other, good/evil, and past/future. These polarities create the relative realities of samsara. They define the reference points of biological life, of individual life, of social life, of morality, and of history. These antithetical pairs give form to a dialectical theater in which self manifests in relation to other, striving in historical time to secure the good life and to avoid evil and death. Carl Jung called this dialectic *enantiodrama,* the drama of opposites.

Tanha, desire, is interwoven with avidya, ignorance, by means of the mistaken presumption that the samsaric dance of opposites is ultimate reality. Ignorance is the mother of greed and hatred because it gives them life. It rationalizes and justifies them. Ignorance also converts our desires into secrets and hides the fact that they are the cause of the sufferings we complain about. Desire is fueled by an ignorant or deluded view of the world and ourselves, namely, the "wrong view" that self and the world are solid, enduring substances which can be grasped, enjoyed, possessed, and preserved, hopefully forever. Wrong view spurs the motivation to preserve and extend the self and its grasp on the world. It is the ideological foundation of all forms of selfishness and selfish cravings, and hence, of all the hatred and violence we cause ourselves.

The cure for ignorance is "right view." Right view converts what appear as secrets under wrong view into an awareness of the basic reality of our situation—an awareness of the three marks of existence.

Right view is the secret of happiness revealed. Right view reveals self and the world as ephemeral appearances, luminescences which are born from emptiness, enter the ceaseless river of samsaric change, and ultimately disappear into emptiness. The secret of happiness is to accept this reality.

The problem is that samsaric mind rejects the reality of emptiness. Dualistic mind perceives emptiness as negative, and therefore frightening. The facts of existence tell us that we will disappear, and the world as we know it along with us. The ego resists emptiness because it resists its own dissolution.

With right view as guide, however, the facts of existence can be seen as having a positive side too. The positive side of suffering is that it provides us with an opportunity to understand the causes of suffering. It creates the possibility of understanding the role of desire and aversion in our lives. Suffering is the first step on the spiritual path. Impermanence and emptiness mean that greed and hatred are also transient, empty phenomena. They too are appearances, illusions. This is good news. This means we can experience them, we can be mindful of them without necessarily acting them out, without permitting their destructive potential to dominate our motivations and our lives.

The Three Desires

When Buddha looked within himself for the cause of suffering he discovered tanha, desire. As he sat, observing his mind, he was able to distinguish three forms of desire: (1) The desire for sensuous pleasure; (2) the desire for life, for continued existence, for happiness, and personal immortality; and (3) the desire for death, for the escape from pain, for personal annihilation and non-existence. Each of us can reflect for ourselves whether Buddha's insight covers the territory. Are there any desires that do not fit into one of these three categories?

These three categories of desire are strikingly similar to Freud's *id*, life instinct, and death instinct. This should not be surprising in view of the fact that Buddha and Freud were examining the same phenomenon. In Freud's terms, the id represents sensuous, lusty, aggressive animal desires. The life instinct is the desire for life, more life, a fuller life, a more defined, substantial and permanent self. The death instinct is the desire to escape from evil, to avoid suffering, to lose oneself and merge with a more powerful, invulnerable entity.[5]

The Desire for Sensuous Pleasure

The desire for sensuous pleasure is obvious, since we all experience it, recognize it, and, to some degree, suffer from it. It is pursued through the six gateways of the body: the five senses—vision, hearing, smell, taste, and touch—and the sixth sense, the mind. Each gateway has its own delights. The most powerful sensuous desires are for food and sex. These two desires strongly motivate thought, feeling, and behavior. The pursuit of food and sex serves biological functions only partly—to nourish and reproduce the body. But the enjoyment of food and sex also serves psychological functions, providing the organism with the subjective reward for the effort to preserve self and the species. Many people pursue food, sex, and other sensuous pleasures compulsively, blindly, and indiscriminately, in order to escape from the suffering, sorrows, and anxieties of life.

Bulimia, or compulsive eating, serves to tranquilize the sufferings of anxiety. Bulimia is epidemic in the Western world today. From the Buddhist point of view bulimia is gluttony, or the greed for food. It is a search for pleasure through eating which is motivated by the desire to repress, deny, and escape suffering. The explanation for this is biological, but this does not mean that bulimia has a biological cause. The cause is psychological, the desire to relieve pain through the experience of pleasure.

The biological basis of bulimia lies in the fact that the nervous systems which regulate eating and anxiety are inversely activated. Anxiety, which is a form of fear, namely the fear of future danger, is mediated by the sympathetic nervous system, the fight-flight reaction. Eating is mediated by the para-sympathetic nervous system.

The sympathetic and para-sympathetic nervous systems are reciprocally innervated. When the sympathetic nervous system is turned on, the appetite is turned off, which is why anxious people suffer from anorexia and loss of weight, and why people use Dexedrine, which activates the sympathetic nervous system, to repress appetite. By the same reasoning, eating tranquilizes anxiety because eating activates the parasympathetic nervous system and relatively deactivates the sympathetic system.

Bulimia is the search for pleasure through eating in order to dull and distract us from the pain of life. The mouth, the oral cavity, the tongue, and pharynx are heavily lined with nerve endings. Eating floods the brain with the most pleasurable and distracting stimulations.

Many people are closet bulimics. They eat to relieve their pain, whether it is anxiety, disappointment, depression, anger, or boredom. They are not defined as bulimics, primarily because they do not care sufficiently about their weight to fast or purge after their binges. But they are overweight because of their emotional binge eating. Many people, especially figure-conscious young women, fast or purge after their binge eating, creating a binge-fast/purge cycle. The binge provides escape into pleasure, but it also adds weight and creates feelings of shame. The function of the fast or purge is to undo the binge. The binge-purge cycle is the alternate indulgence and repression of eating-pleasure consciousness.

Many men tend to use sex the way many women use food—to blot out the pains of existence. Generally speaking, women tend to binge and fast on food while men tend to binge and fast on sex, although there are many examples to the contrary. The classic syndrome of satyriasis, the man with an unsatisfiable sexual appetite, is parallel to bulimia in women. Many men (but women too) use sex as a tranquilizer, to bring relief from the stresses and strains of life. In women the reaction formation against excessive indulgence in food is ascetic fasting, designated by psychiatrists as a form of mental illness—anorexia-nervosa. In men, the reaction formation against excessive indulgence in sex is chastity, a form of sexual fasting which has been institutionalized by patriarchal religions as monasticism.

The desire for sensuous pleasure produces attachments to the outer, material world where the pleasurable stimuli originate. As dogs become attached to the masters who feed them, humans become attached (or addicted) to the sources of their pleasures. The sensualist and the materialist are opposite sides of the same coin. Each wants to possess and enjoy the goods of the material world: good food, comfortable homes, fine clothing, luxurious cars, mechanical conveniences, electronic toys, sexual playmates, and the money and time to enjoy them. This is the motive behind the yuppie mentality, a style of life which is fueled by the desire to escape suffering and the anxiety of death.

To have the money and time to enjoy the sensuous pleasures of life is a political problem, perhaps the most fundamental political problem. The universal desire of humanity is to enjoy life, to love and be loved, to be comfortable, to have fun, to be amused and entertained, distracted and reassured until the moment of death. Those who have power have the power to enjoy themselves. Those who do not have power must go without and suffer. In this sense desire is the most fundamental political problem. Poverty means struggling to exist, without the time or means to enjoy the finer pleasures of life. Wealth provides an opportunity to surround oneself with beauty and pleasure. The desire for pleasure is thus the basic motivation of the pursuit of power. Power corrupts precisely because it provides access to wealth and sensuous pleasure. Buddha said:

> Verily, O Monks, due to sensuous craving kings fight with kings, princes with princes, priests with priests, citizens with citizens, the mother quarrels with the son, the son quarrels with the mother, the father with the son, the son with the father, the brother with the brother, the brother with the sister, the sister with the brother and the friend with the friend.[6]

The animalistic desires for sensuous pleasure are transformed into the human desire for happiness through the process of sublimation. We shall discuss sublimation in greater detail later.[7] Suffice it to say for now that sublimation is a concept drawn from physics, where it refers to the evaporation of a solid into a gas, as when dry ice evaporates into carbon dioxide. In psychology, sublimation is used metaphorically to refer to the transformation of a bodily state or feeling into a mental state or feeling. For example, brute physical hunger is sublimated by civilization into ritualistic eating and elegant dining. Sexual lust is sublimated into tenderness, sympathy, family feelings, and altruism. At the most fundamental level, the desire for sensuous pleasure is sublimated into the desire for eternal life.

The Desire for Life

The desire for life is present in the body at birth, in its homeostatic, hormonal, and reflexive mechanisms. Hunger, digestion, metabolism, excretion, procreation, immunity, and the fight-flight reaction, are mechanisms designed to foster life: to provide nutrition, to eliminate poisons, to resist infection, to repair damaged tissue, to propagate the species, to escape the threat of death.

At the more subtle level of ego, the desire for life is the ego's striving to establish itself, to solidify itself, to gain a secure foothold, to prevail and dominate, and so to enjoy the sensuous delights of the phenomenal world. The desire for life manifests in all of the ego's selfish, ambitious strivings to assert itself, to survive, to endure, to be recognized, to be respected, to be loved, to be successful, wealthy, powerful, and wise. The desire for life energizes the basic dynamic of human social interactions. It is the fuel for our daily soap opera, for our biographies and for history. The desire for life motivates the human drama of conflicts, victories, and defeats of egos in their struggle with each other for more life, a longer life, a richer life, a more meaningful life, everlasting life.

The Desire for Death

The desire for death is, of course, the opposite of the desire for life. As the desire for life is based upon the desire for pleasure and happiness, the desire for death is based upon the desire to escape pain and evil. One is eternalistic, the other is nihilistic. Together they reflect our dual yearnings to be happy forever and to evade suffering forever.

The desire for death is the yearning for relief from pain, from anxiety, from disappointment, despair, and negativity. The motive for the desire for death is most transparent in cases of suicide. Clearly, people with terminal illnesses who commit suicide are motivated by the desire to escape from physical pain and suffering. In so called "altruistic" suicide, such as *hara-kiri*, *kamikaze*, and other forms of socially conditioned suicide, the motive is to avoid mental suffering—shame, humiliation, and disgrace.

Egotistical suicide is also motivated by the desire to escape from mental suffering. Suicide means "self-murder." The motive for self-murder is the unwillingness to face and accept, humbly and gracefully, the failure or futility of one's Happiness Projects. Our sense of self depends upon the possibility of fulfilling our hopes, wishes, plans, schemes, dreams, and expectations. The selfish self strives to find the means to realize its hopes, to preserve, fortify, and expand its meanings, and to seek release and salvation from frustration, disappointment, failure, and loss. Without the life-project, there is no hope. Without Happiness Projects, life loses its purpose and, therefore, its meaning. The loss of hope and meaning shatter the ego. The murder of the body brings it into harmony with the deadened self.

The motive of suicide is to escape from the realities of life, the suffering which is a part of life, the constant changes, the lack of solid, stable, and enduring reference points to hold on to. People commit egotistical suicide when they feel that life will not live up to their hopes, dreams, and expectations, when they feel that their cherished goals and conditioned motivations cannot be achieved, when their hopes for future meaning seem doomed to frustration and failure, when there is no hope of achieving future happiness and peace of mind.

An epidemic of suicide has recently afflicted the youth of the Western world. Our young people have been raised on the undisciplined desires, high expectations, and lofty ambitions of a materialistic society. They yearn for the material pleasures of the world. They long for love, acceptance, freedom, and happiness. Rather than face the nature of existence, rather than accept their deprivation, disappointment, confusion, and fear, rather than accept life as it is, they choose to die. They are dying from their unfulfilled desires, egged on by a secular, materialistic society which mistakenly teaches that happiness is to be achieved through the pursuit and satisfaction of desires.

If not properly understood and skillfully worked with, the three desires generate negativity—unhappiness, pain, disappointment, disillusionment, aggression, despair and depression. The desire for sensuous pleasure, taken to an extreme, leads ultimately to dissipation, deterioration, and death. The desire for life, taken to an extreme, leads to frustration, depression, and aggression. The desire for death leads to a needlessly premature end to the possibility and potentiality of awareness, acceptance, and love.

CHAPTER EIGHT

Self and Identity or Basic Bewilderment

> And Moses said unto God: 'Behold, when I come unto the children of Israel, and shall say unto them: The God of your fathers hath sent me unto you; and they shall say to me: What is his name? what shall I say unto them?' And God said unto Moses: 'I AM THAT I AM'; and He said: 'Thus shalt thou say unto the children of Israel: I AM hath sent me unto you.'
>
> —Exodus 3:13

> We are unknown, we knowers, ourselves to ourselves.
>
> —Friedrich Nietszche, *The Genealogy of Morals*

> Nobody knows who I am or what I do. Not even I.
>
> —Don Juan in Carlos Castaneda's *Journey to Ixtlan*

> This perception of a being, Subhuti, that is just a non-being.
>
> —The Buddha, *The Diamond Sutra*

To the ordinary human mind, "self" seems to be an entity with a definite, reified, unitary existence which dwells at our inner core, persists throughout our conscious lives and possibly beyond, and is the essence of our being and our identity. What is this "self" which is the essence of our being and our identity?

From the Buddhist point of view, self is empty, which is to say that it lacks substance. Self is an appearance without an essence, an "illusion," the repository of our ignorance, and the prime cause of our self-imposed suffering. Zen Buddhist masters are famous for challenging their students with enigmatic questions about the nature of self, such as: "What is your original face?" "Are you your thoughts? Your feelings? Your memories? Your brain? Your heart? Your hands, skin, or bones?" The reader can try these thought experiments. The challenge is to look within and see if you can locate that entity you call yourself. Self-knowledge begins with this search.

From the Buddhist point of view, self is not an independently existing entity. When Buddha searched himself he found a kaleidoscopic bricolage[1] of sensations, feelings, perceptions, thoughts, and the awareness of these. But in this continuous, bewildering flow of mental events, he found nothing he could identify as "self." From this point of view, self is "empty" because it has no definite, distinct, reified essence.

At the same time, it is false to say that self does not exist at all. We all think about ourselves, talk about ourselves, function as ourselves in the social world, and recognize the selfhood of others. In this sense, self exists, but only as an attribution, an ascription, a projection. Self exists as a socially conventional attribution. We attribute the idea of self to the locus of the flowing bricolage of our experiences and to the locus of the presumed bricolage of experiences of others.

Buddha resolved the contradiction that self both exists and does not exist by taking the middle path—the path between eternalism and nihilism. From the view of the middle path it is false to say that self exists, and false to say that it does not. Self exists, but as an *imputation*. We impute or project the idea of self on to ourselves. In other words, the human mind reflexively takes itself as an object and projects a persona onto itself. In this sense, self exists as a self-created fiction. As a fiction, it both is and is not.

From the Buddhist point of view, self, or ego, is ignorance—*avidya*. More specifically, ignorance is the reification of the self. It is the reification of mind's imputation of self onto itself. Self is the source of our ignorance because it mistakenly takes itself and the symbolic field it projects and in which it operates, as real. At the same time, the reification of self and its projections results in the denial and repression of the facts of existence—suffering, impermanence, and emptiness.

Mistaking fiction as fact and fact as fiction creates the conditions of our bewilderment. In the Buddhist view, this confusion is the source of the suffering we impose on ourselves and others.

What is Self?

We can check the Buddhist view by inquiring for ourselves into the nature of self. This is not an academic exercise. It has pragmatic significance. We want to find relief and release from our suffering. To do this we must understand the nature and dynamics of the fictitious self which is the locus of our suffering.

Understanding the concept of self is a daunting task. Who are we, as individuals and as a species? How do we view ourselves? Have we changed over time? Or has only our view of ourselves changed? These questions are deceptively difficult to answer. Self-inquiry is complex, contradictory and obscure: a minefield of traps, dead ends, and illusions. Self is ineffably vague. When we don't think about it, we take for granted that we know what it is. When we give it some thought, it becomes elusive. Trying to know ourselves is like trying to glimpse a shadow in a hall of mirrors.

Self-knowledge requires some preconception of self, or how would we know where to look and what to look for? By what criteria should we distinguish between authentic knowing and illusions we may believe to be true? We want to begin our inquiry on solid epistemological grounds, but what are they? It is not clear even how to start.

What form does authentic self-knowledge take? Is the knowledge we seek scientific? Or is it introspective? Does it consist of facts expressed in logical propositions? Or does it take the form of poetic insights expressed in myth and metaphor? Shall we begin with biology or psychology or sociology or anthropology? And what shall be the role of religion, the traditional source of self-knowledge? If we give some thought to these questions we quickly become aware of the difficulty of understanding the concept of "self."

The apparent solidity of our concept of self seems to be a product of the mind which is itself exceedingly elusive and difficult to grasp because it can only be grasped by itself. A Tibetan Buddhist lama, Jamgon Kongtrul Rinpoche, once asked a group of sophisticated western psychiatrists and psychotherapists—modern experts on the mind—the simple but vexing question, "What is mind?"[2] The response was a resounding and embarrassing silence. They could not, or perhaps would not, dare attempt to answer. Westerners are not comfortable with this question. We do not have a satisfactory answer to it. There is no "official" Western view of mind. There are many "theories of mind," but no commonly agreed view.[3]

The most prevalent Western view of mind is that it is an epiphenomenon of the brain. This view has become popular because Western thought is heavily shaped by science and, as we have observed, science takes the objective point of view and strives to eliminate the subjective. By the rules of its own method, science must deal with mind as an object; so to science, mind seems to be an object, like the brain. Most contemporary Western neurobiologists, psychologists, and psychiatrists take the view that mental events, particularly if they are "pathological," are produced by, and therefore reducible to, neurological events.

This materialist view of mind is attractive because it is reassuring. It gives the impression that the mind, and therefore the self, is solid. Since brain is a solid material object, and mind emanates from brain, then mind is also fundamentally solid. If mind is brain it can be understood through scientific research. If mind is brain it can be managed and manipulated—through psychopharmacology, psychotherapy, the information media, and politics.

From the Buddhist point of view, however, the apparent solidity of the mind is an illusion created by the mind itself. It exists, but only in the mind of the observer. The sense of solid reality of "self" is an illusion, like the Big Dipper. The only connection between the stars of the Big Dipper is the one made by the mind of the observer.

Self has no single, precise meaning. It is a montage of infinitely variable faces and personalities which manifest dually in the subjective and objective dimensions. In one sense, the word "self" denotes the image of my body as an object of my reflexive experience. When I think of myself I think of my particular body which, although it has changed over the years, seems to be continuous with the body of my earliest memories. When I think of others, I think of their particular bodies. In another sense, however, the body is a hunk of matter, an object of scientific investigation which has physiological, genetic, and ecological aspects.

Self also has a behavioral-social component. It refers to the unique behavioral styles and life histories of particular bodies. When we think of ourselves and other selves we think of how we have related to each other, what fun we have had together, and how we have hurt each other. We think of ourselves as heroes and victims in the stream of historical time.

In still another sense, self connotes the thinking subject in reflexive attitude. It refers to the stream of consciousness that is our most cherished personal possession, the focal point of our most urgent questions about the experience and meaning of life. Self is the emblem of the unique human individual, each as distinct from others as a set of fingerprints. Yet, since we each "have" a self, it is a human universal, the totem of the species *Homo sapiens* which is distinguished from the animals by the consciousness of self.

The term "self" has no clear denotative meaning. There is nothing in the world to which we can point as an example of a self, as there are examples of dogs, trees, and stars. We can point to a specific person, but all that we see is the exterior manifestations, and it is the interior life we seek to understand. Even here, the words "exterior" and "interior" are metaphors which distort as well as express the phenomena we are attempting to define. We cannot seem to grasp what it is we are trying to understand without projecting on to it some image to make it comprehensible, only to discover that we then cannot distinguish that image from what we seek to know. How can we know a moving shadow in a hall of mirrors?

Basic Bewilderment

Every beginning on the quest for self-knowledge seems to be an arbitrary intrusion into the enigma. Every beginning explodes into a kaleidoscope of bewildering images, thoughts, and concepts. We have no choice then, but to begin our inquiry into the nature of mind and self from the midst of this confusion. The starting point on the quest for self-knowledge is bewilderment.

Bewilderment is the starting point of self inquiry because it is where we are now. No matter how sure we seem to be of who we are and where we are going in life, there are certain questions we cannot answer: Why was I born? Where did I come from? What is the origin of humanity? What is the nature of the universe? What am I doing here? How am I supposed to live and think? What is the purpose of my life? Why do I have to die? When will I die?

In an episode of Rod Serling's TV series, "The Twilight Zone," Serling's deep baritone introduces the main character of the evening's drama, a hunter who suddenly finds himself on an island, the prey of a hunter he does not know and cannot see. "This man is like all of us," Serling announces quizzically, "he has no idea why he is here or what he is supposed to do. All he knows is that he is condemned to die—time, place, and manner of execution unknown."

Rene Descartes (1596-1650) launched modern philosophy with relentless doubt which questioned every thought, every image, every assertion of the intellect, but could not doubt the doubt. "What, then, can be esteemed as true?" Descartes despairingly asked. His answer? "Perhaps nothing at all, unless that there is nothing in the world that is certain."[4] Descartes could deduce the fact of his own existence only from this doubt. "I think [doubt], therefore I am."

The search for self-knowledge begins in this doubt. Chogyam Trungpa Rinpoche called it "basic bewilderment"—a fundamental, agonizing confusion about who we are and the meaning of our lives.[5] The ordinary human mind is in a continuous state of basic bewilderment and attempts to escape from it into certain knowledge or articles of faith. Basic bewilderment is the starting point on the journey towards self-knowledge and enlightenment.

Very often, my young patients complain to me about their bewilderment. They are confused about what they think, how they feel, or what to do about various important issues in their lives. I sympathize with them and encourage them to acknowledge and accept their confusion. There is no need to fear confusion. I tell them that I too am confused. Everyone is confused because everyone is bewildered about the basic cause, meaning, and purpose of life. I suggest to them that the acceptance of confusion is a step towards clarity. If it is clear that we are confused, then our search has at least begun in a moment of honest clarity.

Who Am I?

The question of identity—"Who am I?"—is the linguistic counterpart of basic bewilderment. "Who am I?" is, supposedly, the perennial question of the neurotic adolescent. When my daughter was a college sophomore she had a poster hanging on her dormitory wall which poignantly expressed sophomoric identity confusion:

> THIS LIFE IS A TEST
> IT IS ONLY A TEST
> IF IT HAD BEEN AN ACTUAL LIFE
> YOU WOULD HAVE RECEIVED
> FURTHER INSTRUCTIONS ON
> WHERE TO GO AND WHAT TO DO

Much of the agony of modern adolescents is the result of the frustrating effort to resolve their basic bewilderment and make sense of life. We all struggle to resolve our confusion by searching for or constructing a view of the world and our place in it which makes sense of our lives. From this point of view, the problem of identity is a philosophical question.

Adults who have adopted some philosophy of life and therefore think they know who they are, tend to regard identity confusion as a symptom of adolescent immaturity. But adults are also vulnerable to identity confusion. In times of social turmoil and instability, when uncertainty and doubt arise about the meaning and purpose of life, many adults tend to revert to the "adolescent" preoccupation with identity. We are reminded here again of the recent resurgence of ethnic wars after the collapse of Communism, which can be viewed as a struggle for identity in a time of social chaos.

In times of rapid change new facts impinge on our sense of self like high energy particles bombarding the nucleus of an atom, splitting the personality apart. Under these circumstances self-contradiction is inescapable and hatches the egg of self-doubt through the eroding shell of which the petrifying specter of the groundlessness of self can be glimpsed.

At the personal level, this kind of identity crisis can occur after a traumatic event, like a personal loss, a death in the family, or being robbed, raped, or injured. It can result from a bad LSD trip when personal reference points are lost and self-image is shattered.

At the social-historical level, self-contradiction can be the result of new scientific discoveries. The history of science, from Galileo and Newton to Darwin and Freud is filled with the discovery of new facts that contradicted a society's image of itself and hurled it into a crisis of identity.

Freud cited three crises of Western identity, each of which was an assault on the collective ego. First was the Galilean revolution in astronomy, which revealed that we Earthlings are not at the center of God's universe. We are a mere detail in it, the inhabitants of a small planet, one of nine, which orbits a medium sized, middle-aged star, one of billions in our galaxy, which is one of billions of galaxies in an unimaginably vast universe.

The second crisis of Western identity was Darwin's revolution, which revealed that we were not created by God on the seventh day but evolved over millions of years from the animals, most recently from the primates. Indeed, we humans *are* animals. Many people take this fact as an insult to human pride, an unacceptable contradiction of the still dominant view of medieval Catholic Europe that humans are God's special creatures.

The third crisis was Freud's own revolution, which proposed that we, insignificant creatures of the cosmos, do not even know our own minds. We do not know ourselves at all! We think we are conscious, but we are unaware. We think we know what we are doing, but we are actually driven by unconscious forces. We are blind to ourselves and bewildered.

The enlightenment philosopher, Blaise Pascal, was aware of this centuries before Freud. "The heart has reasons the mind knows not of," he wrote. The psychoanalytic concept of the unconscious is a modern Western version of basic bewilderment.

Bewilderment is a form of emotional suffering. It is the suffering of confusion and anxiety, of being lost and unable to find home, of feeling alienated, dislocated, and abandoned. Basic bewilderment involves a deep anxiety and insecurity about the precariousness of life and its delicate fabric of meanings.

The insecurity of life is one of the most pervasive and insidious forms of personal suffering. If there is anything like a fundamental human identity, it is *sufferer*, *patient*, and *penitent*. The basic nature of self is suffering. Suffering is intrinsic to the self. It is intrinsic because the basic striving for survival involves the rejection and denial of the ineffability of self, and the search, through a lifetime of frustration, for a stable, secure, and permanent foundation. Yet everything is impermanent and lacks inherent substance.

The Quest for Personal Identity

The quest for self-knowledge is legitimate—if we are to discover the truth that we do not and cannot know who we are—but it is not sufficient if we are to existentially resolve our problem of identity. The problem of identity is not intellectual, it is existential.

Conventionally speaking, personal identity is constructed upon a skeleton of physical, social, biological, and biographical facts, the kind of facts the police might use to track a person down: name, address, telephone number, sex, age, social security number, occupation, DNA profile, fingerprints, etc. These are facts about the self which a scientist or actuary could observe, collect, and classify.

Identity also has a subjective, intellectual component, an auto-reflective interpretation of the facts, a "factual picture" of self. I have constructed a story about myself, as all of us do, based on the objective facts of my life as I interpret them, in which I personify myself to myself. I appear to myself as the hero (or victim) of the story line of my mental life. "I" am the chief character of my personal history. Through my actions and relations to others my character and personality are revealed to myself, although others might see me differently. This bricolage of memories, perceptions, images, constructs, and ideals is a large part of my sense of identity.

The picture I have of myself is partly personal and private and partly public and shared. Every society in every age constructs a guiding myth of the nature of self and its relation to society and nature which serves as a map and compass through the journey of life. In this sense the problem of identity has a social component. The questions of adolescents are not merely sophomoric intellectualizations designed to irritate adults. They are a quest, born of bewilderment, to find their place in society and in the cosmos. The zealous establishmentarian defense of social ideals and ideologies against the critical assaults, heresies, and rebellions of youth serves not only to perpetuate the power of the elders, but also to preserve their identity, their orientation in the world, their particular sense of their place in the sun.

The fragility of self is nowhere better illustrated than in the paradox that, since the self is constructed partly of facts and the interpretation of facts, it can be contradicted by facts. The fraud, the liar, and the secret agent are vulnerable to the negation of their false identifies by contrary facts. But aren't we all?

It takes extreme effort to maintain our sense of self to ourselves and others. One false move, one slip of the tongue, one outburst of anger, one vulgar joke, one sexual indiscretion, one drink too many, and we could be stripped of our reputations, our honor and our hopes. Are we not all vulnerable to acting out of character, to revealing a shameful, secret self that we hide from others, perhaps even from those who know us best? Do we not live in constant fear of being discovered? What if someone could read our thoughts? How many of us could stand up to journalistic scrutiny like politicians must do?

Scientific though they may be, the facts of identity do not exist on solid ground. The guiding myths of both individuals and groups are ideologies—constructions which ignore facts that contradict an ideal image and emphasize facts that promote it. Yet, new facts continuously emerge from the stream of personal biography and public history that may support or contradict who we think we are.

> Who are you? Suppose you're something wrong,
> A plaster cast of Venus in a raincoat,
> A starling with a rooster's song,
> An architect turned into a poet.[6]

David H., a graduate student in a nearby college, consulted me with the complaint that although he felt he loved his wife, he was not in love with her and was not comfortable in his marriage. He felt claustrophobic. He needed space. He wanted to leave his wife and live by himself in order to find out who he was. He phrased his problem as a problem of identity. He wanted to find out who he was. He left his wife and within two months he met another woman with whom he fell in love. He then felt his identity crisis had been resolved. His depression and insomnia disappeared.

The case of David H. illustrates the fact that the quest for identity is not intellectual, it is existential. It is resolved not by finding a set of answers which clarify confusion, but finding a new friend, a new job, a new situation, a new life in which one feels comfortable. The question of identity is then dropped. *It is not answered, it is dropped.* In this sense, the problem of identity is not an intellectual question but a problem of relationship—of the fit of self with others, with community and with life. When we feel we fit, we do not have an identity problem. We know who we are. When we feel we do not fit, the question of identity arises in anguish.

"Who Am I?" is the question of identity, of the relation of self to the world and to life as a whole. The problem of identity cannot be solved intellectually, since self is not a thing. It has no substance. It cannot be objectively described or understood. Self is an appearance we project onto the locus of our subjective experience. This projection creates both self and the problem of identity. This problem must then be solved by fitting the self into the cosmos—by resolving the contradictions between the subjective "I" and the objective world. The question of identity is partly intellectual, partly intuitive, and partly existential. It is a question of harmony, of finding the center, of relaxing into existence.

CHAPTER NINE

Neurosis: An Intersection of Buddhist and Western Thought

> Neurosis is a complex of desires, ignorance, and suffering.
> —Khenpo Karthar Rinpoche

I have often heard Tibetan lamas say that the basic cause of human suffering is neurotic mind or neurosis. They say that because of our neurotic minds we have developed negative, unskillful patterns of thought, emotion, and behavior which eventually cause suffering to ourselves or others.

I found it fascinating that Buddhist masters from a twenty-five hundred year old tradition use the word neurosis as the cause of suffering! I had been taught that neurosis was a relatively modern idea, invented in 1777 by the Scottish physician William Cullen and adopted by Sigmund Freud and modern psychiatry as a category of mental illness. I asked my teacher, Khenpo Karthar Rinpoche, Abbot of the Karma Kagyu Monastery in Woodstock, New York, to clarify the use of the word neurosis according to the Dharma. His answer was concise and stunning. "Neurosis" he said through his translator, "is a complex of desires, ignorance, and suffering."

Desires (meaning both desires and aversions) and ignorance, as we have seen, comprise "the three poisons." By Khenpo's definition, neurosis consists of the three poisons and their consequences, namely suffering. To say that neurosis is the cause of suffering is the same as saying that the three poisons are the cause of suffering.

In the West, the term "neurosis" is used broadly and vaguely. In ordinary language the term is used to denote a wide variety of eccentric, bizarre, apparently irrational or destructive thoughts, feelings, or behaviors. For example, a person might be considered neurotic about money if he or she hoards or squanders it. Similarly, a person might be considered neurotic if he or she binges on food and then vomits (bulimia), or if he or she continuously fasts (anorexia). Excessive jealousy or greed are regarded as neurotic, as are extremes of fearfulness and inhibition. In ordinary language, the term "neurosis" is used pejoratively, as a negative judgment of certain extreme patterns of thought, feelings, and behavior.

Neurosis also has a technical psychiatric meaning with a complex history. It is interesting to consider this history because it reveals an antithetical aspect of the Western mind. It reveals the Western mind in struggle to both reveal itself to itself and to hide from itself. The psychiatric history of the term "neurosis," as I interpret it, consists of a period of discovery and confusion, a clear moment when the Buddhist and Western concepts of neurosis came into alignment, followed by a period, extending into the present, in which the significance of selfish desire in the causation of mental and emotional suffering is denied and repressed.

Neurosis in Western Thought

It is generally accepted that the term "neurosis" was coined by the Scottish physician William Cullen (1710-1790) in 1777.[1] A century earlier the concept of "nervous disease" was introduced into medicine by two English physicians, Thomas Willis (1622-1675) and Thomas Sydenham (1624-1689). This idea of "nervous disease" first occurred at a time in the history of science when biologists were learning about the electrical activity of the nervous system. The accidental discovery of electrical energy in frogs' leg nerves and muscles by Italian physiologist Luigi Galvani (1737-1798) aroused a great deal of interest.[2] This new knowledge of the electrical properties of nerves was incorporated into medicine with the widely accepted idea that disturbances in the electrical energy of the nervous system could cause a wide range of illnesses. Cullen's concept of neurosis was a variation on this theme.

"Nervous energy" replaced the concept of the humors or vapors. Like them, it was thought to flow through the body and, in excess or deficiency, cause a wide variety of diseases in affected body parts.[3] Neurasthenia, for example, was diagnosed for a variety of symptoms thought to be caused by "weak nerves." A large number of poorly understood symptoms and diseases were diagnosed as nervous disorders, or neurosis, including certain neurological symptoms such as paralysis, tremors, and seizures; a wide variety of gynecological disorders; the protean and puzzling symptoms of tertiary syphilis; and many emotional conditions such as apathy, hypochondria, mania, and depression. Many physicians classified a wide variety of symptoms as "hysterical neurosis" if they occurred in women and as "hypochondriacal neurosis" in men. Robert Whytt (1714-1766) was heretically skeptical, however. He suggested that physicians made the diagnosis of "nervous disorder" in cases of symptoms they did not understand.

With few exceptions, the physicians of the eighteenth and nineteenth centuries presumed that neuroses were physical (neurological) illnesses, that is, that they were caused by physical changes in the body (nervous system). This presumption was based on faith alone: faith in science. They were living and working in the strong ideological currents of the Enlightenment, when the power to authorize knowledge was being transferred from religion to science. This transfer involved the abandonment of animistic, mentalistic, spiritualistic, or moralistic explanations of phenomena, including human thoughts, feelings, and actions, in favor of materialistic, scientific, causal explanations.

Physicians of that day, like those of today, strived to be scientific and were therefore motivated to presume that diseases could be explained as physical processes rather than demonic possession, divine retribution, karmic consequence, or moral failure. The overwhelming majority of physicians of the day believed that neurosis had a physical causation in spite of the fact that hundreds of autopsies failed to reveal any supportive evidence.[4] Because of this historical ideological orientation, the discovery of the pathological effects of selfish desire on body and mind were discovered by physicians, but they were mistakenly understood as physical diseases.

Philippe Pinel (1745-1826), the famous hero of the First Psychiatric Revolution,[5] was a notable exception. Pinel was a child of the French Revolution and the Director of the Bicetre, a mental institution for men, and the Salpetriere, a mental institution for women, in Paris. He was aware that hundreds of autopsies on mental patients failed to discover a physical cause of neurosis. Pinel, who was influenced by the moral philosophy of the Enlightenment, was inclined to believe that neurotic symptoms were caused by mental and emotional factors which affected the moral faculties. He advocated a moral etiology of neurosis which he, nevertheless, regarded as an illness. Other physicians in other countries also believed that neurosis was a moral problem in its causation and treatment. They developed small, private, humane, personal "retreats" or "asylums" across Europe and the United States which practiced the so-called "moral treatment of mental illness."[6]

By the latter part of the nineteenth century two competing views on the origin and nature of neurosis had taken shape. On the one hand there were those who believed that neurosis had an organic etiology, either in disturbed electrical energies or some as yet undiscovered neuro-anatomical pathology. On the other hand, "heretical" physicians such as Pinel, Mesmer (1734-1815), Charcot (1825-1892), Janet (1859-1947), Liebault (1823-1904), Bernheim (1840-1919), and Forel (1848-1931) believed in the psychogenic origin of neurosis.

With new scientific discoveries many symptoms that were previously diagnosed as neurosis were discovered to have a physical basis and were classified as medical diseases. As a result, the list of neurotic illnesses shrank over time, giving momentum to the advocates of a moral cause of mental illness. The most influential member of this group was Sigmund Freud, who struggled his entire life to understand the concept of neurosis.

Early in his career Sigmund Freud (1856-1939) accepted both theories of neurosis. He distinguished between "actual neurosis" and "psycho-neurosis." Actual neurosis, Freud believed, was caused by a *physical* damming up of libido in the nervous system. Psycho-neurosis was caused by the dynamic interplay of *psychological* forces—the ego and the unconscious. Later, he lost interest in the actual neurosis and focused on psycho-neurosis, although he was hopeful that a neurological cause of it would eventually be discovered.[7]

Freud's psychoanalytic theory of neurosis became well known and widely applied in Europe and the United States. It was widely accepted by psychiatrists from the 1940s until late in the 1960s. Today it is still widely used by non-medical psychotherapists.

Psychiatry has abandoned the psychogenic theory of neurosis for many complex reasons.[8] The psychogenic theory created a great problem for medical psychiatry in the sixties. It was not only an intellectual problem of understanding the causes of mental and emotional suffering, but also a crisis in psychiatric identity. The psychogenic theory stimulated psychiatrists to becoming intensely interested in the mind and the world of the mind: culture, art, social science, philosophy, and so forth. As a result of these interests, which manifested in psychiatric vocabulary, social style, and thought, psychiatry was losing its medical identity. It was the only medical specialty which was not totally focused on the body.

Another factor was threatening to expose the moral and social functions of psychiatry. Psychiatrists administered a vast bureaucracy of mental institutions which were called hospitals but which had clear social and political functions.[9] As the moral and political underpinnings of psychiatry became more transparent, psychiatrists, longing for a respectable medical identity, began to play down mental and emotional factors in mental illness and instead to search for biological causes and treatments. They fell back in line with the present ideological tendency to rely exclusively upon science for knowledge about our pain and suffering. Today, the medical (neurochemical) model of neurosis prevails once again.

For about sixty years, roughly from the turn of the century to the mid-1960s, Freud's views of the causes of neurotic suffering corresponded closely to the twenty-five hundred year old Buddhist view. There were few competent Buddhist scholars in the West at that time, so this coincidence went relatively unnoticed. Now the number of Buddhist scholars has increased considerably, but the psychoanalytic theory of neurosis has gone out of style.

The psychoanalytic theory of neurosis holds that the cause of neurotic suffering is mental conflict. This conflict occurs in three mental spheres: the *id*, the *superego*, and the *ego*. Briefly summarized, the id is the repository of primitive desires and fears. The superego represents learned moral values. The ego attempts to mediate the conflict between them. In neurosis, the instinctual desires and fears of the id are in conflict with the moral prohibitions and prescriptions of the superego. This intra-psychic conflict causes anxiety because it means that the individual will either have to renounce what it wants or suffer the pangs of conscience and possible social rejection and punishment. The ego mediates this psychic conflict, often becoming a partisan to it, with the aim of reducing anxiety. Neurotic symptoms form as the result of ego's awkward efforts to resolve these psychic conflicts. In classical psychoanalytic theory, neurosis is viewed as a complex of repressed, conflicting desires and aversions, and their painful and disabling symptoms.

The psychoanalytic constructs, id, superego, and ego, roughly correspond to the Buddhist categories of desire and ignorance. Freud defined the id as the "It" or animal, the repository of our primitive sexual and aggressive "instincts," as he called them. If we interpret "instinct" to mean "desire," then the id represents sensual desire. The superego is the locus of our moral aversions to the primitive, sensual, and aggressive urges of the id. The conflict between the id and the superego is a conflict of desires and aversions. Later ego-psychology recognized the importance of our more sublime desires for fame, glory, honor, love, wealth, and immortality, as well as our subtle aversions to failure, defeat, humiliation, deprivation, and death. In the psychoanalytic and the Buddhist view, the cause of neurotic suffering is to be found in this complex of desires, aversions, and ego. Together, they form the neurotic complex.

There are other similarities between the psychoanalytic and Buddhist views, some of which we have already mentioned. The psychoanalytic concept of repression is roughly analogous to the Buddhist concept of ignorance, as we have noted. They are both failures to see, refusals to face and accept reality. Both are defects in awareness, constrictions of consciousness, closings towards the world. As we have seen, this refusal and failure to accept ourselves, others, and the facts of existence as they are, combined with our wishes for eternal happiness, continuity, and solidity, are the major causes of our self-imposed suffering. The Tibetans have a word which describes a mental state which is the opposite of neurosis and, thus, helps to clarify the meaning of it. The word *chokshe* (Tib. *chog shes*) means the acceptance of a simple life, as it is, without the aspiration for more.[10] Neurosis, by contrast, is the rejection of life as it is and the grasping for more pleasure, more happiness, and the escape from pain and death.

The denial of reality causes a kind of blindness that results in a confused, unskillful, awkward, unbalanced, and frustrating traverse of life. This is neurosis in both its occidental and its oriental meanings. Ignorance is negative because it promotes our neurotic desires and aversions, leading to pain for ourselves and others. Instead of relating to the world as it is, neurotic mind projects onto the world its own hopes and fears, and then egocentrically expects that existence will cooperate. When existence does not cooperate, as regularly occurs, neurotic mind becomes anxious, angry, guilty, ashamed, self-hating, or depressed.

Intersections of Buddhist and Western Thought

At one point in history, the Buddhist and Western views on neurosis intersected. There are many other intersections of Buddhist and Western thought, the appreciation of which might help us to triangulate and focus on the basic truths they both grasp, each in their own way.

From the Buddhist point of view the first two noble truths, the fact of suffering and the causes of suffering, are fundamental truths about the human condition. How are they dealt with in our Western traditions? As we shall see they are largely, but poorly, hidden, like nuggets of gold buried just beneath the surface. Occasionally, a nugget will be stumbled upon. If we scrape beneath the surface of our own minds, we shall find suffering, desires, aversions, and ignorance dwelling there. If we analyze the foundations of Western science, medicine, psychotherapy, and politics, we shall find suffering and the three poisons imbedded in them. If we scan Western history, we shall find amongst our greatest prophets, philosophers, and scientists a deep concern with the problems of suffering and the causes of suffering.

Buddhism and Western thought share a common interest in suffering and happiness because they are universal human concerns. Each tradition presents its views in its own prose and idioms. If we could see these themes in western thought more clearly, if we could understand their inner workings, we might gain some insight that could help us in our own struggles for happiness. Inspired by this hope, let us scan the landscape of Western thought for insight into ourselves which may help us to construct more enlightened Happiness Projects.

Western Views of Suffering

CHAPTER TEN

Suffering As a Motive of Mental Life: Science, Medicine, and Psychotherapy

If it is true that the two primary motivations of human behavior are the desire for happiness and the aversion to suffering and death, then these themes should appear in Western thought and social institutions. Buddhism does not have an exclusive claim to the fact of suffering. It is, in my view, stated more clearly and distinctly in Buddhism than in other religions. But the fact of suffering is also basic to the Judeo-Christian tradition, although it is buried in it, like hidden treasure. The fact of suffering and the desire to avoid and transcend suffering are powerful themes in human mental life. Indeed, it would not be an exaggeration to say that they are the basic motive and foundation of religion—as well as of science, medicine, psychotherapy, and politics.

This may seem to be a grandiose claim for such base emotions. How could suffering be the basis of the most sublime achievements of civilization? If we remember, however, that the founding principle of behavioral psychology is that organisms seek pleasure and avoid pain, it may be easier for us to accept that these are the basic motivations of all life. The sublime epiphany of this principle, the highest level of its evolution, is in the two primary motivations of human mental life: the desire for pleasure, significance, and eternal happiness, and the desire to escape from evil—from meaninglessness, pain, and death.[1]

Imagine if life were continuously and eternally pleasurable, with every need, desire, and whim copiously satisfied instantly. What would be the motivation to do anything? Every motivation, every wish would be instantly achieved. Who would ever search for a problem to be solved, or a question to be answered, except, perhaps, for amusement? This would be heaven, where there is no need for science, for religion, or even for thought.

The Western philosopher who comes closest to the Buddhist view that wisdom begins in suffering is William James (1842-1910). James wondered about the evolutionary significance of intelligence. He analyzed it from the perspective of evolutionary biology as a highly developed organ for solving the problems of existence. For living beings the problems of existence are the problems of survival and well-being, and avoiding suffering and death. In James's opinion, the evolution of intelligence, in the individual as well as in the species, is a response to these problems.

Science is a product of human intelligence; this is obvious. It follows from this that the function of science is to understand and find methods for relieving human suffering and unhappiness. As we have previously noted, scientific theories would be unbelievable were they not backed by the "cash value payoff" of technology. The value of scientific knowledge is the power it gives us to bend nature to our needs, to reduce and palliate our suffering, to prolong our lives, to utilize natural resources for the fulfillment of our desires. If science did not tangibly contribute to our happiness, scientific theories would be uninteresting and meaningless.

The Moral Foundations of Medicine

The most concrete and obvious application of science for the relief of human suffering is medicine. Modern medicine may seem to be an objective science which deals with the diagnosis and treatment of disease. The scientific edifice of medicine is so dazzling that it often distracts us from its moral and religious foundations. We reflect upon the ethics of medicine only in extreme dilemmas, such as assisted suicide and the artificial prolongation of life. But the underlying mandate of medicine is moral. It is based on the universal human desires to avoid pain, disability, and death.[2]

The practice of medicine is historically rooted in religion, and even today retains its religious motives and flavor. The physician is perceived as a scientist and technician, but also as an omniscient, sacred authority whose esoteric knowledge and mystifying technical prowess mediate between life and death, between this world and the next. Much of the resentment towards the medical profession is because of its inability to live up to the idealized expectations people have of it.

The religious foundation of modern scientific medicine is evident from the emblem of the physician: the *caduceus*. The caduceus is a bricolage of three ancient religious symbols: the snake, the staff, and wings. In the medical emblem two snakes are coiled in a double helix around the length of a knobbed staff from which a pair of wings emerge below the crown.

In ancient Greece the caduceus was the badge of the king's herald. The staff represents the authority of the king and the wings represent the king's messenger. The staff, or tree, is an ancient symbol which appears in many primitive myths, including the biblical myth of Genesis, as the link between heaven and earth—the Tree of Life. The staff, the tree, and Jack's beanstalk all have the mythical meaning of a connection between humans and their sky gods.

Wings are an ancient symbol of the messenger, like Mercury, god of commerce and communication (so regarded because the planet is closest to the sun and, hence, to the Sun God), and Pegasus, the winged horse, who carries the human spirit to the world beyond. (Some people regard Pegasus as an angel of death—as some people regard physicians.) The serpent, a historical predator of humans, symbolizes, in many cultures, the dual entity Life-Death. The snake sheds its skin, and so dies, only to be "reborn" in its new skin. The caduceus deciphered then, is the religious badge of the physician, intermediary between humans and God, who holds the powers of life and death, between the blessings of a long, healthy life and the curse of suffering and oblivion.

In medicine, the primary factor that distinguishes between health and disease is the universal human desire to avoid pain, disability, and death.[3] Bodily states are classified as diseases because they lead to pain, disability, or death. Of course, some physical conditions which are essentially harmless are classified as diseases because of an anatomical or physiological similarity to more destructive conditions, but this is a secondary and abstract basis for the distinction between health and disease. The scientific superstructure of medicine is rooted in the first noble truth, the fact of suffering.

The Moral Foundations of Psychotherapy

Psychotherapy is regarded in some quarters as a branch of medicine and in others as a religion.[4] Indeed, psychotherapy resembles both medicine and religion in certain respects and differs from them in others. The differences between them, crudely drawn, are that medicine specializes in the sufferings of the body; psychotherapy specializes in the sufferings of the mind; and religion specializes in the sufferings of the soul. To the extent that one believes that mind and soul are similar, psychotherapy has a religious dimension. To the extent that one believes that mind is an epiphenomenon of brain, psychotherapy will be considered as a branch of medicine.

Although both medicine and psychotherapy originated in primitive religion, the modern versions of these three institutions are differentiated from each other by separate areas of jurisdiction—medical disease, mental disease, and moral behavior; by different methods of knowing—measurement, communication, and meditation or prayer; and by different vocabularies—science, psychology, and theology.

Nevertheless, psychotherapy is joined to medicine on one side and to religion on the other by the common theme, indeed, by the common foundation of compassion for human suffering. Even when the differences between medicine, psychotherapy, and religion are sharply drawn on ideological and logical grounds, and even when they are classified separately according to their individual jurisdictions, methods, and language, they are joined at the heart by a common compassion for human suffering.

We can see from this brief sketch how science, medicine, and psychotherapy are motivated by and serve the purposes of the human desire for happiness and the aversion to suffering and death. This is a reflection of the deeper truth that human mental life is motivated by these dual factors. Let us now inquire into how these truths manifest in Western religion.

CHAPTER ELEVEN

Suffering in Western Religion: Genesis and the Lesson of Job

> A good man out of the good treasure of his heart bringeth forth that which is good; and an evil man out of the evil treasure of his heart bringeth forth that which is evil.
>
> —Luke 6:45

The human desire to escape from suffering is the basic motivation and foundation of religion. Every religion provides to its believers a path of life which provides a means for transcending suffering and death and realizing eternal happiness.

The awareness of suffering appears very early in the Old Testament. The first noble truth is enunciated in Genesis. Immediately after expelling Adam and Eve from Paradise, God punishes them with the sufferings of existence:

> Unto the woman He said: 'I will greatly multiply thy sorrow and thy conception; in pain thou shalt bring forth children; and thy desire shall be to thy husband, and he shall rule over thee.'
>
> And unto Adam he said: 'Because thou has hearkened unto the voice of thy wife, and hast eaten of the tree, of which I commanded thee, saying: Thou shalt not eat of it; cursed is the ground for thy sake; in toil shalt thou eat of it all the days of thy life. Thorns also and thistles shall it bring forth to thee; and thou shalt eat the herb of the field. In the sweat of thy face shalt thou eat bread, till thou return unto the ground; for out of it wast thou taken; for dust thou art, and unto dust shalt thou return.'[1]

Genesis is the Judeo-Christian myth of the birth of humanity. Adam and Eve are the first humans and their existence as humans begins in suffering. Otto Rank's claim that the pain of life begins with the pain of birth is affirmed by the myth of Genesis. At the moment of their birth the first humans are cursed with the sufferings of existence. The woman, whose role in biblical times was to bear and raise children, was cursed with painful childbirth and humiliating slavishness to her husband. The man, whose role was to provide the means of survival, was cursed by having to survive in a world indifferent to his needs. In the Garden of Eden Adam and Eve enjoyed instant gratification and eternal life, but after their birth as humans they were condemned to suffering and certain death. From both the Judeo-Christian and the Buddhist point of view, suffering is intrinsic to life, since it begins at the birth of the individual and of the species. This is the first noble truth.

The Link Between Sin and Suffering

The early Hebrews viewed suffering as divine retribution for sin. The sufferings of the first humans, Adam and Eve, are interpreted as punishment for their sin, the "original sin." Some people believe that the original sin was disobedience to God's prohibition against eating the fruit of the Tree of Knowledge. Others, like St. Paul and St. Augustine, think Eve's sin was allowing herself to be tempted by the Devil and Adam's sin was yielding to the sexual seductions of Eve. In both cases the sin is willfulness, or selfish desire. The punishment is a life of suffering. This is an expression of the second noble truth.

The causal relationship between sin and suffering receives its most exalted codification in the Ten Commandments, which is a covenant, or contract, between the ancient Hebrews and their sky god, Jahweh. The Covenant, a foundation stone of Western civilization, states that in return for the faithful fulfillment of their obligations as inscribed on the Mosaic tablets, Jahweh will make the Hebrews (from the Aramaic *haibaru*, "desert wanderer")[2] his "chosen people." If the Hebrews obey the Law (or *talmud*, which means "guidance for life"), God will protect them from suffering and lead them to "the land of milk and honey." Thus, God promised the Hebrews the land of Israel in return for their obedience to the Ten Commandments. The corollary of this contract is that whoever breaks God's law has sinned and shall suffer. God's down payment on this agreement, as it were, was the Exodus of the Jews from slavery in Egypt in the thirteenth century B.C.

The idea that suffering is divine retribution for sin, and its corollary, that happiness is the reward of virtue, is deeply rooted in religious consciousness. It is the basis of moral law. Happiness is perceived as the result of harmony between the individual will and the divine will (the origin of the moral doctrine of "natural law"). Unhappiness is the consequence of discord, which is Adam's sin—original sin—disobedience to God. This view was classically expressed by the eighth century B.C. prophet, Isaiah:

> Say ye to the righteous, that it shall be well with him; for they shall eat the fruit of their doings. Woe unto the wicked! it shall be ill with him; for the reward of his hands shall be given him.[3]

To the ancient, nomadic Hebrews, the sky god Jahweh was the God of Nature, who could be both benevolent and wrathful, generous and demanding. Yahweh was Lord of rain and thunderstorms, of bounty and famine, of fertility and death. Since no one could claim with humility to be perfectly virtuous, suffering was accepted as God's judgment of sinners.

A long series of catastrophes, however, culminating with the destruction of the Temple in Jerusalem in 586 B.C., the end of the Davidic line and Babylonian exile, created a crisis of faith in the Covenant with Jahweh. The problem was not the *fact* of suffering, but *its distribution*.[4] The virtuous and faithful were suffering and dying, it seemed, while the heathen and sinner lived long and prospered.

This appeared to violate God's Covenant with the Hebrews. It contradicted the hallowed idea that virtue is rewarded and that sinners will suffer their just due. How could a just and merciful God punish the righteous and reward the sinner? If God is unjust, then what is the meaning of suffering, and therefore, of life?[5]

The Lesson of Job

These questions are brought to a focus in the Old Testament story of Job. Job is the classical biblical teaching on the first noble truth. I often work with people who are suffering from a great personal tragedy. They cannot accept that such a tragedy was punishment for their sin. They feel betrayed and ripped off by God, as if God had broken his contract with them. They are inconsolable. Nothing I say alleviates their pain to the slightest degree. If they are religious I ask them if they have read the story of Job. Surprisingly, few people have. The story has tremendous therapeutic value. It is an inspirational moral teaching because it offers profound insight and solace to sufferers of every age.

> There was a man in the land of Uz, whose name was Job; and that man was blameless and upright, and one who feared God, and shunned evil.[6]

Job was a great desert sheik, "the greatest of all the men of the east." He owned great herds of sheep, camels, oxen, and donkeys, and fathered seven sons and three daughters. One day, God boasted to Lucifer about his faithful servant, Job. Lucifer, the angel of light, one of God's favorites, who later turned against him and became known as the Devil (Greek, *diabolos*, "slanderer"), said to God: "No wonder Job is faithful to you. Look what wealth you have given him. Take away his wealth and he will curse you."

God trusted Job, and so gave Lucifer permission to take away everything that Job owned as a test of his faith. Job's animals were all stolen or slain, his servants were murdered, and his children were killed by a sudden wind from the wilderness that tumbled their house on their heads. Job fell to his knees and prayed, but "sinned not, nor charged God foolishly."[7]

Once again, God boasted to Lucifer about Job's faith. But the Devil replied: "No wonder he remains faithful. You have not touched his flesh. Afflict him with pain and he will curse you." Again, God gave Lucifer permission to pose the test, and Job was stricken with painful boils from head to toe.

The story of Job was probably written between the third and sixth centuries B.C., during the period of exile and extreme suffering of the Hebrews.[8] Job is a metaphor for Israel. His suffering symbolizes Israel's suffering. If the Israelites were God's chosen people, then why did God make them suffer so much? Since the virtuous suffered along with the sinners, had God not breached his contract with Israel?

The prologue of the story expresses the first noble truth: suffering is a fact of life. Because it is a fact of life, enduring suffering with patience is a test of virtue. In the Judeo-Christian view, suffering is imposed by God as punishment for original sin. Virtuous actions can mitigate original sin and increase one's measure of happiness in this "vale of tears," but virtuous actions cannot prevent suffering. On the contrary, how one endures suffering—humbly or arrogantly—is a measure of virtue. The prologue to Job tells us that God ordains the suffering of those he loves best as a test which the righteous endure and survive. Suffering, thus, is a noble curse, a crisis that creates the opportunity to rise above oneself to a higher level of consciousness. In this view, suffering is a mark of merit in the eyes of God. It is a spiritual cleanser, "the fire that purifies."

The epilogue of the story of Job teaches the virtue of patience. Patience means suffering. The words "patience," "patient," "passion," "pity," and pathology" are probably related through a common Indo-European root to the Latin *pati* and the Greek *pathos*, which means suffering. *Patience is the willingness to suffer without aggression.* Job is a lesson in patience. He suffered serenely, without cursing or rejecting God. Patient suffering brings redemption. God rewarded Job for his patience by restoring to him twice his previous wealth, doubling his honor and reputation, and blessing him with seven new sons and three new daughters, each stronger and more beautiful than the first.

Job lived a long and joyful life of 140 years, and had four generations of grandchildren; everything but eternal life. The Old Testament Hebrews believed that humans are created by God breathing on dust, and that after death dust returns to dust and breath returns to God. (The words spirit and respiration come from the same root.) The idea of personal, eternal life as a reward for suffering does not occur to Job, and is only a minor theme in the Old Testament.[9]

> Man that is born of woman is of few days and full of trouble. He comes forth like a flower, and is cut down; he flees like a shadow and continues not....For there is hope for a tree, if it be cut down, that it will sprout again, and that the tender branch thereof will not cease....But man dies and wastes away. Yes, man gives up the ghost, and where is he?...So man lies down and does not rise. Till the heavens be no more, they shall not awake nor be raised out of their sleep.[10]

Three of Job's friends suggest that a just God does not punish the just. Suffering is God's punishment for sin. Therefore, Job must have sinned. If he would atone and beg God's forgiveness, he would be redeemed and restored to his previous position. Job rejects this advice, not by denying his sins and defending his virtue, but by refusing to defend himself in any way, especially by confessing sins he did not believe he committed. Job believed that to defend himself or make a plea to God for mercy would be vanity. He accepts his suffering as a fact of life. "Let me alone!" he cries, "for my days are vanity. What is man that thou should magnify him?"[11]

With these words Job shows his profound understanding of suffering. He understands suffering not from the narrow point of view of his own selfish strivings, attachments, and losses. He knows it from the cosmic perspective, from the divine perspective of creation as a whole. He understands his suffering as his prideful objection to the universal principle of impermanence.

"How can man be just with God?" he asks. "If one wished to contend with Him, he could not answer Him one time out of a thousand."[12] Like all humans, Job desired long life, health, prosperity, and happiness. But he knew that these are only temporary gifts from God, which are eventually lost when and how God wills. Job sets an example of virtue by enduring his suffering with patience and humility, as befits a creature of God. He does not question God's judgment or mercy. He is neither angry nor bitter. He does not lose faith and does not deviate from the path of virtue. In thundering words of irrefutable authority, Jahweh commends Job by affirming the emptiness and insignificance of the human ego:

> Where were you when I laid the foundations of the Earth? Tell me if you know. Who decided the plan of it, if you know? Who stretched the measuring line across it on which the foundations are fastened? Or who laid the cornerstone when the morning stars sang together and all the sons of God shouted for joy?[13]

The story of Job has consoled sufferers through the ages because, in Horace Kallen's words, it provides "a theory of life, a theory which will define evil's proper place in the economy of nature and the flux of human enterprise."[14] The lesson of Job is that suffering is a fact of life and patience is the virtue of suffering without aggression. To question God's will (to question the facts of existence), to oppose and rage against it, to question his justice, are futile and sinful acts of pride and vanity. Humans are helpless children in the divine lap. The wisdom of Job is the acceptance of impermanence and insubstantiality with patience.

CHAPTER TWELVE

Oedipus Rex: Tragic Hero of the West

> By oneself evil is done;
> By oneself one suffers;
> By oneself evil is left undone;
> By oneself one is purified.
> Purity and impurity belong to oneself;
> No one can purify another.
> —The Buddha

> The greatest griefs are those we cause ourselves.
> —Sophocles, *Oedipus Rex*

The Greeks became aware of the problem of suffering at about the same time as the Hebrews. The classical Greek view of human suffering is expressed in Sophocles' Oedipus Rex, written in the fifth century B.C. The myths of Job and Oedipus express the same nascent awareness of the tragic nature of human life. Sigmund Freud considered Oedipus Rex to be the quintessential tragic hero and made him a symbol of neurotic mind. There is thus, potentially, a great lesson to be learned from the interpretation of Oedipus from a Buddhist point of view. This is not to imply that the Buddhist view is *the* correct one. Works of art, like dreams, have many possible interpretations. There is no one "correct" interpretation. The meaning is in the mind of the beholder. How would the tragedy of Oedipus be interpreted from one Buddhist's point of view?

In my view, the key to Sophocles' tragic view of life is given in Oedipus' answer to the riddle of the Sphinx. The Sphinx is a symbol of the esoteric, a mysterious figure who represents the secrets we keep from ourselves. She is a mythical monster who challenges human ignorance by posing riddles. The punishment for the failure to give the correct answer—the price of ignorance—is a painful death. If the riddle is solved, the Sphinx destroys herself. In Sophocles' story the Sphinx blocks the road to Thebes, posing her puzzle to all travelers: "What creature walks on four legs in the morning, on two legs at noon, and on three legs at night?" In this child-like riddle lies hidden the secret of human life. Those who know it will survive and prosper. Those who do not will suffer and die.

Oedipus answered the riddle correctly and became the hero of Thebes: "Humans are the creatures who walk on four legs as infants, on two legs in the bright sun of their maturity, and on three legs with the aid of a cane in old age." The riddle of the Sphinx is a metaphor for the truths of impermanence, suffering, and death. Humans are born helpless and innocent, grow to maturity filled with hopes and dreams, only to grow old, and die. In words hauntingly reminiscent of the words of the author of Job, Sophocles laments the tragedy of human life in a passage that reveals clearly Sophocles' sense of the truth of impermanence:

> Alas for the seed of men.
> What measure shall I give these generations
> That breathe on the void and are void
> And exist and do not exist?
> Who bears more weight of joy
> than mass of sunlight shifting in images,
> Or who shall make his thought stay on
> That down time drifts away?
> Your splendor is all fallen.[1]

Another translation of the same passage is worth quoting here for the beauty of its lines and the poignancy of its lament:

> Man after man after man, O mortal generations
> here once, almost not here
> what are we
> dust ghosts images, a rustling of air
> nothing, nothing
> we breathe on the abyss
> we are the abyss
> our happiness no more than traces of a dream

the high noon sun sinking into the sea
the red spume of its wake raining behind it
we are you
we are you Oedipus
dragging your maimed foot in agony
and now that I see your life finally revealed
your life fused with the god
blazing out of the black nothingness of all we know
I say
no happiness lasts, nothing human lasts.[2]

From a Buddhist point of view, the story of Oedipus is a metaphor for neurotic mind. Oedipus was the victim of his own grasping ego—of his desires and aggressions. His fate was sealed by his own efforts to escape it. The source of Oedipus's pain and tragedy were his own ignorance, passion, and aggression: the three poisons.

When Oedipus was born, an oracle predicted that he would one day slay his father and sleep with his mother. His parents, the King and Queen of Thebes, desperate to evade the prophecy, ordered their child killed. The shepherd who was assigned the dirty task could not bring himself to kill an infant. Instead, he gave Oedipus to a family in nearby Corinth to raise, thinking the truth would never be discovered. When Oedipus was a young man a drunkard told him of a prophesy that he would slay his father and sleep with his mother. Terrified of fulfilling this prophesy Oedipus tried to evade it by fleeing Corinth.

On the road to Thebes a speeding horse and carriage forced Oedipus off the road. In an egotistical rage he slew the passenger and all but one of the escorts. Unknown to Oedipus, the passenger was his biological father, King Laius, on a journey to enlist help for Thebes in the battle against the Sphinx. After slaying his father Oedipus confronted the Sphinx and solved her riddle, causing her death. He entered Thebes as a hero. Naturally, his fame brought him into the court of the Queen, his mother Jocasta. Oedipus, motivated by lust and the grasping for power, seduced his mother, married her, and became King. Thus he fulfilled the prophesy he tried to evade by unknowingly slaying his father and sleeping with his mother.

Freud interpreted the Oedipus myth literally. He assumed that Oedipus's sin represents a universal (male) unconscious desire to kill the father and sleep with the mother. Taken literally, Freud's "theory" seems absurd. Few people would find such wishes within themselves, even after intensive and honest inquiry. Yet, taken literally, Freud's theory of the Oedipal complex has generated all kinds of bizarre explanations of human behavior as being caused by these forbidden wishes. As a result, many people reject Freud's interpretation as the projection of his own imagination.

On the other hand, there is a profound truth in the Oedipal myth. Oedipus was fated to commit horrible, unthinkable actions which are universally taboo. These actions, and the underlying thoughts and wishes that motivate them, are so repulsive as to be regarded as subhuman. Indeed, it is a mark of the human being to renounce them. But they makes sense as a taboo only if they are also potential wishes and actions. This does not necessarily mean that everyone harbors these wishes. The taboos against patricide and maternal incest are as strong as the taboo against cannibalism. No one has suggested that there exists a universal, unconscious human wish to eat the bodies of others. Yet some people may harbor these urges, as some people may wish to kill their fathers and sleep with their mothers.

There is nothing in Sophocles' play to indicate that Oedipus, consciously or unconsciously, wanted to kill his father and sleep with his mother. On the contrary, Oedipus's actions were tragic precisely because he tried to avoid the horrible fate imposed upon him by the gods.

The Oedipal tragedy seems to make more sense from a Buddhist point of view.[3] On this view, the desire to kill the father and sleep with the mother are *symbols* of human aggression and lust. They are symbols of two of the three poisons. Oedipus was, indeed, carried away by his passion and his aggression, although unknowingly, out of ignorance. It is reasonable, then, to explain the Oedipal myth as representing the causes of pain which Oedipus inflicted on himself and others: the three poisons.

The story of Oedipus is a metaphor, or myth. Taken literally, Oedipus's desires are repugnant. As metaphors, they reveal a hidden wisdom. His crimes were aggression, passion, and ignorance. His ignorance was his failure to appreciate or remember the profound truth of his answer to the Sphinx. The wisdom of the Sphinx, posed as a riddle, was that human destiny is to be born, to grow, and to die. Oedipus wanted more. He was a human being and suffered the flaws of being human. He was burning with the passions of desire and full of pride. When the stranger in the coach drove him off the road, as if he didn't exist, Oedipus was humiliated. He defended his dignity and his pride with anger and aggression. As a result of his egotism, pride, and aggression, he unknowingly killed his own father. When he was welcomed as a hero in Thebes, Oedipus's head swelled. He became full of himself. Now he could sleep with the beautiful queen and himself become king. "Vanity. Vanity. All is vanity."

Ernest Becker viewed Oedipus's allegedly unconscious desires as metaphors for a psychological dynamic inherent in human socialization—the Oedipal transition. Metaphorically, Oedipus's desire to have sex with his mother represents the desire to remain a dependent baby, to continue to relate to the parents physically rather than symbolically, to remain or regress to the polymorphic pleasures of infantile narcissism. Metaphorically, the desire to slay his father represents the desire to resist parental authority, to delay growing up, to avoid renouncing the sensual dependence of the child in favor of the self-control and inhibition required of adults by society.[4]

Everyone experiences and struggles with these two desires—the desire to be taken care of and the desire to be free from the pleasure-denying restrictions imposed by authority. Oedipus's primary taints were not incest and patricide but sexual desire and aggression.[5] Lust and aggression are the twin scourges of humanity. The socialization of the child is designed to repress, modify, and sublimate lust and aggression. Both Buddhism and Christianity teach the repression of sex and aggression. In general, Christianity devotes itself more to the repression of sex and Buddhism devotes itself more to the repression of aggression.

Oedipus wished to be both an infant and a king—a "Baby-King." This is the universal wish represented by the mythical Oedipus. The Oedipus complex, thus redefined, represents neurotic mind's striving for the power to maximize pleasure and minimize pain. We all know people who cannot hide these primitive motivations, who refuse to grow up, who are selfish and demanding, who become aggressive when they are frustrated. To some degree, we all secretly harbor such desires and aggressions ourselves. The desire to be a Baby-King or Queen is the heart of human neurotic suffering. This is, no doubt, what Thomas Hobbes meant when he said, "Evil is a robust child."

The Lesson of Oedipus

Like Job, Oedipus was a wealthy and powerful chief. Like Job, he was pitched from the pinnacle of success into the pits of suffering and sorrow. If Job is a metaphor for suffering—the first noble truth—then Oedipus is a metaphor for the three poisons—the second noble truth. Oedipus is a model of human weakness, sin, and ignorance. Job is a paradigm of heroism and virtue.

Oedipus once knew the truth of the tragic human condition. He showed his wisdom in his answer to the riddle of the Sphinx: "Humans are born, grow old, and die." In other words, life is transient and brief. Ego is an illusion and ambition is futile. Oedipus forgot these essential truths, however, and he forgot that he forgot. Oedipus thought he was a great man who could transcend the limitations of the human condition. In attempting to escape his fate he killed his father in a fit of angry pride, like young gang members in this country kill each other today. He was lustful and ambitious, like any normal modern Yuppie. His desires and ambitions brought him down. His incest with his mother was simply the most outrageous expression of self-indulgence.

When Oedipus learned the truth about himself, when he discovered that the prophesy of sacrilege had been fulfilled in spite of (or because of?) his efforts to avoid it, when he realized his ignorance, he blinded himself, as if to bring an unseeing body into harmony with his unseeing mind. Oedipus's splendor was all fallen. He exiled himself from Thebes and wandered in his old age in the wilderness near Colonnus, a bitter and miserable old man.

Job, by contrast, was and is an inspiration for Israel and for all sufferers. Job provides a model that helps us to endure suffering with abiding faith and patience. Job remembered the cosmic truths of suffering and impermanence. He was grateful for the gift of life, but he accepted suffering gracefully. When Job's splendor was fallen, as he knew it someday would be, he met his fate with courage and humility.

The tragedy of Oedipus is a metaphor for the causes of human suffering. Ignorance is a precondition of the pain we cause to ourselves and others. In our failure to understand the true nature of the human situation we blindly and aggressively struggle for happiness, permanence, and substantiality. When our strivings are frustrated we become aggressive, or depressed. In this sense, Sophocles' insight into human suffering is the same as the Buddha's: The greatest griefs are those we cause ourselves.

CHAPTER THIRTEEN

Jesus

> You have heard that it has been said: 'You shall love your neighbor and hate your enemy.' But I say unto you: Love your enemies.
> —Jesus of Nazareth, Matthew 5:43-5

Of all the religions of the world, the fact of suffering is most transparent at the core of Christianity, symbolized by the figure of Jesus dying on the cross. The life of Christ represents a continuation and fulfillment of the Old Testament interpretation of the problem of suffering. "Think not that I am come to destroy the law, or the prophets," Jesus said. "I am not come to destroy, but to fulfill."[1] Jesus' contribution was original and distinctive, however.[2] Jesus represents an evolution of religious consciousness. As a response to suffering, Moses gave the Hebrews *law*, Job gave them abiding *faith*, and Jesus gave them *love*.

The New Testament explanations of suffering begin with the traditional Hebrew belief that individual suffering is God's retribution for sin. As with the Jews, however, the persecution and martyrdom of the Christians raised questions about the unjust distribution of suffering and, therefore, about the justice, mercy and even the existence of God.

These questions were partially resolved by the concept of original sin, which taints all humans equally. Original sin makes suffering a fact of life for good and evil people alike. The philosophy of Job is also represented in Christianity by the Pauline doctrine that humans cannot, with humility, question or challenge God's will. "Oh man," Paul cried, "who are you to reply to God? Shall the thing formed say to him that formed it, 'Why have you made me so?'"[3]

The Devil is also invoked as a cause of sin and suffering. The Devil is mentioned only three times in the Old Testament.[4] But his personality and functions are fully developed in Christianity where he is blamed not only for original sin because he tempted Eve, but also for all forms of evil in the lives of humans.

The universal and timeless appeal of Christianity, however, is not the power to rationalize suffering but the power of the image of Christ as the victim of suffering and the victor over suffering.[5] Like Job, Christ was innocent and pure, extraordinarily so, having been conceived without sin. Yet he suffered.

Jesus prophesied that he would suffer and die. He accepted this as a preordained fact. Like Job, he faced his fate with courage, weakening only momentarily in Bethany[6] and in the delirium of the passion on the cross, when he cried, "My God! My God! Why have you forsaken me?"[7]

The meaning of Jesus' life is given in his response to suffering. His ministry was for the sinner and the sufferer. "They that are whole" he said, "have no need of the physician; but they that are sick. I came not to call the righteous, but sinners to repentance."[8] Christ's mission was to comfort the poor, the sorrowful, the hungry, and the persecuted, and to admonish sinners who cause the suffering of others. He performed miracles, such as healing the sick and reviving the dead, only to demonstrate his credentials as a healer, which is why only Lazarus was raised from the dead.

Jesus' response to suffering was love. He preached the gospel of love to his flock of sufferers. He taught them unconditional, radical love for every human being, even their enemies:

> You have heard that it has been said: 'You shall love your neighbor and hate your enemy.' But I say unto you: Love your enemies. Bless them that curse you. Do good to them that hate you. And pray for them that spitefully use you and persecute you, that you may be the children of your father in heaven. For He makes the sun rise on the evil and on the good, and sends rain on the just and on the unjust.[9]

This is, perhaps, the most radical and demanding of all the commandments, the most difficult to obey and the most often failed. It seems to strike at the heart of life, against the instinct of self-preservation, against the pursuits of self-interest and self-realization. It seems to require an attitude of passivity towards evil and the readiness to surrender that which is most deeply cherished and desired—life, freedom, and happiness.

Buddhism teaches a similar but even more difficult practice called *tonglen*, otherwise known as "taking and receiving," or "exchanging self with others." It is specifically prescribed for healing anger and aggression. In this practice the meditator progressively visualizes his or her relatives, friends, and enemies and, with mindfulness of breathing, bequeaths all his or her happiness, comfort, and wealth to the others on the outbreath and, on the inbreath, takes the unhappiness, negativities, and pain of the other onto him or herself. This Buddhist practice is as difficult for the ego to practice as Jesus' commandment to love one's enemies.

Jesus, like Buddha, was the exemplary embodiment of his teaching. He lived the gospel of love to the extreme, forgiving even those who taunted, tortured, and murdered him. In his final moments of suffering he cried, "Father, forgive them, for they know not what they do." Although Christians "know" the message of Jesus, it is extremely difficult to follow, so it is repressed into a secret. Nevertheless, Jesus taught that love is the method for transcending suffering. This sublime moral standard is a challenge to anyone seeking higher consciousness.

The Evolution of Consciousness from Law to Love

The Christian gospel of love is not a simple matter of passively turning the other cheek. It represents an evolution of consciousness beyond the Mosaic concern with law and conduct to a concern with the inner, spiritual dimension of experience. Moses gave the Hebrews the Torah, which means "guidance for life."[10] The Torah provides rules of conduct which reduce or prevent the suffering that humans inflict on each other.

Jesus also represents a guide for life. He is called the Shepherd, the Path, and the Door.[11] Jesus is a guide of the *inner* life, a guide to the life of the heart and soul. Jesus represents a solution to the problem of suffering which goes beyond the transformation of conduct from sin to virtue, to a transformation of consciousness from selfish desire to divine love.

The Torah commands: "Thou shalt not kill."[12] Jesus preached that it is not sufficient merely to abstain from physical violence. Hatred, anger, and resentment are also acts of violence, even if they are only thoughts and feelings rather than actions. They are sins nevertheless, and violate the commandment to "Love your neighbor as yourself."[13] Both commandments aim at the relief of suffering, for while violent conduct causes immediate and direct suffering, violent thoughts, feelings, and words create "karmic ripples" which go around and, eventually, come back to afflict the sinner who is their source.[14] In Christ's words:

> A good man out of the good treasure of his heart bringeth forth that which is good; and an evil man out of the evil treasure of his heart bringeth forth that which is evil.[15]

Compare Christ's teaching to the Buddha's:

> You are in slavery to a tyrant of your own setting up:
> Your own deeds, words and thoughts are your own avengers.
> Your acts your angels are for good or ill,
> Your fatal shadows that walk by you still.[16]

Like the Dharma, the gospel of love calls for a personal transformation from a state of consciousness motivated by the desire for self-satisfaction and worldly attainment to one motivated by renunciation, unselfishness, and love. Thus, resentment and anger are to be transformed into compassion and reconciliation. Lust is to be converted into affection, if not into chastity. Greed is to be transfigured into charity. And pride matures into humility.

Jesus and Buddha taught similar solutions to the problem of suffering. Jesus, like Buddha, portrayed himself as a physician. Like Buddha, the disease he sought to treat is suffering—of body, mind, and soul. The medicine is love. The therapy of suffering through love, like dying and being reborn, is not easy. It involves a radical self-transformation. This requires quieting the busy mind and pacifying the desirous heart. To realize this spiritual state Jesus, like the Buddha, prescribes the cessation of thought and the relinquishment of ego-clothing:

> Which of you by taking thought can add one cubit to his stature? And why do you take thought for raiment? Consider the lilies of the field, how they grow: they toil not, neither do they spin.[17]

The state of love, or *agape*, is similar to the state of meditation. It calls for present-centered awareness rather than absorption in memories of the past or visions of the future:

> Take therefore, no thought for the morrow; for the morrow shall take thought for the things of itself. Sufficient unto the day is the evil thereof.[18]

The Christian gospel of love is a spiritual path of redemption from suffering through the figure of Jesus Christ. In his suffering and death on the cross, Jesus is a victim with whom all humans can identify. His Resurrection symbolizes victory over suffering and death. The Resurrection, like the Crucifixion, may be interpreted literally or metaphorically. Taken literally, the Resurrection signifies the transcendence of suffering through actual personal rebirth in heaven after death. This literal interpretation fulfills the individual's desire for personal immortality. It also fulfills Yahweh's promise to the Old Testament Hebrews that virtue shall be rewarded and sin shall be punished. The unequal distribution of suffering on Earth is rationalized by deferring the reward of virtue and the punishment for sin until afterlife. The Resurrection thus permits the restoration of faith in a just and merciful God who actively oversees human affairs.

Taken as a metaphor, the Resurrection symbolizes the victory of love over suffering. The life of Jesus provides a path or way for overcoming suffering and death with love: with compassion, forgiveness and reconciliation; with no thought of personal ambition or satisfaction; with a peaceful heart and a quiet mind, attentively attuned to the unfolding of life; with a humble identification with all God's creatures and works; and with an acceptance of the fact of death. Suffering is thus the mark of discipleship with Christ.[19] Christ's life points out the path to the transcendence of suffering through love, the victory over evil through the perfection of human goodness.[20]

The Spiritual Path

As Christianity evolved through the centuries, the depth and complexity of the human sense of interiority also evolved, and the problem of salvation from suffering came to be formulated in the metaphors of an interior transformation or journey.

Saint Augustine (354-430) fused the intermingling currents of the Christian mystical tradition with the Neo-platonic tradition of philosophical contemplation. Spiritual progress, according to Augustine, moves from nature to mind to God. Sin and suffering occur at the lowest, or material plane of existence. The primary sin, the sin of Adam, is the sexual act, the desire for sensuous pleasure. The "upward path" is an evolution from the body and the senses to rational understanding to wisdom. Wisdom is achieved by turning awareness inward to the soul in search of truth, guided by "divine illumination" and "grace." The greatest good is happiness, defined not as personal fulfillment, but as union with God in love (*agape*) manifested by charity (*caritas*). The spiritual journey is from the earthly city of humanity to the heavenly city, the City of God.

> Accordingly, two cities have been formed by two loves: the earthly by the love of self, even to the contempt of God; the heavenly by the love of God, even to the contempt of self. The former, in a word, glorifies in itself, the latter in the Lord.[21]

Other Christian writers have used different metaphors for the divine journey, some of which bear some resemblance to the Hindu tantric system of *chakras* and the so-called "raising of the *kundalini*." The chakras blend mind and body better than the Christian systems of spiritual development, however. The chakras have physical loci, but are not physical centers. They are subtle bodies, which are states of mind embedded in the body. The chakras are metaphors for the stages of development of cosmic consciousness. The itinerary is basically the same as that specified by Augustine. It is a development from a preoccupation with sex and power, to the opening of the heart of compassion and wisdom and, finally, the attainment of the mystical transcendent consciousness.

Richard St. Victor (d. 1172) used the family of Jacob—his sons, daughters, wives, and servants—as a metaphor for the development of spiritual states of consciousness.[22] By describing the members of Jacob's family in sequence, Richard describes the successive states of self-knowledge and self-discipline which lead to a divine state of inner peace and love.

Some thirteen centuries after the death of Christ on the Cross, St. Bonaventure (1217-1274), a Franciscan friar, described the spiritual journey as a "road to rapture." In *The Soul's Journey into God* he writes about six levels of illumination, each mediated by Christ, from the sensory world of flesh and matter to the inner world of reason and imagination, to the divine world of contemplation and agape—the union with God in ecstasy.[23]

Bonaventure interpreted the Crucifixion as a symbol of atonement for the sin of Adam, the original sin, by which humans are separated from God. Resurrection signifies Redemption. Redemption is the healing of the alienation from God through merging with God. Through the Crucifixion and Resurrection, Jesus, the second Adam, is reunited with God through love. The figure of Jesus on the Cross, and the mystical love consciousness he represents, symbolizes the transcendence of suffering through the reconciliation of opposites. The intersection of the horizontal and vertical limbs of the Cross represents the reconciliation of heaven and earth, of the human and the divine, of life and death, of good and evil, of innocence and maturity, and of suffering and joy.

> For if an image is an expressed likeness, when our mind contemplates in Christ the son of God, who is the image of the invisible God by nature, our humanity is so wonderfully exalted, so ineffably united the first and the last, the highest and the lowest, the circumference and the center, the *alpha* and the *omega*, the cause and the effect, the Creator and the creature, that is, the book written within and without, it now reaches something perfect.[24]

The most famous medieval Christian account of the soul's journey into god is Dante's *Divine Comedy*. In this epic poem Dante depicts spiritual progress as a passage from hell to purgatory to heaven, arranged in a hierarchical sequence from suffering, sin, and ignorance to love, virtue, and knowledge. Dante's guides on the journey are Virgil (70-19 B.C.), the Roman poet who guides him through the inferno and purgatory, and Beatrice, the love of his life, who guides him from earthly love to agape. Like the ancient astronomers of the Mediterranean basin, Dante used the stars to symbolize the goals of the human spirit. Paradise is composed of the seven visible spheres of Ptolemaic astronomy: the Moon, Mercury, Venus, Mars, the Sun, Jupiter, and Saturn. Next came the sphere of the fixed stars, the *primum mobile*, an invisible sphere which is the origin of all motion. At the periphery is the *empyrean—nirvana*—a region beyond space and time, where the soul is united with God in joy.

From the Spiritual Path to the Cure of Souls

By the beginning of the fourteenth century, when Dante memorialized the medieval world view as a Divine cosmic hierarchy with God at the apex and Earth and all its history at the center, the humble mustard seed planted by Jesus had grown into the proud and powerful Catholic Church. Previously, the relief from suffering through the ascent of the soul to God had been voluntary. Redemption was the responsibility of the individual to pursue. Sinners and sufferers, like St. Augustine, took the initiative themselves to renounce their sins and travel the arduous journey of virtue. By the fifteenth century, however, the Catholic Church had usurped the authority to save sinners from themselves—by persuasion, coercion, excommunication, and even death by immolation if necessary.[25]

In the fifteenth century Rome established an Office for the Cure of Souls whose aim was to save sinning, errant, and lost souls from eternal suffering.[26] What began as the symbolic salvation from suffering through the mythical figure of Christ on the Cross, was transformed into a social institution of pastoral counseling. The Cure of Souls, like modern psychiatry, had a coercive side too. Officers of the Church were charged with the responsibility of defending the faith by identifying sinners, sufferers, and heretics and, by persuasion and coercion, inducing them to confess and reform.[27] The *Malleus Malificarum,* or *Witches Hammer,* was an elaborate manual which assisted the priest in diagnosing witches and determining the proper means of their reform and "cure," by death if necessary.[28]

From the spiritual point of view, the Cure of Souls, and the figure of Christ on the Cross which is its foundational icon, is the predecessor of modern psychotherapy. The psychoanalyst Otto Rank (1884-1939) called psychotherapy the "grandchild of religion" because the common ground of both is the desire to escape the pain of life which Rank believed begins at birth.[29] Modern psychotherapists do not think of themselves in the tradition of Christ. They like to think of themselves as a branch of medicine that deals with the diagnosis and treatment of mental illness. But the appeal of Christ on the Cross, like all religious icons, has the same motive as psychotherapy. Indeed, religion, medicine, and psychotherapy are joined at the heart by the desire to relieve and transcend suffering.

CHAPTER FOURTEEN

Suffering and Politics

> Thus the criticism of heaven turns into the criticism of the earth, the criticism of religion into the criticism of right, and the criticism of theology into the criticism of politics....
>
> —Karl Marx

> He who does not understand that politics is religion and religion is politics understands neither politics nor religion.
>
> —Mahatma Gandhi, *An Autobiography*

By the fifteenth century the Catholic Church, in an uneasy alliance with aristocrats and monarchs, dominated the social, economic, and political life of Western Europe. The medieval social structure consisted of a class hierarchy with nobility at the top, followed by clergy, land owners, tradesmen, and peasants and serfs at the bottom. This unequal class structure was explained and justified as a manifestation of the divine hierarchy, ordained by "natural law." The unequal distribution of suffering between the upper and lower classes was rationalized as a manifestation of the divine cosmic plan.

The medieval world of Europe was on the wane, however. The old feudal order was usurped by monarchies who consolidated economic and political power as their self-proclaimed "divine right." The voyages of discovery of the fifteenth and sixteenth centuries opened new continents for trade, exploitation, and colonization. This inaugurated the "age of empires" and produced a new and powerful *bourgeois* class (burghers, or city dwellers) which upset the old hierarchy.

Discoveries in mathematics, physics, and astronomy between the fifteenth and eighteenth centuries undermined the Ptolemaic geocentric astronomy upon which medieval Christian cosmology was based. The Catholic Church, which had been corrupted by the greed for secular power, began to lose it. Challenged by monarchs, heretics, and reformers, it resorted to the desperate, bloody purges of the Inquisition to save itself. Instead, it lost its claim as the noblest vehicle for the relief of human suffering.

By the eighteenth century Europe was in turmoil. The new science and mathematics had revolutionized the view people had of their world and themselves. The class conflict between the upper classes and the bourgeoisie and peasants culminated in 1789 with the French Revolution. This was only one of a long series of democratic revolutions which continue today against the tyranny and injustice of feudalism, totalitarianism, and class exploitation.

In this great historical transformation, the traditional reliance on the dogmatic and sacramental powers of the Catholic Church for the rationalization and redemption of suffering was eroded by doubt and cynicism. The European Enlightenment (c. 1650-1800) saw the transfer of responsibility for human suffering and unhappiness from reliance on the authority of religion to reliance on science and democracy.[1] The problem of suffering came to be addressed not in terms of salvation after death through faith and piety, but in terms of social progress on Earth through democracy and science.[2]

The Roots of Communism: Jean Jacques Rousseau on the Problem of Suffering

In 1755 the French Academy of Dijon sponsored a contest for the best essay on the perennial question in which we are vitally interested: "What is the origin of unequal human suffering, and what is the best remedy for it?" Jean Jacques Rousseau (1711-1778) submitted the winning essay. His contribution marks the beginning of modern thought on the problem of suffering.[3] Rousseau proposed that the problem of suffering should be addressed by science rather than by religion, by a critical inquiry into human nature rather than by an appeal to traditional dogma about the personality and motives of God:

> For how shall we know the source of inequality between men, if we do not begin by knowing mankind? And how shall man hope to know himself as nature made him, across all the changes which the succession of place and time must have produced in his original constitution? How can he distinguish what is fundamental in his nature from the changes and additions which his circumstances and the advances he has made have introduced to modify his primitive condition?...For it is by no means a light undertaking to distinguish properly between what is original and what is artificial in the actual nature of man, or to form a true idea of a state which no longer exists, perhaps never did exist, and probably never will exist, and of which, it is nevertheless, necessary to have true ideas, in order to form a proper judgment of our present state.[4]

Rousseau sought the causes and cures of unequal human suffering by means of a historical inquiry into human nature. By understanding primitive humans in their original state (*l'homme naturel*) in contrast to civilized humans (*l'homme artificiel*) Rousseau hoped to formulate an ideal type of human society that could serve as a basis of social criticism and social progress.

For this, the great Immanuel Kant (1724-1804) revered Rousseau as the Newton of the human sciences. A picture of Rousseau was the only decoration in his ascetic study.[5] Inspired by Rousseau, Kant believed that the purpose of science is not merely to discover facts and general laws, but to reveal the fundamental order of the universe on which to base a universal morality. The ideal is the Enlightenment ideal of replacing a religious view of the world with a scientific view as the basis of morality. Kant envisioned as the purpose of science to reveal not only "the starry heavens above," but also "the moral law within." To understand the nature of good and evil, Kant believed, it is necessary to understand "what is enduring in human nature, and the proper place of man in creation."[6]

Neither Rousseau nor Kant had any knowledge of Darwinian evolution, of course. The first hominid fossils, which were Neanderthal skull fragments, did not come to the attention of scientists until 1856; ironically, only three years before the publication of Darwin's *Origin of Species*. Rousseau's concept of primitive humanity was a fantasy shaped by personal idiosyncracies and strong historical currents.

Rousseau was a solitary, idealistic, recklessly independent and critical spirit who was happiest away from Parisian society, wandering alone in the woods.[7] He lived in the era of ocean sailing and the exploration of continents and civilizations unknown to the Europeans. Ocean voyagers brought back romantic reports of paradisiacal cultures with no violence. Rousseau attributed the peacefulness of these societies, or "primitive communities," to the absence of private ownership of property. By comparison, the turbulent class wars of European society seemed to be a retrograde fall. Rousseau sought the root causes of this fall so he could formulate a political program of Utopian reform. Reflecting radical perceptions of the class structure of his time, Rousseau concluded that the dividing line between primitive and civilized humans, the original sin and root cause of the fall, was the ownership of private property:

> The first man who, having enclosed a piece of ground, bethought himself of saying, "This is mine," and found people simple enough to believe him, was the real founder of civil society.[8]

Rousseau's reliance on primitive peoples as a contrast for understanding modern society won him the honor of being regarded as the father of anthropology.[9] His idea that the ownership of private property is the root cause of unequal suffering because it creates an unequal class structure which keeps the poor in chains, strongly influenced Karl Marx (1818-1883) and shaped the ideology of future communist societies. The word "communism" refers to communal primitive societies, as opposed to the individual ownership of private property as exists in modern society.

The word "radical" means "root." Rousseau's concept of the root cause of social evil became the cornerstone of radical critiques, protests, and revolutions of the past three centuries which sought to correct the evils of capitalism by eliminating what was supposed to be its root cause: private property. The now discredited Marxist ideal of a classless society in which people live in harmony and dignity is a version of Roussseau's Utopian fantasy about pre-civilized society. For this reason some people also regard Rousseau as the father of modern totalitarianism.

Karl Marx on the Problem of Suffering

Philosophers of the Enlightenment, like Rousseau, were inspired by the hope that democracy and science would provide a rational and equitable solution to the problem of suffering. By the middle of the nineteenth century, however, it was becoming disappointingly evident that the new scientific-industrial revolution had intensified the problem of the unequal distribution of suffering. It had given rise to a new class system in which the upper, capitalist class had accumulated great wealth and power while the lower, working classes lived in poverty and misery, sharing little of the wealth produced by their labor.

These conditions spawned a new formula for the alleviation of suffering: the Utopian Communism spawned by Karl Marx. Like the religious figures who preceded him, Marx was concerned primarily with the problem of suffering. John Bowker writes:

> ...Marx concentrated not on suffering as a theoretical problem, but on the actual facts and occurrences of suffering as he observed them. Suffering lies at the foundation of Marx's thought because he was first stirred to his vehement and passionate appeals for revolutionary action by his observations of the appalling conditions in which working people lived and died.[10]

Marx's analysis of human suffering, as we have noted, traces back to the European Enlightenment and Jean Jacques Rousseau. Accordingly, his solution to the problem of self-imposed human suffering was the abolition of private property and private production. Since his ideal society was the primitive community where the means of production are shared, his political system was called "Communism."

Marxist Communism is a blend of religion and science. We don't usually think of Marxism as scientific, but Marx was one of the first to apply the methods of "the new science" to politics and government. Karl Marx is regarded by sociologists as one of the founders of modern social science because he used facts, statistics, and theories to describe and explain social conditions, and to formulate policies for the relief of suffering and the pursuit of happiness on earth.

If Marxism is science, however, it is science with a mission, the same mission that animates religion—the desire to escape from suffering. Marxist faith is not in God, but in the power of science and politics for deliverance. Marxists use political power and science to achieve their ideological aims. They clothe themselves in the authority of science to extract obedience from their followers. In its authoritarian structure and its demand for obedience, Marxism resembles religion. Lewis Feuer called Marxism "the first secular world religion," with its own sacred texts, saints, heretics, and holy city.[11]

In the tradition of the Enlightenment, Marx believed in a religion of humanity, a secular humanism based on practical social-political action to relieve suffering. He condemned traditional religion as "the opium of the people."[12] Marx argued that a movement which believes in salvation from suffering after death is itself a projection of existing class contradictions which repress dissent, lull people into passivity, and prolong their suffering.

Marx's aim was to devise a political system which could relieve the suffering caused by poverty, slavery, exploitation, injustice, and alienation. Marx and his friend and collaborator, Friedrich Engels (1820-1895), were well aware of the similarities between Communism and Christianity, as these words of Engels demonstrate:[13]

> The history of early Christianity has notable points of resemblance with the modern working class movement. Like the latter, Christianity was originally a movement of oppressed people: It first appeared as the religion of slaves and emancipated slaves, of poor people deprived of all rights, of peoples subjugated or dispersed by Rome. Both Christianity and the workers socialism preach forthcoming salvation from bondage and misery. Christianity places this salvation in a life beyond, after death, in heaven; socialism places it in this world, in a transformation of society.

To Marx, suffering is suffering, whether expressed in religious or social terms. "Religious distress," he wrote, "is at the same time the expression of real distress and the protest against real distress." It is "the sigh of the oppressed creature, the heart of a heartless world."[14] In Marx's program to secularize religion, devotion to the "holy family" is viewed as a diversion from the distress of the "earthly family." "Once the earthly family is discovered to be the secret of the holy family," Marx wrote, "the former must then itself be criticized in theory and revolutionized in practice."[15]

Marx believed it is futile to rely on religion for relief from suffering. Philosophy relied futilely on analysis and understanding. Marx's revolutionary approach relied on political action. "The immediate task of philosophy," he wrote, "which is at the service of history, once the saintly form of human self-alienation has been unmasked, is to unmask self-alienation in its unholy forms. Thus the criticism of heaven turns into the criticism of the earth, the criticism of religion into the criticism of right, and the criticism of theology into the criticism of politics."[16]

Although the Communist societies inspired by him have failed, Marx revolutionized the traditional view of suffering in the modern world. God is no longer the originator and administrator of suffering. Society is. God is no longer the agency of relief from suffering. Politics is.

It is often said that Marx turned Hegel on his head. Marx argued, persuasively to many, that Hegel's claim that "all that is real is rational and all that is rational is real," was a projection of the existing class structure and served to rationalize, justify, and perpetuate it. Marx insisted that the basis of consciousness and of suffering is not God but society. History is not an idea in the consciousness of God, as Hegel thought. On the contrary, the material conditions of life—the means of production—generate history and give thought its form. According to Marx, consciousness does not cause social conditions, social conditions determine consciousness.[17]

Karl Marx viewed the task of philosophy, of science, and of politics as not merely to understand the world, but to transform it in the service of human interests. "The philosophers have only interpreted the world in various ways," Marx wrote in another famous passage, "the point however, is to change it."[18]

Marxism has undergone radical transformations in the past fifty years. The Marxist-Leninist Communism of the Soviet Union grew into a world super-power and then collapsed, as all tyrannies must collapse under the weight of the demoralization of their people. Communism has collapsed in the Soviet Union and Eastern Europe, and is failing or struggling elsewhere. But Marxism has left its imprint on modern politics. Most modern political ideologies, whether they admit it or not, are blends of Marxism and Capitalism. They are derivatives of Marxism in that they place their faith in science and politics for redemption from suffering. Modern politicians may not realize it, but their reliance on scientific advisors and scientific facts to rationalize their policies and strategies stems from Karl Marx.

Modern liberals stand on the platform that the causes of human suffering are to be found in evil social conditions and that the cure of suffering is political action to eliminate those evils. By contrast, modern conservatives mistrust government and believe in old-fashioned pre-Marxist religion. They believe that people are responsible moral agents and that suffering is caused by moral failure. The relief of suffering, therefore, relies on moral reconstruction and enlightened self-interest rather than state action. This is why Christian fundamentalists are politically conservative and why they often think of liberals as influenced by Marxist thought. It also explains why liberals think of conservatives as blind and callous to the social conditions which contribute to human misery.

The Betrayal by the Saviors

The great historical appeal of both the Judeo-Christian tradition and of modern politics is based on the same pure, primary motive: the relief of human suffering. Religion offers redemption from suffering through life after death. Politics promises it through state action to change existing social conditions. In both cases the original pure motive has been often betrayed by disciples who became devils, who caused suffering rather than relieved it.

Wise people through the ages have been aware of the danger of the helper who tries to relieve suffering and instead, causes it. An old Chinese proverb recognizes the harm that helpers do: "Why are you angry with me?" the proverb asks, "I never tried to help you!" Recall the famous, ironic justification for an act of war: "We had to burn the village to save it." Unwanted help is a form of tyranny.[19]

Buddhists have long recognized misguided efforts to relieve suffering as a cause of it. This is "the pain of pain," *duhkha duhkhata*, the suffering caused by the desire to be free of suffering.[20] Reflections on recent history may alert us to beware of the person who flashes the badge of the healer and promises paradise. This is an irresistible bait that few humans can resist. Here, Buddha's advice is invaluable: "The wise person knows that the bait is hooked."[21]

When the Catholic Church launched the Inquisition and the Cure of Souls against the threats of rebellion and heresy, St. Thomas Aquinas (1225-1274), the great "doctor of the Church" who is still honored today for his reconciliation of Christianity and Aristotelian philosophy, proposed a "final solution" to the problem of heresy. These are his words: "From the point of view of the heretics themselves," he wrote, "there is their sin, by which they have deserved not only to be separated from the Church, but to be eliminated from the world by death."[22] The Church condemned Bruno, Galileo, and many other heretical scientists, but it honors Aquinas.

The Catholic Church is not alone in its hypocrisy. Most of today's wars, mass violence, and bloodshed are committed by religious factions fighting each other: Moslems and Jews in the Middle East; Protestants and Catholics in Northern Ireland; Christians and Moslems in the former Yugoslavia. It is an irony fundamental to the nature of the human ego that the institutions to which we look for relief from suffering are the main causes of it. The cause, of course, is not in the institution, but in the self-grasping of people who use the institution for the satisfaction of their own egotistical Happiness Projects. Everyone's particular formula for happiness and the escape from suffering becomes the rationalization for their violence.

Politicians, from Lenin and Stalin to Mao and Pol Pot, including liberals and conservatives from around the world, have pursued their ideal of reducing human suffering by inflicting it. They have defended their power and hegemony through bloody purges, inquisitional torture, prison camp archipelagos, psychiatric prisons, official discrimination, and legal repression.

The desire to relieve suffering which is the common ground of both Marxism and Christianity is, ironically, also the basis of their mutual animosity. Each accuses the other of causing suffering. In the last century, Karl Marx condemned religion as a cause of suffering. In this century, Pope John Paul II criticized communism as the enemy of human freedom and the human spirit.

This mutual condemnation illustrates how suffering is the basic standard for evaluating our social institutions. We judge governments, parties, and bureaucracies by how well they serve our personal strivings for happiness, and how well they ameliorate the problems which cause our pain.

Western Views of Desire

CHAPTER FIFTEEN

The Evolution of Desire into the Happiness Project

> We need, in fine, a metaphysic which recognizes both the continuity between man and animals and also the discontinuity.
>
> —Norman O. Brown, *Life Against Death*

As the root of the word implies, *emotion* is the feeling that moves us. As we previously have discussed, there are two basic or primary emotions: desire and fear. Fear manifests in behavior as aversion. Desire and fear, or aversion, are two of the three poisons of Buddhism. Every act, every wish, every judgment, every plan and hope for the future is energized by our desires and our fears. As we have previously established, we shall call them both desire, because one is the desire to have, the other is the desire to get rid of.

The sweet poison of desire profoundly permeates the human psyche. Of all the kaleidoscopic aspects of human nature, none is as vital nor as bewildering as desire. Desire, particularly the desire to escape from suffering, is the driving force of life, the motive of all our hopes and ambitions. It fuels our thoughts and feelings. Our personalities and characters are shaped by our encounters with desires: by our strivings to satisfy them; by our slavish submission to them; by our sublimations and symbolic gratifications of them; and by our struggle to control and repress them.

Culture too is shaped by desire. Culture is the emanation of the collective human character, as are the institutions which form the foundation of society. Religion, science, and medicine are shaped by our desires for pleasure and happiness and our desires to escape from suffering and unhappiness. Without looking squarely at desire, self knowledge, and inner peace are not possible.

We love, cherish, and defend our desires because we think that satisfying them will bring us pleasure and happiness. We act as if we have a stubborn faith, more unshakable than our most unquestioned religious beliefs, that if our desires are satisfied we will be happy. Yet, for all the delight it promises, desire has a fearsome quality which makes us shudder and look away, blinding us to the nature of our being. To paraphrase George Bernard Shaw: "There are two great tragedies in life. One is not to get what one's heart desires. The other is to get it." We are caught in this paradox: The more we want something the more we are afraid we will not get it. And as we are about to achieve it, we become frightened by the loss of pursuit of it which has given our lives meaning. Our desires are the root of our suffering. Hence desire is tinged with anxiety, and there is a systematic tendency—by both the individual and society—to avoid a full awareness of it.

For all its positive life force, desire has fatal flaws. Another complication is that our desires are not always desirable. Some are worthy and others are not. This conflict of desires should bring us to pause and reflect. The trouble with desire, however, is that it does not pause to reflect. It urges us to act and is not easily ignored, resisted, or repressed. More often than not it plows ahead, unheeding of reason's caution, bashing us into a wall and taking others down with us in its wake. Desire is at the heart of our pain. It is the root of our deepest personal and social problems. Resisting the awareness of our desires and failing to take responsibility for our desires are the sources of our greatest confusion about ourselves and about the meaning and purpose of our lives.

In sum, desire is the most basic element of human nature and personal identity. It is the driving energy of life, the essence of motivation. It is the fountain of our happiness and unhappiness. It generates religion, science, medicine, psychotherapy, and art. It comprises the central problem of ethics and morality. It is the key to the kingdom of heaven and the ticket to hell. Desire is the essence of neurosis. Understanding our desires is the key to the secret of happiness.

The Physics and Biology of Desire

To understand desire and its impact on our lives and emotions, we must develop what Norman O. Brown calls a metaphysic which "recognizes both the continuity between man and animals and also the discontinuity."[1] Animals have desires, but like their suffering, their desires are simple and direct. Doggie dreams are made of hunting and eating, of secure territory and play and, in season, of sex. In animals, there is no essential difference between desires and instincts. The two words denote the same basic phenomena. Instincts are bodily mechanisms, shaped by genetic instructions, which define organismic techniques and lifestyles. The desire of the spawning salmon to swim upstream is shaped by physiology, as are the bee's desire to dance and the lion's desire to hunt. The desires for food and sex, for self-preservation and the propagation of the species, are built into the structure and function of the animal body.

Desire is the impulse though which nature fulfills her destiny. It is the energy through which the universe differentiates itself, the motive for the creation of the individual. So defined, desire can be traced back to the first signs of change in the primordial featurelessness of the cosmic fireball. It was born in the first ten seconds of creation, according to the modern scientific myth, when homogeneous energy began to cool, congeal and differentiate into the charged sub-atomic particles which gradually combined to form protons, neutrons, electrons, and eventually, atoms and molecules.

Desire is the potential of individualized energy particles to bond and form a new entity. The magic of desire manifests when protons and neutrons marry to form the nucleus of atoms and when atoms unite to form molecules. The bonding of oxygen and other atoms around carbon created organic compounds which are the basis of life as we know it. Desire evolved further when organic molecules in the prehistoric ooze replicated themselves, giving birth to evolving living systems. Primitive, virus-like substances developed into unicellular organisms which, in turn, divided and multiplied up the evolutionary scale until desire eventually flowered in the sexual urge of complex organisms to copulate and procreate.

Desire is the striving of the universe to fulfill its potential, to grow, change, and differentiate. It is the energy of evolution. Mythologically, desire is represented by Eros, the Greek god of love and fertility, who personifies the harmony, order, and completion of the world. This aspect of desire, simply stated, is signified by *Go!*

But life is not incessantly on the go. There is also a time to stop: for reconnaissance and reappraisal, for sleep and vacation, for renewal and meditation, and inevitably, for death. The universe is a blend of *Go!* and *Stop!*, of activity and rest, of generation and decay. Living systems are a dynamic balance of action and inhibition.

The nerve impulse is a depolarized *Go!* surrounded by a polarized *Stop!* It is a traveling wave of excitation with a quiescent membrane ahead and a refractory membrane behind. The mammalian cerebromotor *Stop!* mechanism was dramatically demonstrated years ago by the Spanish neurobiologist, Delgado, who surgically implanted electrodes in the inhibitory brain centers of a live bull and then, as the bull charged at him in the center of a ring, calmly pressed a button and electronically brought the raging bull to a sudden *Stop!*

If spring and summer represent *Go!*, then autumn and winter represent *Stop!* This is the tendency of the universe to rest, to run down, to disintegrate and return to primordial featurelessness. It is Thanatos, the Greek god of death, personification of chaos and conflict. In its extreme human form, the desire to *Stop!* is the death wish.

Like the desire to *Go!* the desire to *Stop!* can be zealously pursued, with the anticipation of great satisfaction. Homicide and suicide call for great passion. Asceticism, Puritanism, and self-discipline require strong motivation and determination. *Go!* and *Stop!* cannot exist without each other. They are *Yang* and *Yin*, life and death, the archetypical antithetical pair that reflect the *On / Off* cybernetics of the universe.

The Sublimation of Desire By Language

Humans are animals, and human desire is, in part, animal desire. Hunger, lust, the will to live, the urge to socialize and play and, on the other hand, the desire to rest, to sleep, to retreat, and the final destiny of death are all built into the human body. But there is an aspect of human desire which is markedly different from animal desire. When humans appeared on earth desire took on a new dimension. Scholars and scientists generally agree that one of the most important differences between the minds of animals and humans is language. The evolution of language, which polarized thought into a subject-object dualism, also polarized desire.[2] The development of linguistic consciousness transformed animal desire into uniquely human desire.

The biological axiom, "ontogeny recapitulates phylogeny," reflects the fact that the development of the individual mirrors the development of the species. To say the same thing another way: The evolution of the human species is repeated in the evolution of every individual. The development of a child into an adult involves the evolution of desire into its human form.

The infant is primarily a physical organism whose mind is suffused with sensations and perceptions of its body. The infant's desires are purely sensual, like those of the animal. As the infant matures it learns to substitute symbolic actions for sensuous actions. Instead of grabbing food with the hands and shoveling it into the mouth, the child learns to ask politely and use a knife and fork. Table manners represent a hallmark difference between humans and the animals. Animals eat, humans dine. As lions teach their young to hunt, human parents teach their young table manners. As the child develops, sexual lust is sublimated into affection and cooperation. The development of the human mind, like the evolution of human civilization, involves the repression and inhibition of impulsive sensuous desires and their transformation into refined, socially acceptable desires. This, in a nutshell, is the process of socialization through which a human child becomes a social adult. Socialization, essentially, is the social modification of desire.

The social modification of desire is the core of the psychological process of "sublimation." Sublimation is fundamental to human identity because it represents the essential distinction between animal and human desires. Sublimation is a metaphor drawn from physics where it refers to thc transformation of a solid into a gas, as when dry ice evaporates. It is a beautiful metaphor. Sublimation is the evaporation of the sensuous body into the subtle body, of sensuous animal desire into sublime human desire. It is the evolution of the desire to eat into the desire to dine, of the desire to fornicate into the desire to make love, of the desire to kill in battle into the desire to defeat in sport. In the life of the species as well as the life of the individual, sublimation is the transformation through language of animal *Go!* into human motivation, aspiration, and ambition; and of animal *Stop!* into human prohibition, repression, and guilt.

As the child grows and develops, the body and the desire for sensuous pleasure are relatively repressed and sublimated into the self and the desire for self-esteem. Self-esteem is the sublimation of body pleasure into ego-pleasure. The desire for self-esteem is the yearning to feel good about one's self in relation to other people, in relation to life, and in relation to existence. The desire for self-esteem is the longing to fit into the *samsaric* world, to be accepted and admired as an object of value in the world of shared social meanings.

The socialization of the child involves a relative transformation of body-sensuous consciousness into mind-meaning consciousness.[3] This evolution occurs by means of the repression of the desire for sensuous pleasure and its sublimation into the desire for happiness—the desire for life, for meaning, for purpose, for success, for victory, for transcendence, for spiritual union with the godhead in eternal bliss.

In this transformation the child renounces the primacy of the body, represses the desire for sensuous pleasure, and identifies with the parents by undertaking a life-project: the Happiness Project.[4] The Happiness Project involves the renunciation of present sensuous pleasure for the sake of future happiness. The Happiness Project converts sensual desire into ambition. Influenced by parental repression and guidance, the child formulates a life purpose or goal—to marry and raise a family, to become a doctor, a lawyer, a business executive; to become rich or famous; to enjoy success and the accumulation of objects; to climb the highest mountain; to attain enlightenment. This life-project, or life-goal, gives life purpose and meaning. It is the embodiment of the desire for life.

The Happiness Project is the vehicle through which self transcends the physical body. Through sublimation, self establishes itself as separate from the physical body and above it. This sublimation is the original alienation, the original sin. It occurred the moment Adam and Eve were expelled from Eden. At that moment of the Fall into historical time they became ashamed of their bodies. Their shame of their bodies is their rejection of the body and the affirmation of the reality of dualistic mind. The Fall into historical time is the Fall into samsara. The same transformation occurs when the infant must give up hope of being Baby-King forever and formulate a Happiness Project through which social identity is established.

Through the vehicle of the Happiness Project self becomes a disembodied locus of meaning and value in the social body from which it draws its significance. The social body, which is a product and a projection of mind, lives on beyond the death of the physical body and, therefore, becomes for the individual an immortality vehicle.[5] By identifying with the samsaric world of socially shared symbols and meanings, self acquires a social significance which may live beyond the death of the body. This is what Durkheim meant when he said that society is the essence, the source, and the object of religion.[6]

Sublimation As the Evolution of Consciousness

The evolution of sublimation is depicted in the Old Testament myth of Eden. The prehominids Adam and Eve, the not-yet-fully-human first humans, lived with and like the animals, with two exceptions: God gave Adam and Eve the power to name the animals. This symbolizes the human domination of the animals through the power of language. Words are not purely symbolic. They have tangible social reality. They enable us to communicate with each other to manipulate the physical world. Science and technology would not be possible without language. Those who have the power to label people also have the power to dominate them.[7]

The second exception was that God prohibited Adam and Eve from eating the fruit of the Tree of the Knowledge of Good and Evil:

> Of every tree of the Garden thou mayest freely eat; but of the tree of the knowledge of good and evil, thou shalt not eat of it; for on the day that thou eatest thereof thou shalt surely die.[8]

This archetypical taboo, "Thou shalt not..." is the beginning of the Fall. Eden was paradise because desires could be satisfied with impunity, without punishment. The taboo, or prohibition, meant that at least one desire could not be satisfied with impunity. By God's commandment, the violation of the taboo is punishable by death. This implies that Adam and Eve already had the foreknowledge of death, or else Yahweh's threat would not have been a deterrent. Their ability to name the animals and the awareness of death signifies that Adam and Eve had already evolved a level of consciousness beyond the animal.

The significance of the archetypical taboo is the human struggle with desire in the aspect of life and death. In this struggle the question arises: "Should I or shouldn't I?" This question marks the beginning of moral consciousness. Primordial sublimation is the Fall, in which unreflective and uninhibited desire is repressed and transformed into reflective and inhibited desire. The desires to feel good, to please oneself and to propagate the species are sublimated into the desires to be good, to please God, and to be happy forever.

Sublimation in Psychoanalysis

The evolution of sublimation is depicted in the psychoanalytic tradition by two myths authored by Sigmund Freud under the guise of psychological theories. Freud was intensely interested in the evolution of conscience, guilt, shame, and morality. One of the myths he proposed may seem silly if taken literally as a scientific fact or theory. As a myth, however, as a metaphor, it is a profound representation of psychological reality.

Freud suggested that the first step towards civilization, the domestication of fire, was the result of the repression and inhibition of "urethral eroticism" and its sublimation into socially useful ambition. Freud imagined that primitive men put out fires by urinating on them, as little Viennese boys probably did.

According to Freud, the inhibition of the desire to put out fires by peeing on them resulted in the domestication of fire. "Whoever was the first to deny himself this pleasure and spare the fire," Freud wrote, "was able to take it with him and break it in to his own service."[9] While Freud's "theory" may seem ridiculous as scientific fact, it makes sense metaphorically. In the life of the individual as in the life of the species, infantile and primitive desires are repressed and transformed into socially acceptable adult and civilized desires. Urethral eroticism is replaced by a Happiness Project. The urethral erotic boy may become a fireman. The bossy child may become a cop. The dreamy preadolescent may become a writer.

In another myth of the evolution of sublimation, Freud suggests that guilt and morality evolved from an archetypical crime of the primal horde.[10] The primal horde were a group of young, robust, prehistoric men motivated by rampant desire, not unlike the modern teenager on a "wilding" expedition.

In a lusty rage, the primal horde killed the tribal father, ate him, and took his females. Freud assumed that the primitive, like the neurotic, has ambivalent (polarized) feelings of tenderness and resentment toward the father. Following the primal murder, the primal horde were horrified at what they had done. Their tenderness towards the father was sublimated into remorse and guilt. The desire for the father's females and the patricidal resentment were thenceforth renounced and repressed. In Freud's view this archetypical renunciation and repression of sexual and aggressive desires marks the submission to law and authority and the inauguration of the incest taboo. Hence, it marks the beginning of civilization and is the basic foundation of both character and culture.

Freud proposed that this mythical prehistoric event is repeated in the life of the (male)[11] child. Like the primal horde, the child lusts for the mother and resents the father. As we have seen, Freud called this constellation of desires the Oedipus complex. If these desires are not adequately sublimated, they form the seed of neurosis.

The successful resolution of the Oedipus complex requires the sublimation of sex and aggression. The desire for the father's woman (the mother) is repressed and sublimated into the socially acceptable desire to have one's own wife and children. The desire to kill the father is repressed and sublimated into the desire to be like him, to cannibalize his image and become a good father, a good worker, and a good citizen.[12] Individual character is formed in the struggle to sublimate animalistic desire (sex and aggression) into a form which is morally acceptable to father, family, and society.

The sublimation of desire, Freud believed, determines the structure of culture as well as of the individual. The repression of the desire for the mother is socially manifested as the incest taboo. In its sublimated form the incest taboo is extrapolated into rules governing sex, marriage, and kinship, which comprise the basic structure of society.

The incest taboo is a set of rules regulating with whom one can and cannot have sex. This may be why some people perceive homosexuality as a threat to the family. The taboo against homosexuality is a variant of the incest taboo. By transgressing one taboo, no matter how peripheral, irrelevant, or obsolete it may be, the homosexual threatens all taboos. Homophobia, in other words, is the first line of defense against incest. The fear of the "fag" or "les" out there may be an inverted projection of the fear of the "mother-fucker" (or daughter-fucker) within.

The taboos against incest and parenticide are the primordial prohibitions, the *Thou shalt nots* that initiate conscience and the moral order. These taboos give family and community their structure. The repression of aggression towards the parent is the root of social authority. Through sublimation and the Happiness Project resentment towards the authoritarian parent is transformed into social conformity. This conformity is given social form through the worship of the totemic figure (or flag) which is the foundation of legitimate authority, law, and morality.

We can now see how, in both the Judeo-Christian and the psychoanalytic myths of the evolution of desire into the Happiness Project, sublimation is represented as the transformation of sensuous desire into moral desire under the impetus of a prohibition or taboo with the significance of life and death.

The Sublimation of Pleasure into the Happiness Project

To review: From the point of view of evolutionary biology, sublimation is the evolution of sensuous desire into the Happiness Project. It began with the evolution of language, when the primate eye-brain-hand system was wired for speech.[13] The moral faculties originate with the word, and the word is *No!, Stop!, Thou shalt not*. *No!* antithetically implies *Yes!*. The dialectic between *No!* and *Yes!* is moral discourse.

The evolution of the Happiness Project signifies the metamorphosis of the sensuous animal into the moral human, as if the solid hungers for food and sex evaporate into the ethereal hungers for self-esteem and immortality. This metamorphosis does not solve the human problem; it poses it. In humans, the desire to *Go!* and the desire to *Stop!* exist at two different levels: at the level of the body and at the subtle level of the ego and society. And out of the cauldron of these conflicting and contradictory desires, ego is born.

CHAPTER SIXTEEN

Religion and Law: Desire As Sin and Crime

> As ye sow, shall ye reap.
>
> —Galatians 6:7

> Beings are the owners of their deeds, heirs of their deeds....Whatever deeds they do—good or evil—of such they will be the heirs...and wherever beings spring into existence, there their deeds will ripen; and wherever their deeds ripen, there they will earn the fruits of those deeds.
>
> —The Buddha

In the Judeo-Christian tradition suffering is believed to be willed by God as punishment for violating divine law. The violation of divine law is sin. Suffering, therefore, is the punishment for sin.

This language, while accurate and logical, omits and obscures the role of desire as a cause of suffering. It renders desire invisible and converts the truth about desire into a secret that we hide from ourselves. Divine law, after all, is established by divine will, which is an expression of divine desire. Divine desire is in contrast to, and ordains the renunciation of, selfish desire. Selfish desire is the root of sin because it contradicts divine desire. Therefore, it would seem more appropriate to say that, in the Judeo-Christian tradition, suffering is punishment inflicted by God on humans who indulge in forbidden desires.

This rephrasing brings the Judeo-Christian and Buddhist views on the causes of suffering closer together. It is consistent with both traditions to say that suffering is caused by indulgence in selfish desires. There is still a significant difference, however. In the Western tradition the tendency is to think of suffering as caused by an external agent, God, as punishment for disobedience to divine law. In the Buddhist tradition the tendency is to view suffering as self-caused—as the natural consequence of indulging in selfish desires.

We can distinguish two kinds of religion. One relies upon an external power for salvation; the other relies on one's own efforts. It is not an invariable rule that religions are purely either one or the other; the major world religions are mixtures of both. But the distinction will help us to understand better the relationship between desire, sin, crime, and suffering in Buddhist and Western traditions. The Western concepts of sin and crime resemble the Buddhist concept of negative karma in that all three are linked to selfish desire. However, in the Western view the suffering which is the bitter fruit of sin is inflicted by an external agency, while in Buddhism the suffering is self-inflicted.

Karma

Karma is the Buddhist law of moral cause and effect. The Sanskrit word *karma* literally means "action," and in Buddhism it is interpreted specifically as intentional action. It refers to actions born in desire and executed by means of intentional efforts. In the West, the word has come to be used to mean "fate." When something bad happens to a person people will say "it was his or her karma." In this sense, karma refers not only to the actions themselves, it refers also to their consequences. An action and its consequences are inseparable. To say that a certain fate is a person's karma means that person's predicament is the consequence of his or her past desires, intentions, and actions. In this sense, character is fate, as the Greeks believed.

The "law of karma" means that our deeds create the circumstances of our future suffering or joy. In the Buddha's words:

> Beings are the owners of their deeds, heirs of their deeds, their deeds are the womb from which they sprang, with their deeds they are bound up, their deeds are their refuge. Whatever deeds they do—good or evil—of such they will be the heirs...and wherever beings spring into existence, there their deeds will ripen; and wherever their deeds ripen, there they will earn the fruits of those deeds.[1]

Buddha was one of the first humans to enunciate the law of causality as the principle that determines events of the phenomenal world.

Before the Buddha people believed that events were shaped by the will and magical power of the gods. Many people still believe this today. Buddha taught that all phenomena are conditioned, that is, they are determined by previous events. On this principle modern scientists would agree.

Buddha's "law of dependent origination" states that everything is conditioned. Within that web of conditionality, however, individuals retain free will to make moral choices. Karma, which is *intentional* action, implies choice. To intend an act means to prefigure its consequences and do the deed wanting those consequences, or at least not wanting to avoid them. Our intentional actions create a chain of moral cause and effect, action and reaction; the consequences of our actions are determined by our actions. Nevertheless, we are free to choose whether to act or not. The intentional act is freedom's door into the determined world. It is the vital point at which we may intervene and alter the fate ordained by past actions.

The principle of karma shows both that our fate is determined by our actions and also that, through choosing our actions, we are free to shape our own fate. The law of karma is simultaneously the principle of causality through which our past determines our future, *and* the freedom and power to shape the future. It is not merely fate, it is the power to create the conditions for our future happiness or unhappiness.

The law of karma thus contains within it the seeds of redemption, the possibility of purification. This requires accepting personal responsibility for the conduct of our lives. Buddhist's believe that the details of the results of karma are difficult, if not almost impossible, to comprehend. The consequences of our actions may not be apparent to us, or we may refuse to acknowledge and take responsibility for them. This is why one of the first and most often repeated teachings a novice Buddhist will hear is the importance of understanding and remaining mindful that future happiness and unhappiness depends on what we choose to do now on our journey through this life!

In the Buddhist view, each of us is responsible for our own happiness or unhappiness. Personal responsibility and self-reliance, hence, are among the highest virtues. In the Buddha's own words:

> By oneself evil is done;
> By oneself one suffers;
> By oneself evil is left undone;
> By oneself one is purified.
> Purity and impurity belong to oneself;
> No one can purify another.[2]

Buddha's views on personal responsibility are quite strict. We are responsible not only for our own happiness and unhappiness but, by logical extension, for our own thoughts, desires, intentions, choices and actions; for it is upon these that our future happiness or suffering depend. In the Buddhist view, we are responsible for what we think and believe. This view was well expressed by the French existentialist philosopher Jean Paul Sartre, who believed that personal choice and responsibility are inescapable. Even if an angel appears to us bearing a commandment from God, Sartre suggested, we should first have to choose to believe in the authenticity of the angel before submitting ourselves to the will of God. The same sentiment was expressed by the Buddha twenty-five hundred years earlier:

> Save his soul's light overhead,
> none leads man, none ever led.[3]

This means that an understanding of selfish desire as the cause of our self-imposed unhappiness cannot be imparted by one person to another. It *can* be learned, however. It can be learned by a method so similar to Plato's that one must wonder about the influence of Buddhism on Platonic thought. Truth is discovered not through scripture or the appeal to authority but through seeing the inner light—through awareness and reflection upon one's own experiences. These haunting words of Buddha might well have been written by Plato more than a century later:

> Truth is within ourselves; it takes no rise from outward things, whate'er you may believe. There is an innermost centre in us all, where truth abides in fullness; and around, wall upon wall, the gross flesh hems it in, this perfect clear perception which is truth. A baffling and perverting carnal mesh binds it and makes all error: and to know rather consists in opening out a way whence the imprisoned splendor may escape, than in effecting entry for a light supposed to be without.[4]

The moral principles of personal responsibility and self-reliance necessarily follow from the view that suffering is intrinsic to desire rather than caused by an external agent. One cannot do as one pleases and then pray to a merciful god for salvation from suffering. The punishment for sin is inherent in the desire itself. Suffering is inherent in desire, as we have seen, because desire itself is a state of deprivation, and because existence does not readily yield to human desires.

The tragedy of sin is that we mistakenly believe that pursuing our selfish desires will make us happy. We think that sensuous pleasure and self-satisfaction will fulfill us. In this belief even the allegedly sane are stubbornly deluded. The irony is that, by definition, sin is both something we desire and, at the same time, something that will cause us to suffer. As the Buddha said:

> Pleasure is a bond, a joy that's brief,
> Of little taste, leading to drawn-out pain.
> The wise know the bait is hooked.[5]

The Ten Commandments and Mosaic Law

In the Judeo-Christian tradition, the law of karma is expressed in the biblical admonition: "As ye sow, shall ye reap." This aphorism implies that the sufferer has some responsibility for his or her future happiness or suffering. To be sure, God is the intermediary between the desire and the suffering. God judges the believer's motivations and actions and executes the punishment. Nevertheless, the concept of individual responsibility is strong in the Western tradition. The Judeo-Christian version of the law of karma was expressed well by the biblical prophet, Isaiah, whose words reiterate the teachings of the Buddha:

> Say ye to the righteous, that it shall be well with him; for they shall eat the fruit of their doings. Woe unto the wicked! It shall be ill with him; for the reward of his hands shall be given him.[6]

When God commanded Adam and Eve to avoid the forbidden fruit, he gave them the power and the responsibility of free choice. If God did not want to give them free choice, he needed only to make the fruit bitter. Instead, he made it sweet and forbade them to eat it. Taboo implies choice. If Adam and Eve did not have free choice, it makes no sense for God to give them a commandment. The myth of Eden, thus, metaphorically represents the evolution of choice in the pre-dawn of human history.

The capacity to choose means the capacity to decide whether to indulge a desire or to renounce it, to confront a fear or to avoid it. Talmudic scholars, pondering why a merciful God would permit evil to exist in the world, concluded that evil is the price of free choice. God's commandment implies that Adam and Eve could choose to disobey. Otherwise, why not build repugnance of the forbidden fruit into their bodies? The behavior of all the other animals is shaped by genetics and physiology. Choice requires a higher state of consciousness. Choice means choosing between good and evil, right and wrong. Desire and choice are the twin foundations of ethics, morality, and law.

The Ten Commandments symbolize a contract between the Hebrews and their Sky-God, Jahweh, a contract that is the foundation of modern Anglo-American law. The Ten Commandments could be called the "Ten Choices." This contract with Jahweh stipulates that if the Hebrew's choose to follow God's Commandments they will be rewarded with a happy life in the land of milk and honey. If the Hebrews choose to violate God's Commandments they will be condemned to pain and misery. In this contract God reveals to the "chosen people" (that is, to the "choosing people") the secret of their fate. The reward for obeying the law is happiness. The punishment for breaking the law is pain.

The power of choice is unique to the human mind. Animals do not possess it. Making responsible choices requires the mental capacity to understand the law and the consequences of one's actions. Responsibility means *the ability to respond* to the task at hand, namely, the consciousness of freedom, of the law, and of the consequences of conforming to or violating the law.

A certain level of consciousness is therefore a precondition to entering this contract with God. A person must have the capacity to form conscious intent which implies the ability to understand the law and the moral quality of actions. Excluded from this burden of responsibility, obviously, are people who do not have the capacity for conscious intent, such as children, the mentally retarded, the senile, and those who are delirious as the result of physical illness. This principle is the basis of the concept of criminal responsibility in Anglo-American law.

The Concept of Criminal Responsibility

In Anglo-American law, a person is held criminally responsible if they have the capacity for *mens rea*, for conscious intent. If a person is not believed capable of forming conscious intent they may be judged insane and excused. The modern insanity defense evolved from this principle.

One of the early definitions of insanity was the so called "Wild Beast Test," which states that a person shall be excused from criminal responsibility if they have no more capacity to reason than a wild beast.[7] From the standpoint of this principle the child, the mentally defective, and the senile are morally equivalent to a wild beast.

The concept of criminal responsibility was expanded by McNaughten's Rule, an article of English law which defines insanity.[8]

According to this criterion, *a person shall be held criminally responsibile if they have the capacity to know the nature and consequences of their actions and whether they were right or wrong*. If a person is judged to lack the capacity for conscious intent then that person is excused from responsibility and not punished. The modern insanity defense thus has its origins in Mosaic law.[9] Intent, or conscious desire, is the mark of guilt. Innocence, on the other hand, is literally the lack of desire or intent and/or the absence of moral consciousness.

The concept of criminal responsibility has been obscured and complicated by American psychiatry, which has lobbied to change the rules so that the test of competency in most jurisdictions now depends upon a diagnosis of mental illness, with all its conceptual confusions, rather than on the capacity to form conscious intent. This has further eroded the public sense of personal responsibility for one's actions; it has also obscured the idea that desire and choice are the roots of sin and crime.

The Buddhist concept of karma and the Western concept of criminal responsibility are roughly similar, although the former applies to all behavior, not just criminal. Each is a distinct cultural formulation of the problem of distinguishing bad desires from good ones. Both sin and crime are the undesirable consequences of the indulgence in selfish, destructive desires. Sin is the religious name for desires which cause suffering. Crime is the secular name for it. Sin and crime are, thus, both manifestations of the causal relationship between desire and suffering.

CHAPTER SEVENTEEN

Desire: The Basis of Ethics and Morality

> Ethics is necessary because men's desires conflict. The purpose of ethics is first, to find criterion by which to distinguish good and bad desires; second, by means of praise and blame, to promote good desires and discourage such that are bad.
>
> —Bertrand Russell, *A History of Western Philosophy*

If everything that felt good were good, then neither morality nor ethics would be necessary. People would simply do what they want, as animals do, without the constraints of conscience, morality, or law. The problem of ethics would be resolved by hedonism, and the "pleasure principle" would be the highest moral good.

This is a fantasy of paradise, however, not a fact of life. The dream of paradise is a sublime projection of the pure pleasure principle. The problem with the pleasure principle is that our desires are not always desirable. In the life of the individual and of the species, paradise is lost when our selfish desires lead to suffering for ourselves or others.

To avoid the pain and punishment of sin, our moral intelligence compels one desire to yield to another. The desire for pleasure submits to the desire for self-preservation in its sublimated forms: the desire to be good, to be protected, to be approved, and to be loved forever.

When the desire to indulge yields to *No!* the source of the *No!* is perceived as a superior, god-like force. The *No!*-sayer is regarded with both fear and fascination. The Ten Commandments, which are all

"Thou shalt nots," are prohibitions which stimulate the development of considered, responsible choice and, hence, stimulate the development of moral consciousness. Parental commandments create guilt and inhibit behavior in the child as the divine commandments do for the human species. The god-like aura of society is derived from its power to enforce prohibitions and taboos.

The renunciation of base desires under the force of the *No!* prohibition, and the substitution of another, "higher" desire, gives desire a conflicting and dialectical form. This tension amongst desires is the basis of ethics and morality.

Philosophy, like medicine and psychotherapy, is a child of religion. It is the intellectual residue of religion. It seeks to understand through reasoning the path away from pain and death towards happiness and immortality. As the ancient religious traditions declined, philosophy arose from their ashes, like the phoenix, as a source of wisdom and guidance. In this context philosophical ethics is the heir of religious ethics.

The main problem of ethics and morality is to choose among desires. Bertrand Russell understood this most clearly. "Ethics is necessary," he observed, "because men's desires conflict." Ethics has two main purposes according to Russell: "First, to find criterion by which to distinguish good and bad desires; second, by means of praise and blame, to promote good desires and discourage such that are bad."

Ethics in Western Philosophy: Plato

After studying Buddhist philosophy and coming to some understanding of the four noble truths, I undertook to review the writings on ethics of some major figures of Western philosophy to see how they corresponded to the Buddhist view. I was startled to find how the issues of desire and choice are the basic problems of Western ethics. In a brief panoramic view, here are some thoughts to ponder.

Plato (428-348 B.C.), whose writings are so reminiscent of the Buddha, appears to have been the first Western thinker to recognize that the problems of ethics derive from the dialectic of desires. Referring to pleasure but applying equally well to desire, Plato said:

> She has one name and yet takes many forms.
> For do we not say that the intemperate has pleasure,
> And the temperate has pleasure in his very temperance?[1]

In this distinction between the pleasures of indulgence and the pleasures of temperance and/or renunciation, Plato identified the two poles of desire. At one pole are the animal desires for the pleasures of the flesh: to eat, to drink, to fornicate, to play, and to fight. At the other pole are the sublime human desires for the pleasures of the spirit: to be happy, to have a clear conscience, to love, to feel fulfilled, to live by the highest meanings, to be whole and holy. Ethics, as a philosophical category, was generated by the polarization of desire into the desires of the flesh and the desires of the spirit, the desire to indulge and the desire to renounce. The history of ethics is a dialogue on this dialectic.

In Plato's time, ethics was defined more broadly than Russell defined it in this century. The Greeks viewed ethics as the supreme business of the mind: to tend the soul in its journey through life. The purpose of ethics was to answer the question: "What is the good life and how can it be achieved?" To Plato, the purpose of life is obvious. It is to be happy, to live happily. The function of ethics is to evaluate Happiness Projects in order to discover the path to happiness. The central questions of ethics therefore are: "What is happiness and how is it achieved?" Good and evil were not major considerations in Plato's ethics.[2] What leads to happiness is good; what interferes with happiness is evil. We have forgotten this fundamental, life-centered principle of ethics.

In his dialogues Plato explored the two extremes—the pole of indulgence and the pole of renunciation. In his day, these two extremes were represented by the Sophists and the Cynics. Callicles expressed the Sophist view with the advice, "He who would truly live, ought to allow his desires to wax to the uttermost." At the other extreme, the Cynics' view of ethics was expressed by Antisthenes: "Better madness than a pursuit of pleasure."[3]

Plato, like the Buddha less than a century before him, rejected both extremes in favor of the famous "golden mean." Buddhists call the golden mean, the "middle way," best expressed in Madhyamika philosophy. The golden mean avoids the extremes of indulgence and renunciation through balance and harmony.

Plato depicted the golden mean through the metaphor of the celestial chariot drawn by two magnificent horses. The horse on the left, unruly and ugly, represents passionate desire. The horse on the right, obedient and beautiful, represents spiritual desire. In Plato's view, neither horse alone could drive the chariot. Neither path alone will lead to happiness—neither the uninhibited gratification of desire nor the ascetical renunciation of it. The path to happiness lies in a balance between the two. In Plato's celestial metaphor the charioteer, who is

Reason, brings balance to the team. In Plato's ethics, similar to Buddhist ethics, happiness is found with the guidance of reason in the middle ground between indulgence and renunciation.

To live happily thus requires an inner transformation—the development of a rational moral consciousness and moral character. This transformation involves bringing the contrapuntal elements of human nature into balance. The Greeks believed that this inner, moral harmony must be synchronized with the harmony of the heavenly spheres. Virtue consists in achieving this balance; it is not, as many modern interpreters insist, an absolutist list of right and wrong actions. To Plato and the Greeks, the virtuous person is in balance with the universe. Such a person is centered in the midst of creation, moderate, prudent, morally aware, and possessed of the wisdom and courage to follow the golden mean.

Pondering the pleasures that might bring true happiness, Plato observed that not all pleasures are equal. Some are greater and some are lesser. Also, some are preceded by desire and some are not. One might enjoy drinking beer, for example, even when not thirsty. But the joy of a cold beer after a fierce thirst is incomparably greater. But so is the pain: the pain of thirst.

Desire is thus haunted by pain. The desire for water is haunted by the pain of thirst. Like the desire for water, all desires are bipolar and contradictory: at the one pole is the exciting prospect of drink; at the other pole is the painful absence of water. For all its positive life force, desire is cursed by a dark underside of emptiness and deprivation. It is an aggressive deprivation in quest of tranquil fulfillment. Plato recognized well the frustration of desire:

> Then he and everyone who desires, desires that which he has not already, and which is future and not present, and which he has not, and is not, and of which he is in want.[4]

This insight has great significance which is not easy to grasp. It is one of the vital secrets we keep from ourselves. The problem is not that this secret is too difficult to understand; it is too simple.

The fact is that whatever we want, we feel deprived of. Just as thirst, the desire for water, is a lack of water, the person who desires power suffers from feelings of powerlessness; the person who desires material wealth suffers from feelings of poverty; the person who desires fame or attention suffers from feeling ignored; the person who desires to be good suffers from feelings of guilt; and the person who desires happiness suffers from unhappiness.

This is not merely a cute Freudian dogma: that everything is really the opposite of what it seems to be. The fact is that the human mind functions by contrasts. Up has no meaning except in relation to down. Right and left, good and evil, past and future are dependent upon each other for their meaning. In the same way, presence and absence, desire and deprivation are codependent upon each other for their existence.

The sobering implication of the insight that desire is haunted by deprivation is that happiness cannot be won by desiring it. The pursuit of happiness is a tragic quest because happiness is not possible in the presence of desire. Desire is contaminated by precisely those painful feelings of deprivation which are the obstacle to our happiness. This tragic state of affairs, which the faint-hearted stand no chance of understanding, means that our Happiness Projects are the main cause of the sufferings we impose on ourselves and others. In the words of Gendun Rinpoche:

> Only our searching for happiness
> prevents us from seeing it.[5]

Plato understood this irony well. The Platonic image of happiness is free from the taint of desire. That is why Platonic love is pure and innocent. Not because there is no sex in it, which is the mistaken popular idea, but because there is no desire in it. Plato believed that the highest and most perfect pleasures are those not accompanied by desire. They are spontaneous and complete without the vices of insufficiency or excess. Indeed, the best things in life are free. The greatest pleasures are accessible through reason rather than through desire, by being aware rather than by striving and craving. Plato defined this state of happiness as "love." Platonic love is not the craving for sex, solace, or romantic succor. It is an inner transformation, the development of inner harmony which quiets the soul and opens the mystical doors of perception to the truth and beauty of creation.

Christian Ethics: Saint Augustine

Plato's idea of the virtuous soul's journey through life was incorporated into Christian ethics, largely through the efforts of Saint Augustine (354-430). Augustine struggled his whole life with the conflict between the desires of the flesh and the desires of the spirit. He regarded the desires for sensuous pleasure as bondage, the same bondage from which enlightenment is liberation. Augustine revealed his inner unrest in *The Confessions*:

> For of a forward will, was a lust made; and a lust served, became custom; and custom not resisted, became necessity. By which links, as it were, joined together (whence I call it a chain) a hard bondage held me enthralled. But that new will which had begun to be in me, freely to serve Thee, and to wish to enjoy Thee, Oh God, the only assured pleasantness, was not yet able to overcome my former willfulness, strengthened by age. Thus did my two wills, one new, and the other old, one carnal, the other spiritual, struggle within me; and by their discord undid my soul. Thus, I understood by my own experience, what I had read, how the flesh lusteth against the spirit and the spirit against the flesh.[6]

Augustine's devoted mother, Monica, was a faithful Catholic, and wished her son would pursue a religious calling. From his youth, however, Augustine was devoted to play and frivolity. As a young man he consorted with actors, writers, and students. He lived a bohemian life and had many loves and concubines. "To Carthage I came," he wrote, "where there sang all around me in my ears a cauldron of unholy loves."[7]

Augustine was blessed with a sharp mind and a gifted tongue. He was a student of rhetoric, and was familiar with the philosophic and religious thought of his times. For a while, he was a "hearer" or auditor in a Manichean sect. The Manicheans, like the Christians, taught that suffering and sin were the result of the pleasures of the flesh. But Augustine was reluctant to give up these pleasures. He prayed to God for relief from compulsive concupiscence, but his prayers were ambivalent. "Give me chastity and continence," he cried, "only not yet. For I feared lest thou shouldest hear me soon, and soon cure me of the disease of concupiscence, which I wished to have satisfied, rather than extinguished."[8]

After years of inner conflict, Augustine experienced a religious conversion at the age of 32, in which spiritual desire conquered sensuous desire. While walking in a Milanese garden, watching lovers embracing, he despaired that he could ever renounce the love of women for the love of God. In the midst of his self-pity he heard a child's voice calling "*tolle, lege; tolle, lege,*" "take up and read; take up and read." He opened a volume of the Apostle Paul and read the first words on which his eyes fell: "Not in rioting and drunkenness, not in chambering and wantonness, not in strife and envying; but put ye on the Lord Jesus Christ, and make not provision for the flesh in concupiscence."[9] From that moment on, he recalled, "light and serenity" infused his heart, and all doubt vanished."

Augustine agreed with Plato that desire is evil because it is defective and imperfect and leads to bondage, misery, and sorrow.[10] He blended the Platonic ideal of "the good" with the Christian idea of God. God is the perfect plenitude of pure *being*, lacking no virtue and containing no vice; absolute in *truth* and *beauty*; mighty, just, and incorruptible. Compared to God, human carnal desires are the essence of corruption.

Like Plato, Augustine sought happiness. "Although then one obtains this joy by one means, another by another, all have one end, which they strive to attain, namely, joy."[11] Like Plato, Augustine believed that the greatest good, the greatest pleasure, and the greatest happiness are one and the same: union with God in joy. "How then do I seek Thee, O Lord? For when I seek Thee, my God, I seek a happy life."[12]

Augustine believed that the chief obstacles to happiness and to God are the three lusts: the lusts of the flesh, the lusts of the eyes, and the ambition of the world.[13] They are the evils which obstruct the momentary glimpses of God that, with the gift of grace, are possible in this lifetime. But the final realization of mystical fulfillment is not to be achieved by earthly creatures. It is the reward after death for a virtuous life. And this path of Christian virtue, the way to the heavenly City of God, is the renunciation of desires.

Augustine was more antagonistic towards sensuous desire than Plato, perhaps because he was more tempted by it, and hence, more fearful of it. As a result, he did not embrace Plato's golden mean, but sided instead with the puritanical horse at the pole of renunciation. Plato allowed reason to moderate the antithetical desires to indulge and to renounce. But Augustine viewed Plato's golden mean as a dangerous flirtation with desire. To give limited permission for the satisfaction of desire, as temperance does in moderation, is to assent to corruption and sin. It gives the Devil all the room he needs to do his dirty work.

Like the typical convert, Augustine went from one extreme to the other, from the desire to indulge to the desire to renounce. Before his conversion Augustine was compulsively indulgent. Afterwards, he was militantly puritanical, so puritanical that he opposed the ceremonial use of wine for fear that it might provide his monks with an opportunity for drunkenness.[14]

Like the child who rebels against the parent, thinking he will be free of them while actually making them the negative standard for his values, Augustine's puritanism kept him as absorbed by the battle against desire as he previously had been by the pursuit of it. He struggled constantly with his desires for sex, drink, and food. He fasted frequently, striving to subject his body to his will. He complained to God that although he ate merely to stay alive, concupiscence overcame him as the food passed from his plate to his belly. He was apparently more successful in his battle against sex and drink than he was against food, for as he confessed to his maker, "Full feeding sometimes creepeth upon Thy servant."[15] From this confession, a modern psychiatrist might diagnose Augustine as bulimic.

Saint Paul

In his puritanism, Augustine was closer to Paul than to Plato. Like Augustine, Paul was a convert. Before his conversion Saul, as he was then known, was a hunter of Christians. He breathed out "threatenings and slaughter against the disciples of the Lord."[16] After his conversion he became, with equal ferocity, a hunter of sinners.

In his *Epistle to the Galatians*, Paul itemized the sins he condemned with the vitriolic piety of a fire and brimstone preacher: "adultery, fornication, uncleanness, lasciviousness, idolatry, witchcraft, hatred, variance, envyings, murders, drunkenness, revellings and such like: of the which I tell you before, as I have also told you in time past, that they which do such things shalt not inherit the kingdom of God."[17]

Although this list is not composed exclusively of sensuous desires and pleasures, Paul believed that sexual desire is the primal sin, "original sin," because it precipitated the Fall from innocence and immortality to concupiscence and death.[18]

Augustine subscribed to Paul's concept of virtue and sin which, compared to Plato's are extremist on the side of renunciation. This extreme polarization of sensuous and spiritual desires is the foundation of Christian ethics and the consequences of virtue and sin are projected into the afterlife as the polarization of heaven and hell. Those who pursue the pleasures of the flesh live in the City of Man and will be condemned on "judgment day" to eternal suffering. Those who renounce them and pursue the Christian path of renunciation will dwell on judgment day in the "eternal sabbath" of the City of God.

The religious ethics of Saints Paul and Augustine resemble the ethics of Plato by recognizing desire as the source of evil. They diverge from Plato by rejecting sensuous desire completely and striving for the ascetic ideal of converting it into spiritual desire. They also diverge from Plato by rejecting reason as the method for resolving the problem of desire and achieving happiness. Christian happiness is not achieved through reason, but through faith, love, and charity.

Faith is the key to Pauline Christian ethics. Faith is the identification of self with the perceived "will of God." It is the method by which body and ego are transcended and the joy of selfless spiritual love is achieved. The problem with faith, however, is that it often becomes confused with obedience to authority. In Catholicism there is a tendency to confuse the faithful identification with the suffering, loving Jesus with faithful obedience to Church dogma. This confusion facilitated the establishment of a powerful, political Church, whose Pauline ethics have dominated Western civilization, by fire and by sword, for more than a thousand years.

Modern Ethics

With the advent of the "new science," the secular authority of the Catholic Church began to crumble, and reason was reintroduced as the most suitable method for defining and pursuing the good life. Philosophers of the Enlightenment differed in their views on the good life. They all seemed to agree, however, that the fundamental problem of ethics is to clarify which desires are good and permissible and which are evil and, therefore, taboo. What follows is a brief survey, touching on the highlights of a few important philosopher's ethical visions. The interested reader can study the text's themselves to see how profoundly the theme of desire is woven into Western ethical discourse.

Thomas Hobbes (1588-1679) was among the first to apply "natural philosophy," as science was called in his day, to the study of human behavior.[19] Following the mechanistic science of his time, Hobbes regarded motion as the underlying basis of both physical and mental phenomena. He called animal motions "endeavors." Remarkably coincidental with the Buddhist view, Hobbes considered endeavors to be bipolar, consisting of desires and aversions—two of the three poisons.

Hobbes defined desires as the striving towards objects and aversions as the striving to avoid objects. Evil, in Hobbes' anthropoid metaphor, is a robust child. Evil is done by people whose desires and aversions are obnoxiously uninhibited and uncivilized, like those of a highly strung boy. Hobbes concluded from his observations of human behavior that people are primarily concerned with the gratification of their desires, many of which are just barely under control. The only sensible solution to the problem of rampant desire, he reasoned, is for the people to give common consent to the "leviathan state" to control destructive desires, by force if necessary, so citizens can live peaceably amongst themselves and be protected from others. Hobbes' philosophy helped to rationalize and justify a social contract with the people in which the state becomes the arbiter of ethics through law and police power.

Benedict Spinoza (1632-1677), like Rene Descartes (1596-1650), sought the key to ethics in the certain logic of geometry. Like other thinkers, Spinoza sought in ethics the secret of supreme, lasting happiness. After a long personal struggle, not unlike Saint Augustine's, Spinoza rejected the pursuits of fame, wealth, and sensuous pleasure as vain and futile. He resolved to discover whether the geometric method could define a principle of *good* through which lasting happiness could be achieved. After long and deep reflection, Spinoza decided that desire is the central problem of ethics and of human nature—"the essence itself of man."[20]

> By the word 'desire,' therefore, I understand all the efforts, impulses, appetites, and volitions of a man, which vary according to his changing disposition, and not infrequently are so opposed to one another that he is drawn hither and thither, and knows not whither he ought to turn.[21]

In his classical essay on human bondage, Spinoza defines desire as the bondage that leads to unhappiness. (This is a totally Buddhist idea; Spinoza may have been one of the first of a long line of Jewish Buddhists!) Desire is bondage. Happiness is liberation from the bondage of desire. The path to happiness is liberation from desire through reason and through the intellectual love of God, which enables the blissful contemplation of nature in the aspect of eternity.

Immanuel Kant (1724-1804) also sought the basis of morality in reason. Indeed, he advocated the subjugation of desire to reason. Kant believed that moral law, like natural law, must be rational, universal, and necessary. The indulgence of desire is the contrary of rational moral action. Reason dictates, therefore, that personal desire should be renounced in favor of the "categorical imperative," the highest moral law, which substitutes dutiful goodwill for personal interest.[22]

In the nineteenth century the utilitarians sought the basis of morality in mathematical calculation. They believed that the purpose of ethics and morality is to promote the greatest happiness for the greatest number. The greatest happiness is defined as an optimum balance of pleasure and pain. They sought to determine this balance using the new science of mathematics, through a calculus of desire and suffering—the "hedonistic calculus."

Arthur Schopenhauer (1788-1860), unlike his predecessors, did not invoke science, mathematics, or reason as the basis of his ethical system. As a young man, Schopenhauer was introduced to the sacred literature of Hinduism. His philosophy of ethics is pure Vedanta in Western dress. Revolting against the prevailing Hegelian idea that reason is the primary force in nature and history, Schopenhauer regarded *will* (desire) as the force that moves matter and life. Will creates around itself the illusion of goodness, while actually being the root of evil. Listen to Schopenhauer for echoes of Buddha and Plato:

> For all effort springs from defect—from discontent with one's estate—is thus suffering so long as it is not satisfied; but no satisfaction is lasting, rather it is always merely the starting point of a new effort.[23]

Like the Buddha and Plato, Schopenhauer believed that desire is inherently defective and painful. All things are occupied by the striving after existence, but the basis of all striving is need and deficiency, and thus involves suffering.[24] "All suffering," he wrote in what could be the motto of the wise psychotherapist, "proceeds from the want of proportion between what we demand and what we get."[25]

The basis of morality according to Schopenhauer, and the Vedanta, is the ascetic renunciation of desire, including the very desire to exist. This renunciation is achieved by means of a higher wisdom that quiets the will:

> Thus it may be that the inner nature of holiness, self-renunciation, mortification of our own will, asceticism, as here for the first time expressed abstractly, and free from all mythical elements, as denial of the will to live, appearing after the complete knowledge of its own nature, has become a quieter of all volition.[26]

Contemporary Ethics

From this brief survey of the history of ethics it should be evident that the basic problem of ethics is choosing between competing and conflicting desires in order to find the optimum path to happiness in life. This is not how ethics is ordinarily perceived today, however. The role of desire in ethics is repressed, thus making our public and private moral dilemmas more difficult to understand and resolve.

In the twentieth century we have lost the sense of ethics as a means for the achievement of happiness. The popular notion of ethics tends to be of a more or less fixed code of right and wrong behavior to which people must adhere in order to be regarded as good people. Professional philosophers, in particular, have lost the traditional sense of the connection between ethics and happiness. Instead, they think of ethics intellectually, as a problem of finding a logical or scientific basis for moral action or, failing that, rejecting ethics as a fuzzy psychological zone.

With the advent of modern scientific psychology, the ethical dimension of human suffering has been denied and repressed. Psychology does not concern itself with ethics or ethical behavior. Even psychotherapists have, by and large, ignored or repressed the fact that people suffer from the consequences of their moral conduct and, consequently, that therapy must involve some kind of raising of moral consciousness. The irony, as we shall presently see, is that the conflict of desires, which is the central problem of ethics, is also the central problem of neurotic suffering and psychotherapy.

CHAPTER EIGHTEEN

Psychotherapy: The Psychology of Hidden Wishes

> The nature of the patient's nature is redefined so that, in effect if not by intention, the patient becomes the kind of object upon which a psychiatric service can be performed.
>
> —Erving Goffman, *Asylums*

Religion, ethics, and psychotherapy emerged at different stages of the evolution of the human ego. In religion the problem of desire is addressed in the rhetoric of sin and salvation. In ethics it is posed in the language of good and evil. In psychotherapy it is expressed in the semantics of mental health and illness. Nevertheless, the central problem of all three is the same: how best to live with the contradictions and conflicts between our desires to indulge in pleasures, and our desires to renounce them.

As human consciousness has evolved, the relationship between suffering and desire has become more abstract, indirect, and obscure. In religion the themes of desire and suffering are just under the surface of sin. In ethics they are eclipsed by the concepts of good and evil. In psychotherapy they are obscured by the language of health and illness. By viewing the patient's pain as caused by mental illness, desires are disguised as instincts, drives, impulses, and biochemical imbalances; virtue masquerades as mental health; the priest impersonates the psychotherapist; and the spiritual journey is distorted into the treatment of psychopathology.

Diverse and astute observers such as Otto Rank, Allan Watts, and Thomas Szasz have noticed the close relationship between psychotherapy and religion.[1] The fact that psychotherapy is vulnerable to being compared with religion, rather than undermining it, reveals its value. The function of psychotherapy is the same as that of religion—to relieve mental pain and light a path to well being.

Theories of psychotherapy are profuse. In my view, people seek psychotherapy not because they believe they are mentally ill, but because they are in mental and emotional pain from which they seek relief. Similarly, the success of psychotherapy does not depend upon the abatement of psychiatric symptoms as defined by the medical model,[2] since many of these symptoms are not necessarily painful. Delusions, for example, may be perfectly ordinary, acceptable, and even socially conventional from the patient's point of view, but disturbing to the spouse, the employer, or the psychiatrist.[3] The true success of psychotherapy depends upon the abatement of the patient's distress and unhappiness, and the enhancement of the capacity to enjoy life. Psychotherapy begins in the confusion and suffering of the individual and its aim is the relief of that suffering. With these thoughts in mind, let us now reflect upon the role of desire in psychotherapy.

What Did Freud Desire?

Modern psychotherapy began with psychoanalysis. The founder of psychoanalysis, Sigmund Freud (1856-1939), is largely ignored and disparaged these days, except in university departments of literature. Many psychiatrists and psychologists consider his work to be obsolete. Nevertheless, his ideas have helped shape our present thinking on mind and suffering. Whether one agrees with Freud or not, he is one of the seminal thinkers of the twentieth century. Many of his views on the dynamics of the mind have been so completely integrated into our language and thought that we often forget that they originated with Freud. Freud may have presented his views in the obsolete style of nineteenth century biology, but they reflect fundamental insights into the dynamics of the human mind. Examining Freud's work "*doch noch ein mal*,"[4] yet one more time, may help to us to see more clearly the hidden role of desire in modern psychotherapy.

Freud cloaked his ideas in the medical model, thus obscuring the role of desire as a cause of suffering. To understand why he did this we must consider the irreverent question posed by Jacques Lacan: "What was Freud's desire?"[5] By posing this question Lacan acknowledged that desire is the central problem of psychoanalysis and psychotherapy. To understand the ethical dimensions of modern psychotherapy, therefore, it is helpful to understand the desires of its founder. Freud's desires, and the desires of its modern practitioners, shape the language of psychotherapy in the same way that the patient's desires shape his or her character and neurosis.

Like most people, Freud had many conflicting desires. He tells us in his own words that he never felt "any particular predilection for the career of a physician."[6] He wanted to be a scientist, and was motivated by curiosity directed more towards human concerns than towards nature.

Freud was moved to study medicine by the theories of Darwin and a reading by one of his professors of Goethe's essay on nature. He did not take his medical degree until 1881, and worked with great satisfaction from 1876 to 1882 in the laboratory of the neurophysiologist, Ernst Brucke. Freud did some outstanding work in Brucke's laboratory, the scientific validity of which endures today. He described some microscopic anatomy of the brain; he explained how certain central nervous system ganglia establish contact with peripheral sites; and he was amongst the first to propose the unitary nature of the neuron, a landmark discovery for which another neurologist deservingly got credit.[7] Freud also came close to describing the anaesthetic qualities of cocaine, but abandoned his research in order to visit his fiance. Before leaving, he suggested to his friend, the ophthalmologist Dr. Koller, that he investigate the anaesthetic properties of cocaine on the eye. The discovery of ophthalmic anaesthesia was credited to Koller rather than Freud.[8]

In spite of his good work and growing reputation as a competent scientist and neurologist, Freud was advised by Brucke in 1882 to abandon research and enter medicine. The prevailing anti-Semitism of the day made it unlikely that Freud would advance in academic research; and the pay of a scientist was poor—too little for him to support his expanding family. So Freud became an "aspirant" or resident in neurology under Theodor Meynert, and studied cerebral anatomy and its relation to diseases of the nervous system.

Freud became one of the leading medical authorities in Europe on neurological paralysis of childhood.[9] His expertise in paralysis led to a fortuitous chain of events culminating in the invention of psychoanalysis. As his writings and reputation spread in Europe and abroad,

Freud's yearnings grew for success, honor, and power. His ambition was to become a world famous "biologist of the mind," in Frank Sulloway's apt phrase. Freud's desire was to become the renowned and honored patriarch of a new science of the mind.[10]

The Invention of Psychoanalysis

Freud discovered psychoanalysis in 1893, when he was called by his colleague, Joseph Breuer, to consult on a young woman who displayed apparent paralysis and other neurological symptoms, but showed no confirming signs of organic disease.[11] Freud saw a number of similar patients with Breuer—women with crippling neurological symptoms, but no identifiable organic basis. This was a challenging puzzle to the renowned diagnostician. Freud had studied with the premier neurologists of his day, including Rene Charcot, who held a chair in neuropathology at the Salpetriere in Paris. He had learned well one of the fundamental axioms of the new scientific neurology: that there is a causal relationship between lesions of the nervous system and the symptoms of organic neurological disease. Freud summarized this axiom, which is still valid today, as follows:

> Every clinical detail of a representation (organic) paralysis finds its explanation in some detail of cerebral anatomy and, vice versa, we can deduce the structure of the brain from the clinical characteristics of the paralysis. We believe that a perfect parallel exists between these two series of facts.[12]

The fertile paradox presented by the women who were Freud's early psychoanalytic patients is that they all violated this axiom. They displayed paralysis and other neurological symptoms, but no evidence of any underlying organic lesions could be found. Freud was familiar with such patients, diagnosed as "hysterics," from his training with Charcot and his reading of the neurological literature which he often reviewed for professional journals.[13]

The problem of hysteria was considered one of the most perplexing "medical" puzzles of the day. Charcot abandoned his practice of organic neurology to specialize in the problem. One of the intriguing facets of hysteria was that there seemed to be a link to hypnosis. Other neurologists, such as Mesmer and Morel, had demonstrated that hysterical symptoms could be caused and cured by hypnotic suggestion. It was Freud's good fortune that a group of patients with the most daunting neurological problems of the day fell into his hands.

Psychoanalysis and modern psychotherapy began with Freud's attempts to solve the paradox of hysteria—apparent physical paralysis with no confirming neurological signs.

The Neurotic Lesion

Freud's first step was to concede the obvious. Based on the observable facts and the accepted axiom that neurological diseases are caused by physical changes in the nervous system, Freud was forced to the conclusion that his patients did not have neurological lesions: "I maintain on the contrary that the lesions in hysterical paralysis must be entirely independent of the nervous system."[14]

What does this statement mean? If the lesions are not in the nervous system (or some other part of the body) then where are they? And if they are independent of the body, is it proper to call them "lesions," since the term conventionally refers to damaged tissue?

Freud's use of the term "lesion" was shaped by his desire to be a scientist and, hence, by the scientific *lingua franca* of his day, which was Newtonian physics and Darwinian biology. To be a scientist one hundred years ago meant, among other things, the conscious rejection of religion and philosophy as explanations of phenomena. Although hysterics did not demonstrate any lesions of the nervous system, Freud nevertheless had to find a lesion or be led into the unacceptable realm of mind and spirit. This is the motive for disguising the problem of desire in the language of medicine.

It is not difficult to translate Freud's pseudo-scientific "lesions" of hysteria into the language of desire. Lesions are unacceptable wishes. They are independent of the nervous system because they exist in the mind. They are not things but thoughts. Freud called unacceptable desires "lesions" because they are painful. Indeed, desires are painful, as we have seen. These *desire-lesions* are, in Freud's own words either "alarming or disagreeable or shameful by the standards of the subject's personality."[15] To indulge them is dangerous; to repress them is frustrating. The wish must therefore be hidden from oneself in order to manage the suffering. But the secret can only be partly hidden, and the neurosis is the symptomatic eruption of that painful secret into thought, speech, and action.

The classical Freudian example of a hidden wish, the "emotional lesion" which is the universal cause of neurosis, is the Oedipal wish. Freud imagined that the (male) child desires exclusive claim to the love and attention of the mother. To accomplish this, however, he must get rid of his competitor, his father. The life of the individual, thus, begins in tragedy. The child's desires are sins and crimes: incest and patricide. The helpless infant is thus doomed to suffering. He must either commit unspeakable crimes or renounce his wishes and be doomed to frustration.

To indulge in the wishes to kill the father and sleep with the mother is unacceptable. To manage the pain which is the result of these desires the forbidden wishes must be repressed—denied and ignored. But they can be only partially repressed. They continue to press for fulfillment. The best the normal male can do with his Oedipal wishes, according to orthodox psychoanalysis, is to identify with the father and marry a mother substitute. From a less sectarian point of view, one might say that the adult, in his or her relationship to sexual partners, must work through the unsatisfied wishes and unresolved fears of one's earlier relationship to the parents. In the neurotic individual the neurotic symptom or neurotic character is a compromise formation—a partial repression and partial indulgence of the repressed, forbidden wishes.

The Hiding of Hidden Wishes

Freud described his patient's problems in the language of science instead of religion or ethics because he wanted to be seen as a scientist. The following quotation from an abstract of one of Freud's early papers illustrates how psychoanalytic language obscures the problem of desire which, nevertheless, remains a powerful but hidden presence in psychoanalytic theory. The quote is from a paper entitled "A Case of Successful Treatment By Hypnotism." The patient is a married woman whose neurotic "symptom" consisted of her "difficulty" breast feeding each of her three children. The "symptom" was cured by hypnosis and explained by Freud as follows:

> There are certain ideas which have an affect of expectancy attached to them. They are of two kinds: intentions and expectations. The affect attached to these ideas is dependent on two factors: first on the degree of importance associated with the outcome, and secondly on the degree of uncertainty inherent in the expectation of that outcome. The subjective uncertainty (the counter expectation) is itself represented by a collection of ideas which are called distressing antithetic ideas. In neuroses, where primary presence of a tendency toward depression and low self-confidence exists, great attention is paid by the patient to antithetic ideas against his intentions.[16]

Translated loosely into ordinary English, this starchy, pseudo-scientific passage means that Freud's unhappy patient had unfulfilled desires, and suffered from a depressingly persistent pessimism that her desires would ever be satisfied. As we have seen, intentions and expectations are both forms of desire. The feelings of longing and deprivation are more intense depending on the degree of importance assigned to their satisfaction. The degree of uncertainty of the satisfaction of desires shapes the feelings of pessimism and gives rise to pessimistic thoughts, which Freud, in his attempt to sound scientific, calls "distressing antithetical ideas."

Most likely, Freud's patient "could not" nurse because she did not want to nurse. She had an aversion to nursing, or to her child, or perhaps she disliked her husband but could not say so and could not leave him. Perhaps she would have preferred to have been able to choose not to raise children and to pursue a career instead, as many modern women do. In the moral climate of her times, however, she had no respectable choice but to fulfill her wifely and motherly duties. She could not rebel and maintain a respectable social identity. And she would not docilely comply. Her depression and low self esteem were the result of the "distressing antithetical idea" that she could not have what she wanted. Her resentment surfaced in her "inability" to nurse her infants. This "neurotic symptom" which was defined as a mental illness because it contradicted the male-defined conventions of the day, was relieved by assuming the sick role, which exempted her from blame.

Most of Freud's early patients were cut from the same cloth. They were women with apparent neurological symptoms but no physiological basis, who objected to their designated role in the patriarchal Victorian social system of the European continent. They could not rebel without being cast out of their society; and they would not conform. The only acceptable form of protest was "counterfeit illness"[17] which partially hid and partially expressed their moral dilemma while preserving, indeed, enhancing their social status as tragic young women stricken by a mysterious "neurological" disease—conversion hysteria.

Freud's explanation of neurosis focused on an idea "with an affect of expectancy" attached to it; in other words, a wish, or desire. Bluntly stated, without the distortion of pseudo-scientific euphemism, this fundamental psychoanalytic axiom states that the cause of neurosis is unacceptable or frustrated desires—unacceptable or frustrated Happiness Projects. If the desires are strongly held and uncertain of success, negative, pessimistic thinking arises which predispose to depression and low self-esteem. This is a perfectly feasible explanation of the psychological causes and dynamics of depression which is consistent with both psychoanalysis and Buddhism.

The Medicalization of Desire

As Freud developed the language of psychoanalysis he medicalized it. What he first called "ideas with an affect of expectancy" were later described as instinctual drives or impulses. The "distressing antithetic ideas" were described as "resistances." Drawing from the concept of neurosis of his day, Freud attributed to the "expectant idea" a charge of nervous energy, or cathexis, similar to an electrical charge. The resistance to the charged instinctual drive was called a counter-charge or anti-cathexis. In these concepts Freud had the basic structure of his theory of neurosis, which I quote at length because it demonstrates how the ethical issues surrounding desire are obscured by the medical-biological language of psychoanalysis:

> It was now easy to reconstruct the pathogenic process. Let us keep to a simple example, in which a particular impulsion had arisen in the subject's mind but was opposed by other powerful tendencies. We should have expected the mental conflict which now arose to take the following course. The two dynamic qualities—for our present purposes let us call them "the instinct" and "the resistance"—would struggle with each other for some time in the fullest light of consciousness until the instinct was repudiated and the charge of energy withdrawn from it. This would have been the normal solution. In a neurosis, however...the conflict found a different outcome. The ego drew back, as it were, after the first shock of its conflict with the objectionable impulse; it debarred the impulse from access to consciousness and to direct motor discharge, but at the same time the impulse retained its full charge of energy. I named this process repression; it was a novelty, and nothing like it had ever before been recognized in mental life. It was obviously a primary mechanism of defence, comparable to an attempt at flight, and was only a forerunner of the later-developed normal condemning judgment.
>
> The first act of repression involved further consequences. In the first place the ego was obliged to protect itself against the constant threat of a renewed advance on the part of the repressed impulse by making a permanent expenditure of energy, a counter-charge or anti-cathexis, and it thus impoverished itself. On the other hand, the repressed impulse, which was now unconscious, was able to find means of discharge and of substitutive gratification

> by circuitous routes and thus to bring the whole purpose of the repression to nothing. In the case of conversion-hysteria the circuitous route led to the nerve supply of the body; the repressed impulse broke its way through at some point or other and produced symptoms. The symptoms were thus results of a compromise, for although they were substitutive gratifications they were nevertheless distorted and deflected from their aim owing to the resistance of the ego.[18]

In this passage Freud has described a moral conflict in medical-scientific language. The attentive reader will have no difficulty in interpreting the moral content of the subtext. John Dewey once said that it is incorrect to say that an individual thinks, that is, that an individual's thoughts are independent of the society in which he or she lives. It is more correct to say that an individual gives unique expression to the thought of his or her times. The language and concepts that Freud used to describe his patient's conflict of desires were patterned on the template of the dominant modes of thought of his day.

The dominant thought of Freud's era (and ours) was science, particularly the conceptual frameworks of the developing sciences of physics and biology and their progeny, medicine, and in Freud's case, neurology. One of the aims of science, as we have discussed, is to remove all traces of religion and moral thought from scientific knowledge. Reading Freud, it is necessary to remember that he tried to describe and explain the symptoms of his "patients with no organic disease" scientifically, on the model of the biology, medicine, and neurology of his day.

Freud conceived of the mind as a machine, much as Newton conceived the cosmos as a machine. Freud's mind machine consists of three primary forces: the id, the superego, and the ego. The id and superego are in direct opposition to each other. The ego regulates these two titanic forces, striving for a homeostatic balance.

It is evident that Freud's metaphor of the *machine* and Plato's metaphor of the *two-horse chariot* refer to the same phenomenon. They both refer to the dialectic of desires. Each metaphor uses the power symbols of its day to represent the mind: one, a two horse chariot, the other, a machine. The desire to indulge in pleasure is the id, the unruly and ugly horse on the left. The desire to renounce pleasure is the superego, the obedient and beautiful horse on the right. The charioteer (or master machinist) is the ego, who tries to steer the warring titans on the middle path.

Freud himself noticed and was troubled by the incongruities between his "clinical data" and his attempts to explain them with the medical-scientific model. His patient's language and behavior resembled soap operas more than mechanical systems. Freud complains about this inconsistency in *Studies in Hysteria;* in the case of Frau Elizabeth von R. he writes:

> I have not always been a psychotherapist, but like other neuropathologists I was educated to methods of focal diagnosis and electrical prognosis, so that even I myself am struck by the fact that the case histories which I am writing read like novels, and as it were, dispense with the serious features of the scientific character. Yet I must console myself with the fact that the nature of the subject is apparently more responsible for this issue than my own predilection.[19]

Freud never pursued this awareness of the contradiction between his clinical data and his theories. Indeed, it was not in his interests to pursue these inconsistencies, for Freud wanted to be a scientist, not a novelist, and certainly not a philosopher or a priest.

Freud's colleague, Joseph Breuer, was much more forthright in acknowledging that the issues that emerged in their work with hysterics were social and psychological rather than scientific. In *Studies in Hysteria* Breuer wrote:

> In these discussions there will be little talk of the brain and nothing at all of molecules. Psychic processes will be dealt with in psychological language, for it cannot really be done in any other way. If instead of "idea" we should say "cortical irritation," the latter expression will only convey some sense through the fact that we will recognize in the disguise our old acquaintance, and thus quietly restore the "idea." For while ideas with all their nuances are familiar to us as objects of our experience, "cortical irritations" impress us more as a postulate, as an object of future and hoped for cognition. Such substitution of terms seems only an aimless masquerade.[20]

Breuer and Freud agreed on the facts, but admitted that their "interpretations and assumptions did not always coincide."[21] Both men found it difficult to accept the idea that sexuality played a prominent role in hysteria. Breuer responded by withdrawing from his association with Freud. He withdrew partly because of his personal difficulties in dealing with the sexual issues. Breuer's wife was jealous of the time he spent with his young, attractive female patients. Breuer also withdrew, however, because he could not in good conscience translate and disguise problems of sexuality and desire into problems of nervous energy, discharge, and repression.

Freud, by contrast, was not deterred by the scandalous suggestion that repressed sexuality is the cause of neurosis. His desire to be a scientist justified his intellectualizing and translating his observations and ideas into the language of science. This linguistic distortion changed his perceptions of the phenomena he was working with so that his patient's problems fit the conceptual models and clinical techniques that he preferred to use.

CHAPTER NINETEEN

Neurosis: The Dialectic of Desire

> The symptoms of neurosis, as we have learnt, are essentially substitutive gratifications for unfulfilled [sexual] wishes.
>
> —Sigmund Freud, *Civilization and Its Discontents*

To get a better idea of how the language of desire has been transformed into supposedly value-neutral psychiatric language by the medical model, let us look at one of Freud's classic case histories.

When Freud confessed that his patient's illnesses sounded more like novels than medical histories, he was talking about the case of Frau Elizabeth von R., who was referred to him because of pain in her legs and *astasia-abasia*—the inability to stand or walk. Freud examined her carefully and could find no organic basis for her symptoms. Following Charcot's criteria, of an apparently neurological illness with no objective signs, he diagnosed her as suffering from conversion hysteria.

Freud then engaged Elizabeth von R. in what he admitted was "sham treatment" while Breuer prepared the soil for the "psychic treatment" they were using at the time, which was catharsis.[1] Freud viewed catharsis as analogous to archeological excavation in which successively deeper layers of the mind are uncovered. His theory was that as the archaic strata are exposed, the emotions are vented and become conscious, thus relieving the symptoms.

The Life Drama of Frau Elizabeth von R.

Under the influence of Freud's suggestions and quasi-hypnotic techniques, Frau von R. told a story which, in its general features, is typical of Freud's cases of conversion hysteria. She was the youngest of three daughters of a prominent, affluent family. When she was young her mother fell ill. Perhaps because of this, she developed an especially close relationship with her father to whom she became extremely devoted. He was also fond of her, boasting of her proudly as "pert and disputatious." As a young woman she was very willful and ambitious, wishing to study music. At that time she was revolted by the idea of sacrificing her ambitions and her freedom for marriage.[2]

One summer her father became acutely ill with a heart condition. Elizabeth assumed full responsibility for nursing him. She slept in his room, at his beck and call every minute of the day and night. When her father died she concentrated her full attention and care on her mother, whose health was failing. Her pain and inability to stand and walk began during this period of nursing her parents.

While she was nursing her parents her eldest sister married "a talented and ambitious man of notable position." He was selfish and rude, however, and provoked Elizabeth's antagonism, particularly when he moved his family to a distant city, increasing Elizabeth's burden of caring for her mother. Elizabeth's second sister then married a man of whom Elizabeth grew fond. After an operation on mother's eyes, the three families enjoyed a reunion at Bad Gadstein, a summer resort. Elizabeth's symptoms began here. As Freud put it: "From now on Elizabeth became the patient in the family."[3]

Towards the end of that summer the second sister unexpectedly died from complications of pregnancy. Her husband moved away with their child to live with his family. Elizabeth, who had sacrificed her own ambitions for the sake of her family, felt abandoned and demoralized by her lonely and inescapable obligation to care for her dying mother. "Resentful of her fate," Freud wrote in prose that won him the Goethe Prize for literature, "embittered over the failure of her little plans to restore the family luster; of those dear to her, some were dead, some away, and some estranged—without any inclination to seek refuge in the love of a strange man, she lived thus for a year and a half, away from almost all social relations, nursing her mother and her pains."[4]

During this period Freud experimented with modifications of hypnosis, which was the standard but unsatisfactory treatment of hysteria. He devised the technique of placing his hands on his patient's forehead and asking her to tell him everything that came to mind as he applied pressure. Amongst other things, Frau von R. told Freud about meeting a man at a dance that she reluctantly attended while her father was ill, only to return to his sick room to find him in serious condition. She berated herself for neglecting her beloved father and renounced any interest or further attention to this man, of whom she was fond and who pursued her until he became discouraged. Freud also discovered that Frau von R. was very attracted to her second sister's husband. After her death she confessed to Freud a thought which "flashed like dazzling lightning through the darkness...'Now he is free again, and I can become his wife.'"[5] These contradictory thoughts revealed Frau von R.'s inner conflict between her obligations to her family and her desire for her own happiness (which Freud regarded as equivalent to sexual desire.)

The Medicalization of Moral Conflict

Freud was disappointed with Frau Elizabeth's story, which he called "a history of banal mental shocks."[6] As a physician, he was not interested in this "soap opera." Nevertheless, it was the only data he had upon which to base his conjectures about the cause of Elizabeth's conversion reaction.

Motivated by his curiosity and his ambition, Freud hoped to discover a scientifically respectable cause of her hysterical symptoms, which would make him famous and rich. This is not meant as a condemnation of Freud, since he was human and, like all of us, yearned for success and recognition. It is meant as an insight into his motivations. Much as he tried to translate Elizabeth's story into a scientific-medical theory of a mental disease, Freud could not escape the fact that the cause of her hysteria was a conflict between her desire to be happily married and her desire to serve her family. The cause of her neurosis, in other words, was a conflict of desires. On the one hand, she wanted a career and/or a marriage. On the other hand, her conscience would not permit her to abandon her sick father for the sake of her own happiness in marriage—to her dead sister's husband or any "stranger."

This moral dilemma caused her extreme mental pain because neither side of the conflict could be satisfied without great cost. To marry and abandon her parents was defined by her times as an unacceptable evasion of her moral responsibility. To give up a satisfying career or marriage was an unacceptable sacrifice of her personal happiness. To deal with this impasse Elizabeth tried to put the dilemma out of mind.

Freud recognized Frau von R.'s unwillingness to be aware of her moral dilemma, and thus "discovered" the unconscious. The effort to put the painful moral dilemma out of mind he called "repression." The unwillingness to become aware of the offending desires he called "resistance." Freud believed that his theory of the unconscious, repression, and resistance was a great scientific discovery, arrived at by "the very same procedures adopted by the older sciences."[7]

Although Freud could not avoid seeing his patient's moral dilemmas, he also could not afford to describe them as moral dilemmas and expect his theories to be accepted by the scientific community. The scientists of Freud's day, we may recall, wanted to purify knowledge of all traces of the defilements of religion and philosophy. For the Vienna Circle of positivist philosophers who were Freud's contemporaries, this meant especially ridding science of all traces of ethical ideas.[8] Freud himself was, thus, confronted by a daunting moral dilemma.

Freud articulated his ideas about the basic cause of neurosis with varying degrees of awkwardness. At first, in *Studies in Hysteria*, published in 1895, Freud could not avoid talking about Frau von R.'s moral dilemma, although he attempted to be indirect about it. In one circumlocution he wrote that Elizabeth's hysterical symptoms began "in a moment during which the ideas of her duties towards her sick father came into conflict with the content of her erotic yearning...."[9] He came closer to recognizing the moral quality of this mental conflict when he said, "Again, it was an erotic idea which came into conflict with all her moral conceptions...."[10]

In his later writings Freud deemphasized the moral dilemma inherent in neurosis in an effort to create acceptable scientific concepts and language. He focused on the *energy* of the affect of desire rather than on the desire itself.

In his *Autobiographical Study*, which appeared in 1925, Freud described the conflict of desires as "a particular impulsion opposed by other powerful tendencies."[11] In normal people, Freud wrote, "the two dynamic qualities—for our present purposes let us call them 'the instinct' and 'the resistance'—would struggle with each other for some time in the fullest light of consciousness, until the instinct was repudiated and the charge of energy withdrawn from it."[12] In neurosis, however, the ego barred the impulse from access to consciousness, the process which Freud called "repression." This required the ego to protect itself from the "repressed impulse" by means of a "counter-charge or anti-cathexis." The mechanism of conversion hysteria, in Freud's discourse, is the impulse breaking through the repression and causing symptoms which were a compromise formation between the impulse and the opposing resistance.

Out of these metaphorical physico-mental forces Freud developed his now famous "structural" view of the mind, consisting of the id, the superego and the ego. Freud called the id the "reservoir of instinctual energy." The superego is a metaphor for conscience, the desire to be good. The mediator between these "psychic forces"—in ordinary language the mediator between these conflicting desires—is ego.

Neurosis As a Moral Problem

In the latter part of the twentieth century critics of psychoanalysis began to realize that the problems of conversion hysteria and other psychoneurosis are problems of language and desire. Long before Jacques Lacan declared that the unconscious is a language, Thomas Szasz interpreted hysteria and other so called "mental illness" as problems of language and communication.

"Briefly, my thesis is," Szasz wrote in 1961, "that Breuer and Freud's observations on hysteria, though couched in medical-psychiatric terms, are statements concerning certain special patterns of human communication."[13] On this view, neurosis is not a medical problem but a problem of (interpreting) language and (moral) choices. Neurosis is a problem of choosing between the conflicting desires to indulge and to renounce, a dilemma which is made more difficult to resolve because of the refusal to be aware of and take responsibility for it.

In the rhetoric of Freud's pseudo-scientific discourse, Frau Elizabeth von R. suffered from conversion hysteria because of a clash of "psychic forces." In the language of morals, her illness was itself a language. Frau von R. was presented with the excruciating moral dilemma of choosing between her desires for a career and marriage and her desires to care for her family. Instead of confronting this dilemma directly she hedged, compromised, hinted, and symbolically acted out her dilemma.

Her counterfeit neurological disease was her way of finding a compromise for her moral dilemma, a compromise for which she did not take responsibility. If she could not have a career or husband, then, out of the willfulness and disputatiousness that her father admired, she would escape from her role as servant by becoming a patient. She experienced ("converted") her mental pain as feelings of physical pain. Her emotional and social helplessness became her counterfeit physical helplessness. Her "illness," thus, provided her with an excuse from the servile duties which required her to sacrifice her happiness. The tragic life of Fräulein von R. is a memorium to the fact that neurosis is a conflict of hidden wishes, a conflict of desires for which the individual does not take responsibility.

CHAPTER TWENTY

Desire and the Discontent of Civilization

> One feels inclined to say that the intention that man should be 'happy' is not included in the plan of Creation.
> —Sigmund Freud, *Civilization and Its Discontents*

Although Freud liked to think of himself as a scientist and shaped his language to the scientific paradigms of the day, he spoke explicitly about desires and their vicissitudes on a number of occasions. Indeed, he could not avoid giving desire its due attention since it is at the heart of the mental suffering he was attempting to understand and to heal.

In *The Interpretation of Dreams* (1900) Freud analyzed and explained dreams as expressions of wish fulfillments and fears.[1] This has become common knowledge. Wishes are desires, and Freud's theory of dreams says, in effect, that desires, particularly repressed desires or "hidden wishes," give dreams their motive and content.

In *The Psychopathology of Everyday Life* (1901) Freud explained a wide range of *faux pas*—slips of the tongue, lapses of memory, seemingly irrational actions—as motivated by hidden desires. His example of the Viennese parliamentarian who opened an unpleasant session of the legislature by banging his gavel and announcing that the session was hereby closed, appealed to the public's sense of humor as well as their intuition about human nature. In these works and others, Freud formed the foundation of his thought in the proposition that desires shape the waking and sleeping mind, although he did not enunciate it so clearly.

Ironically, although Freud was an outspoken and controversial critic of religion, his views on desire coincide astonishingly with the Buddhist paradigm. It is no coincidence that Buddha's and Freud's views on desire and suffering coincide, since they were both astute observers of the same universal human phenomena. We may recall that the Buddha distinguished three fundamental classes of desire: the desire for sensual pleasure, the desire for life, and the desire for death. Freud classified desires in much the same way.

From the beginning of his work, Freud recognized that the driving forces of the mind are the animal urges for sensual pleasure—for food and personal survival (the ego instincts) and for sex and species survival (the object instincts.) Following Nietzsche and Groddek, he identified the "psychic entity" which is the reservoir of these sensuous desires as the *id* or "it."

Later, when he was compelled to explain a wider variety of human behavior with his psychoanalytic theory, particularly sadism and aggression, Freud enlarged his classification of instinctual drives into two basic types: sex and aggression, *eros and thanatos*, the life instinct and the death instinct.[2] These two basic Freudian instincts correspond closely to the Buddhist categories of the desire for life and the desire for death which we previously discussed.[3] Although Freud modified his views on each of these fundamental desires, he maintained this basic instinctual dualism to the end.

Freud's most forthright discourse on desire and its relation to suffering appears in his mature work *Civilization and Its Discontents* (1930).[4] Ironically, Freud begins this marvelous book, which I would rank as one of the most important of this century, with a discussion of *nirvana*. An esteemed friend, the Vedantic scholar Romain Rolland, wrote to Freud after the publication of *The Future of An Illusion* (1927) to suggest that the source of religious feeling was not, as Freud had proposed, the Oedipal wish of a helpless humanity for the protection of a benevolent father, but rather the mystical feeling of oneness with the universe.

Try as he might, Freud could not discover such a mystical feeling within himself. He recognized the validity of the idea of the fundamental identity of self and cosmos, quoting with approval a line of a contemporary dramatist: "Out of this world we cannot fall."[5] But Freud did not believe that an idea could be a source of religion and he could not find within himself the desire to lose his ego boundaries in mystical union with the cosmos. He conceded that other people might experience such a feeling, which he traced back to "an early phase of ego feeling" and called it "oceanic narcissism." But he rejected his friend's claim that this could be the source of religion because, "After all, a feeling can only be a source of energy if it is itself the expression of a strong need." In other words, Freud believed that only a desire could be the source of religion; in his view, the infantile wish for parental protection was such a desire.

Although Freud rejected religion as an infantile illusion, he recognized the universal human need for it, quoting lines from Goethe acknowledging its ubiquity:

> Who possesses science and art also has religion;
> Who has neither science nor art needs religion.[6]

In a thesis which coincides with the Buddhist view, Freud maintained that religion springs from the desire for relief and release from suffering. "Life as we find it is too hard for us," he wrote, "it brings us too many pains, disappointments, and impossible tasks."[7] To bear the pain of life we need palliative measures. Of these there are three types: (1) "powerful deflections," such as religion and science; (2) "substitutive satisfactions," such as art; and (3) intoxicants, which, Freud argued, are universally necessary to numb humans to the pain of life. The aim of religion, Freud believed, is to palliate the suffering of life and provide a hope of future happiness, like the narcotic Marx believed religion to be.

Freud on Happiness and Suffering

In his relentless curiosity about the causes of human discontent, Freud asked the perennial question: "What is the purpose of life?" He concluded that only religion can answer this question. Undaunted by this limitation, and unwittingly demonstrating that his "new mental science" of psychoanalysis is more of a religion than a science, Freud then proceeded to answer the question by inquiring into what people show by their behavior is the purpose of their lives. He concluded, as Buddha, Plato, and Aristotle did before him, that people strive to be happy, and that the purpose of life is the pursuit of happiness. "This endeavor has two sides," Freud wrote, "it aims, on the one hand, at an absence of pain and unpleasure, and, on the other, at the experiencing of strong feelings of pleasure."[8] This is the psychoanalytic "pleasure principle," and it describes two of the three poisons.

Freud's insight into the causes of psychic pain are astonishingly Buddhist. Freud attributes the cause of human psychic pain, in effect, to egotistical desire in the face of impermanence. This view is inherent in Freud's classification of the three main sources of suffering: (1) the body; (2) nature; and (3) relationships. The body causes suffering because it is impermanent and is doomed to sickness and death, while we long for health and immortality. Nature causes suffering because it is unpredictably indifferent to our desires and periodically inflicts pain and destruction upon us. Interpersonal relationships are painful because we all want our own way.[9]

Freud gave the same answer as Buddha and Plato did to the question, "What is happiness?" Happiness is the satisfaction of desires. The more intense and urgent the desire, the more gratifying the pleasure of satisfaction. The problem, as Buddha and Plato also recognized, is that certain desires may have unpleasant consequences. In an axiom that well expresses the Buddhist law of karma Freud wrote, "An unrestricted satisfaction of every need presents itself as the most enticing method of conducting one's life, but it means putting enjoyment before caution, and soon brings its own punishment."[10]

Freud proposed that the human effort to evade pain and find pleasure shapes both personality and culture. One approach to avoiding pain he mentions is that of Eastern religion, particularly *yoga,* which Freud understood as the ascetical renunciation or "killing off" of the instincts or desires. Another technique, which we have already considered in detail, is less radical, namely, sublimation. Through sublimation desires are given limited, substitutive satisfaction, such as through artistic expression, sexual love, imagination, and, at the extremes, neurosis. All attempts to find happiness are unsatisfactory however, because pain can not be avoided, and because pleasures are delayed, diluted, partial and, at best, transient.

The purpose of life is the program of the pleasure principle, Freud wrote, and this is why civilization is discontented. The pleasure principle, the desire for pleasure, cannot be satisfied: "its programme is at loggerheads with the whole world.... There is no possibility at all of its being carried through; all the regulations of the universe run counter to it. One feels inclined to say that the intention that man should be 'happy' is not included in the plan of Creation."[11]

The Enantiodrama of Desire

Aside from the impermanence of the body and the capricious forces of nature, the main cause of the discontent of civilized humans, Freud believed, is civilization itself. The underlying basis of this cause, however, is in the human mind, of which civilization is a projection.

According to Freud, the energy of the mind and the course of human history are generated by the interplay of the antithetical instincts (or desires) of eros and thanatos, the life instinct and the death instinct, which symbolize the desire for pleasure and the aversion to pain. Eros is the desire for pleasure, including sexual pleasure, life, love, and convivial association with others. Thanatos, which Freud saw as a separate instinct, is the source of aggression and hatred. For peaceful association to be possible, for civilization itself to be possible, the sexual and aggressive drives must be controlled. This creates the conditions for psychological and political repression and frustration.

Freud saw that the requirement of civilization to repress sex and aggression gives rise to guilt, because these feelings cannot be completely repressed. The feelings of guilt include the anxiety and inhibition which accompany the struggle to repress a forbidden desire. The inhibition necessary to control a forbidden desire may become generalized. The anxiety is the subtle, nagging fear that the desire may be acted out, or, that it may go ungratified. The sense of guilt, which is produced by civilization itself, appears as a malaise or discontent. "The price we pay for our advance in civilization," Freud wrote, "is a loss of happiness through the heightening of the sense of guilt."[12]

The link between Buddha and Freud is complete. It is evident that they share the same fundamental views on human suffering. Suffering is an inevitable and inescapable aspect of life. The cause of suffering is selfish desire, specifically, the competing and conflicting desires to indulge and to renounce sensuous and ego pleasures. The orthodox psychoanalytic view thus coincides with the Buddhist view that the combination of ignorance (*avidya*) or repression, which occludes intelligence and makes the rational conduct of life impossible, and selfish desires, which lead to feelings of deprivation, frustration, aggression, and violence, are the chief causes of the suffering we humans impose on ourselves and others.

Narcissism and Compassion

The hidden similarities between psychotherapy and religion are nowhere better revealed than in the contrast between narcissism and compassion. Narcissism is regarded as a personality disturbance, a symptom of mental illness. Compassion is regarded as a sublime religious virtue. What could possibly be the connection between the pathological state of narcissism and the religious state of compassion?

Freud was a scholar of classical cultures, as was his father. He took the name "narcissism" from a story in Greek mythology of a young shepherd boy who, while drinking water from a clear pond, became entranced by his own image, fell headlong into the pond and drowned.

The psychoanalytic understanding of narcissism is phrased in the language of Freud's theory of the instincts. Freud believed that sexual desire, what he called "object cathexis," could only be satisfied by attachment to an external object. Gradually, he realized that the ego itself could become the object of desire, or what he called "libidinal cathexis." Freud gave the name "narcissism" to the libidinal cathexis of one's own ego.

If we translate the psychiatric theory of narcissism into ordinary language, it is apparent that narcissism is the traditional religious concept of selfishness rediscovered and renamed. All religions teach that self-absorption and selfishness are sinful and potentially destructive. Narcissus was so selfishly absorbed with himself that he drowned. In the concept of narcissism Freud discovered the obvious fact that people have a tendency to become selfishly and destructively absorbed with themselves and the satisfaction of their own desires.

Today, psychiatrists regard narcissism as a pathological condition. The basis of this diagnosis is the distinction made between"healthy narcissism" and "pathological narcissism." In other words, society accepts a certain degree of self-absorption, selfishness, and self-interest, which it calls "healthy narcissism." The desire for money, for example, is considered "healthy narcissism," or enlightened self-interest, if done legally, and pathological if done illegally. "Pathological narcissism" is a socially defined excess of selfishness which inflicts unacceptable pain on others and is, hence, diagnosed as a symptom of mental illness.

Ernest Becker regarded narcissism as a key concept for understanding the tragic nature of human life.[13] In his view, the source of narcissism is our animal nature. Narcissism developed through aeons of evolution as a mechanism for protecting the individual's survival, integrity, and identity. For Becker, narcissism is an epiphany of the individual organism's desire to survive, prevail, and flourish:

> Through countless ages of evolution the organism has had to protect its own integrity; it had its own physiochemical identity and was dedicated to preserving it. This is one of the main problems in organ transplants: the organism protects itself against foreign matter, even if it is a new heart that would keep it alive. The protoplasm

> itself harbors its own, nurtures itself against the world, against invasions of its integrity....But man is not just a blind glob of idling protoplasm, but a creature with a name who lives in a world of symbols and dreams....His sense of self worth is constituted symbolically, his cherished narcissism feeds on symbols....And this means that man's natural yearning for organismic activity, the pleasures of incorporation and expansion, can be fed limitlessly in the domain of symbols and so into immortality.[14]

Becker suggests that this narcissistic striving for immortality is the cause of humanity's self-inflicted suffering. This corresponds to the Buddhist view that the primary cause of suffering is an attachment to self—to an interest in the satisfaction of one's own desires and one's own Happiness Projects without regard for the consequences to others.

In the Buddhist view, self-attachment, or egotism, is the result of ignorance of the fact that self is an illusion, a projection of itself onto itself. Self is an illusion, like the Big Dipper in the night sky, which is a projection of a pattern onto stars which have no intrinsic connection and are actually disconnected and light years apart. The illusion of self supports and justifies the pursuit of selfish desires, the consequence of which is the sufferings we impose on ourselves and others. Thus it is that narcissism, or selfishness, is at the root of self-imposed human suffering.

The traditional Buddhist remedy for selfishness is compassion. Selfishness and compassion are opposites. Compassion means unselfishness. Compassion is necessary for the realization of the egoless bliss of nirvana. But both compassion and egolessness are misunderstood in the West.

Compassion is not merely an occasional feeling of sympathy for less fortunate people. Compassion is a discipline which requires, in the words of Khenpo Karthar Rinpoche, "the diligent mindfulness of a keeper of a flame." The development of compassion means taming and training the mind. It involves an analysis and acceptance of the facts of existence. It calls for the development of a keen moral consciousness. And finally, it involves a renunciation of selfishness and self-centeredness in favor of a policy of kindness towards others.

Some people think that the state of egolessness means the disappearance of the person who thinks and acts conventionally in the social world. As Chogyam Trungpa Rinpoche said, "We cannot be a guest at our own funeral." We cannot become egoless and then go get a pizza. Our egos cannot disappear while we are still here, working, drawing a paycheck, and watching television.

Egolessness is not a glamorous mystical state. The basic form of egolessness is unselfishness, which is the basic qualilty of compassion. Compassion is the ability to empathize with others, to understand that others, like ourselves, desire happiness. The realization of this fundamental law of human psychology creates in us the opportunity to realize for ourselves the suffering of others, and to care for them. This is the *bodhisattva* ideal. The bodhisattva ideal is the opposite of selfish, dualistic, neurotic mind. One of the secrets of happiness is that compassion is the antidote to narcissism. It is the skillful means by which we may free ourselves from the pain of our own egocentric strivings and sufferings.

Western Views of Self

CHAPTER TWENTY-ONE

The Evolution of Self: The First Humans

> To explain Adam's sin is therefore to explain original sin, and no explanation is of any avail which explains original sin and does not explain Adam. The deepest reason for this is to be discovered in the essential characteristic of human existence, that man is an individual and as such is at once himself and the whole race, in such wise that the whole race has part in the individual, and the individual has part in the whole race....Adam is the first man; he is at once himself and the race....Therefore what explains Adam explains the race and vice versa
>
> —Søren Kierkegaard, *The Concept of Dread*

In the Buddhist view, the basic causes of suffering and, therefore, the main obstacles to our happiness, are the three poisons—passion, aggression, and ignorance. Passion and aggression represent the two poles of desire, the desire to possess and the desire to repel, which we call desire and aversion. Ignorance refers to the failure to realize, accept, and integrate the three facts of existence—suffering, impermanence, and emptiness. This complex of desires and ignorance—the neurotic complex—frustrates our Happiness Projects and causes the suffering we humans impose on ourselves and others.

Ignorance is not the mere absence of knowledge, however. It is not simply the denial of or failure to understand the facts of existence. Ignorance also has the quality of projecting onto the world something which is not there. This is why ignorance is sometimes also called "illusion." Ignorance is not only the denial of or failure to realize the facts of existence, it is also the projection onto the world of the illusion that these facts are the opposite of what they actually are. Illusion, in other words, is the projection onto the world of the wish for, and the possibility of, eternal happiness, permanent fixed reference points, and a solid, substantial field of phenomena inhabited by solid substantial selves.

At the center of ignorance is the wish for a solid, substantial self. The idea that the sense of self should be at the core of our ignorance is strange and somewhat frightening to Westerners. It is frightening because we rely on our sense of self for our orientation to life. A strong sense of self connotes a resolute, confident traverse of life. We Westerners think we know who we are, or at least *that* we are. Our sense of ourselves is our most precious possession, our emblem, or totem. We each identify ourselves with a particular algorithm, or totemic pattern, of world, local, and family history, *with* specific people and groups and *against* others, and with definite values, ideals, and images of reality. A poor sense of self connotes confusion, awkward blundering, ineptitude, hesitation, conflict, and pain. We regard people who are confused about their identity as mentally ill. To spotlight the self as the source of our suffering seems to threaten the foundations of our existence.

One of the sharpest apparent contrasts between the Western and the Buddhist view of reality is that in the West we take self as real and substantial, while Buddhists view self as illusory and empty of substance. This is a misconception, however. From the Buddhist point of view, it is incorrect to say either that self exists or that it does not exist. The truth lies somewhere in between, which is one reason that Buddhism is called the "path of the middle way." In the Buddhist view self does not exist as a discrete, concrete, independent, autonomous substance. It does exist, however, as a fiction, as the false attribution of an independent substantial "I" on to the stream of consciousness and the body.

The idea that self is a reflexive fiction is neither new nor foreign to the West, although it is far from the popular conception. Confusion about human identity is a consistent undercurrent in Western thought. As Sigmund Freud has reminded us, the Western sense of identity has undergone three distinct periods of crisis, confusion, and change.[1] The first crisis of identity occurred when the heliocentric astronomy of the sixteenth century undermined Catholic cosmology which placed the earth at the center of God's creation. The second crisis was precipitated by Darwin's theory of evolution, which contradicted the sacred belief that humans are the special creations of God. The third crisis was one Freud believed he had caused himself with his theory of the unconscious which states, in effect, that we humans live in a state of ignorance, unaware of our own thoughts and feelings.

One cannot find anywhere in Western literature a clear and concise description of the nature and essence of the human self. No one can tell us what it is because it does not exist, or rather, it exists only as a figment of our imaginations. Nevertheless, the popular belief in a substantial self persists as an article of faith. Nietzsche challenged this conception with the counter-claim that we humans don't really know who or what we are. We only think we do. "We are unknown, we knowers, ourselves to ourselves," Nietzsche said.[2] The idea that self is manufactured, that it is a "human doing," is at the heart of existential philosophy, which claims, as Buddhists do, that self is not a substance but an "existence" which is created and continuously transformed by its own actions and projections. Modern structuralist and post-structuralist thought posit self as a *linguistic* creation which comes into being only through linguistic reference to itself.

If the Buddhist view is true, that the fictional self who mistakes itself for a substantial reality is the source of its own suffering, then the project of the European Enlightenment, to understand the origins of unequal human suffering from the point of view of science, deserves to be rethought. Rousseau's inquiry, as we may recall, led him to the conclusion that private property is the root of evil, that the first man who enclosed a piece of ground saying, "This is mine!" is the real founder of class exploitation and social suffering. The idea that social conditions and arrangements determine human consciousness and behavior has become a powerful and influential political ideology, but it is only a half-truth. No one could deny that society plays a role in shaping the human experience, and that social evils such as oppression, injustice, exploitation, and poverty cause enormous human suffering. But society itself is a projection of the human mind and a product of human activity.

No matter how repugnant social conditions may be, by themselves they are an insufficient and incomplete explanation of human evil. For the question remains: Is there an evil dwelling in the human heart that motivates people to seize property for themselves and to enslave, oppress, and torture others? Is there a factor in human nature that produces the social conditions that cause unequal suffering? Perhaps we shall find, as Buddhists believe, that the basic cause of self-created human suffering is the selfish thought, "This is mine!", rather than the private property it appropriates. If society is a projection of the human mind, then private property is a product of the selfish self.

Rousseau's analysis of the problem of unequal suffering relied upon the new knowledge brought back to Europe of peaceful primitive communities. Rousseau himself had no knowledge of evolution. If he had, he might have traced human evil back to the animal's selfish strivings to survive and expand. Any search into the nature of the human self will inevitably encounter the imposing presence of the animal. Modern evolutionary biology teaches that humans are evolved animals, similar to other animals in certain respects and different in others. Rousseau's answer to the Academy of Dijon needs to be updated in the light of modern evolutionary biology.

Traditional Buddhism has also yet to face the challenge of reconciling its views with evolutionary biology. Buddhism is an ancient Asian religion. It was formulated with no knowledge of evolution. As it spreads into the West, opportunities occur for dialogues between Buddhists and western scientists. The Fourteenth Dalai Lama has encouraged these dialogues.

The interesting and relevant questions are: What is the scientific view of the evolution of self and its relation to nature? Does the scientific evidence of evolutionary biology support the Buddhist view of self as a self-created fiction? What follows is an interpretation of the facts of human evolution which supports the Buddhist view.

The Evolution of Humanity

As Rousseau, Kant, and Kierkegaard understood, if we are to understand specifically human suffering, then we must first understand what is basically human. What are the fundamental similarities and differences between humans and animals. How did the human sense of self evolve and how is it related to self-imposed suffering? In other words: Who were the first humans? And, what was their sin?

The date at which the first humans appeared on earth is an open question. It will always be an open question. The archeological evidence of the evolution of the human species is fragmentary and incomplete, consisting of scattered, fossilized bones, stone tools, and refuse heaps dating from widely discontinuous periods over the past twenty million years or so.

Even if we had a complete and continuous record of the evolution of the human species, with no "missing links," the first humans still could not be identified on the basis of scientific evidence alone. Evolution is a continuous process from generation to generation. The dividing line between the animal and the human is a matter of human perception and interpretation. How can we distinguish the first humans from their non-human ancestors without first knowing, or deciding what is basically human?

Various criteria have been proposed to mark the mythical transition from the animal to the human, each invariably reflecting a particular preconception about human nature. At one end of the spectrum is the view that humans are not fundamentally different from the animals. This view, represented by modern scientific psychiatry and psychology, maintains that the important determinants of human behavior are biological mechanisms, and that human aggression and neurotic suffering are caused by "biochemical imbalances." At the other extreme is the intriguing claim that humans are "divine animals" who have not yet become fully human. Perhaps Buddha or Christ were the first fully human beings and our species as a whole has not yet completely evolved to that degree of divine maturity.

Between these polar extremes is a long list of criteria for identifying the first humans. One set of criteria is anatomical, based, for example, on the shape of the vertebral, pelvic, and leg bones, from which the possibility of erect posture can be deduced. Another anatomical standard is the volume and shape of the skull, from which the level of intelligence may be inferred. Other criteria are cultural, based on archeological artifacts, such as stone and bone tools, remnants of hearth-fires and postholes, carved bones, painted pebbles, pottery, jewelry, and the like. From these artifacts, the possibility of tool using, fire making, house building, art, and religion can be gauged. Other criteria of the first humans are more speculative. Some are based on theories of the origin of language, consciousness, and free choice. Others stipulate the emergence of agriculture or civilization, like Rousseau's criterion of the first private ownership of property.

Answers to the question, "What is human nature?" seem to be as varied as human self-perceptions. How can we make sense of this diversity? Kierkegaard has given us guidance by proposing that questions about fundamental human nature are questions about both the first humans and about ourselves. Whatever marks the first humans as different from the animals also marks us.

Inquiries into the first humans can be approached in several ways. They can take a diachronic form which attempts to order the facts in historical time. The basic diachronic approach is evolutionary biology. From the point of view of evolutionary biology, the relevant questions are "Who were the first humans, and what biological characteristics distinguish them from the animals?"

Questions about the first humans and basic human nature can also take a synchronic form. This is the form of myth, legend, and story which attempts to grasp psychological realities in the language of metaphor. We will now first consider the scientific facts about the emergence of the first humans and then try to make sense of them in the light of myth.

The Criterion of Humanness

Evolutionary biologists agree that the primate line began around seventy million years ago when the dinosaurs were becoming extinct. At that time, a mouse-like creature climbed from the forest floor into the trees in search of food. To survive in the trees, this creature, over tens of millions of years, developed a prehensile grasp and the agility of a tightrope walker. The human hand, which alone in the animal kingdom can oppose the thumb and index finger in the sign of perfection,[3] evolved from these tree dwellers who used their hands for locomotion. Climbing trees, walking on branches, and swinging from branch to branch in search of food is greatly aided by stereoscopic and color vision. And so, over tens of millions of years, as adaptive variations were rewarded with survival and reproduction, the eyes of this creature swung slowly to the front of the face.

For about fifty million years this proto-primate line dwelled in the trees perfecting a complex system of eye-brain-hand coordination. About fifteen or twenty million years ago, probably under pressure of population growth, cooling climate, and receding forests, these creatures began to climb down from the trees to search for food on the savannahs at the edge of the dense primeval forests. With their athletic agility, stereoscopic and color vision, manual dexterity, and superior intelligence, these creatures, called Ramapithecines, were powerfully suited for survival. Studies of bone fragments from a few dozen individuals suggest that Ramapithecines could stand upright and peer over the tall savannah grass in reconnaissance for food and predators. Their erect stride freed their hands, possibly for carrying food back to the troop, or for carrying their young on portages in search of new supplies. In contrast to apes, Ramapithecines had small incisor teeth, suggesting that they may have used unmodified sticks and stones as weapons and tools. If erect posture is taken as the criterion of humanness, then Ramapithecus is the patriarch of the human line. But they had a brain size of only 450 cc or so, and by this criterion they were not yet human.

There is an archeological gap of some three million years between the most recent Ramapithecines and the next hominid in the line of human descent, the Australopithecines, of whom there are traces dating to five million years ago. Australopithecus walked more securely upright than its predecessors. Their tools were more advanced, consisting of stone cutters, bashers, and choppers. The Australopithecines seem to have split into two separate lines, the robust form which became extinct, and the gracile form which may have evolved into later species

If tool making is taken as the criterion of humanness, then perhaps the gracile australopithecine was the first human. Quite possibly, however, the criterion of tool making is a projection of modern peoples enchanted by technology. As Lewis Mumford shrewdly observes, "There is nothing uniquely human in tool making until it was modified by linguistic symbols, aesthetic designs, and socially transmitted knowledge. At that point the human brain, not just the hand is what made the difference."[4] The Australopithecine tools are more advanced than the modern chimp's, but by the criterion of brain size, this hominid was not yet fully human. Its cranium carried only about 500 cc of intelligence, only a little more than the chimp's.

Next in line of descent is Homo habilis, the first *homo*, the "handy man" who roamed the African plains more than three million years ago. They walked erect and had a more advanced tool kit, consisting of flint scrapers, cutters, and hand axes made by hammering chips from hand sized rocks. But they had an average braincase of 750 cc or so, not yet in the human range.

Homo erectus—the famous Java and Peking man, and later, Heidelberg man—roamed across Africa, Asia, and Europe more than one million years ago. They were larger than their predecessors, almost human in appearance. In a great quantum leap of evolution their brain size grew to about 1000 cc, more than double that of their Australopithecine ancestors. Homo erectus were clever tool makers and hunters. They were the mythical Prometheans who domesticated fire, perhaps by cultivating a flame caused by lightning or molten lava, or perhaps by accidentally igniting dry leaves while manufacturing their flint tools. Possibly they invented cooking. But they left no traces of symbols, art, or religion, and by these criteria had not yet become fully human.

If brain size is used as a measure of intelligence and taken as the criterion of humanness, then the first humans may have appeared around 250,000 years ago. The Swanscombe and Steinheim fossils, which date from that era, have skull volumes of 1300 cc, well within the range of modern humans. In certain respects these creatures are intermediate between Homo erectus and Homo sapiens. On the whole, with the exception of relatively minor features, such as body hair, skull shape, and facial contours, their gross anatomical appearance was probably similar to ours. They were the earliest Homo sapiens, "man the wise." But their wisdom was not yet fully human. In spite of their full-sized brains early Homo sapiens were very primitive. They could build fires, cook food, and manufacture a few varieties of stone tools. But there are no embellishments or decorations. They were nomadic hunter-gatherers who lived in bands of around fifty and left their dead where they fell.

Unfortunately, the archeological record is barren for the next 150,000 years until the appearance of the Neanderthals. The Neanderthals initiate a remarkable set of changes in the record—the appearance of symbols. One of the most remarkable features of human evolution is that for sixty million years the primate brain increased in size, developing a sophisticated eye-brain-hand coordination suited to the manipulation of objects. Yet, not one symbol appears in the archeological record until 150,000 years after the brain had reached its present volume. Then, suddenly, with the Neanderthals, there appear carved bones, painted pebbles, and ceremonial burials with corpses sprinkled with red ochre and laid to rest facing east, towards the rising sun. If language, art, and religion are taken as the criteria of humanness, then the first true humans were these Neanderthals, whose traces suggest that they may have been the first creatures aware of their existence in the midst of creation.

The Neanderthals were robust and athletic cave dwellers. They hunted wooly mammoths, giant bear, and sabre-toothed tigers. Yet, all traces of them mysteriously disappeared about thirty thousand years ago. They seem to have been assimilated, replaced, or possibly eradicated by the Cro-Magnon peoples who migrated to Europe from the Near East and Africa.

The Cro-Magnon were skilled hunters, fishers, artists, and tool makers. They painted their caves with astoundingly beautiful pictures of animals and hunters, embellished with undeciphered symbols, some of which were possibly lunar calendars. They adorned themselves with jewelry and developed to a fine art the craft of making tools out of stone, bone, antlers, and ivory. Very likely, the Cro-Magnons or their descendents settled down, raising livestock and farming in the first villages along the fertile banks of rivers of the Near East about ten thousand years ago.

If the beginning of agriculture is taken as the criterion of full humanness, then these Homo sapiens sapiens, "man the doubly wise," were the first humans. But if civilization and writing are taken as the criteria, then the first humans are only about five thousand years old, for that is when the great kingdoms of the Nile, the Tigris and Euphrates, the Indus, and the Yellow rivers began to take form. By some criteria, however, the people of the earliest civilizations were not yet fully human. Julian Jaynes believes that the first humans did not appear until after the Homeric era, with the emergence of self-consciousness, the awareness of the subjective "I."[5]

The Homeric epics probably originated around 1200 B.C. and were passed down from generation to generation by a tradition of oral recitation until around the eighth century B.C. when Homer, or his scribes, set them down in writing. Jaynes compared Homer's Iliad and the oldest book of the bible, Amos, which were written at about the same time, and contrasted them with Ecclesiastes, the most recent Book of the Old Testament, which dates to the second century B.C. By comparing the degrees of subjectivity expressed in Homer and Amos to Ecclesiastes, the reader may get some feeling for the pace of the evolution of subjective consciousness over six centuries of human history. Amos shows no sense of interiority, no mental images or metaphors, no self-motivation or self-reflection. He is a very primitive human. By contrast, the preacher in Ecclesiastes tells us that everything is ego: "Vanity of vanities, all is vanity."[6] Over six centuries, the brutish prophet had become a sensitive poet!

Jaynes concludes from this comparison that the Homeric peoples had no egos. They were ruled by their bicameral minds which hallucinated verbal commands from their gods and kings.[7] He believes that subjective consciousness, the consciousness of self, does not appear until after the sixth century B.C., the age of Confucius, Buddha, and Thales, when the bicameral mind broke down and the hallucinated commands were attenuated into the "inner newsreel," the "supratentorial chatter," the constant narratization of experiences that characterizes human mental life. Even if we shift Jaynes' timeline backwards five hundred years, or a thousand years, or five thousand years, it would be fair to surmise that the human ego, the sense of self-consciousness, emerged more fully during this period.

Ecclesiastes does not represent the final flowering of human self-consciousness, however. It is a continuous process of evolution. Michel Foucault believes that humanity did not appear until it appeared to itself by entering the field of knowledge for the first time. Foucault dates this to the seventeenth century, when the scientific study of nature was turned reflexively on to human nature. In Foucault's view, humanity is a fragile existence, indeed:

> Taking a relatively short chronological sample within a restricted geographical area—European culture since the sixteenth century—one can be certain that man is a recent invention within it....man is an invention of recent date. And one perhaps nearing its end. If those arrangements were to disappear as they appeared...then one can certainly wager that man would be erased, like a face drawn in the sand at the edge of the sea.[8]

Foucault's metaphor applies to every human generation and to every human being. We are all self-portraits drawn in the sand at the edge of the sea. Human nature is a product of the human mind reflecting on itself. If we imagine ourselves as upright animals, then the human line began about fifteen million years ago with Ramapithecus. If we imagine ourselves in the images of technology, then perhaps the first human tool makers were the five million year old Australopithecines. If we imagine ourselves as artists, then the first humans were the Neanderthal artisans who carved stones and painted pebbles. Perhaps, thirty-five thousand years from now, a new species of Homo sapiens will classify our cruel and brutish species, which has mismanaged the world, as not yet fully human, an intermediate species between Neanderthals and themselves.

The Evolution of Self-Consciousness

If the idea of human nature is a product of the human mind reflecting on itself, then the consciousness of self is a primordial human quality. The primordial self-image is the archetypical image of the double, self reflecting on itself as other, creating itself out of the experience of that duality—out of no one, so to speak.

If self-consciousness is taken as an overarching criterion of humanness, then we must ask when humans first appeared in evolutionary time by this criterion. When, in other words, did we first become aware of our existence as creatures in the midst of creation? In the context of biological evolution this question suggests another. What biological transformation occurred in the structure and function of the hominid organism to produce a creature capable of self-consciousness and its associated manifestations: the "supernatural environment of society and the extrasomatic evolution of history?"[9]

Objective evidence from a wide range of disciplines suggests, or at least is consistent with, the interpretation that the first humans emerged between the time the brain reached its present size and the time symbolic activity first appeared in the archeological record. By present accounting, this would be sometime between 50,000 and 250,000 years ago.

The precise date probably can never be given because we are talking about a transformation, a *rite de passage*, rather than a particular historical event. Indeed, the precise date is unimportant. What is important is the nature of the process that occurred during this period. It is a process which has its roots in the deep, primeval past and grows continuously into the future. This transfiguring process, the evidence suggests, involved the reorganization of the preexisting primate eye-brain-hand system for the development of speech.

The evidence for this interpretation is in the archeological record. For sixty million years or more the primate brain grew in size and complexity, developing a sophisticated neural system of eye-hand coordination suitable for the location and manipulation of objects in space. Until about 100,000 years ago this neural system deposited only a few varieties of primitive, practical, and undecorated tools in the archeological record. Then, suddenly, there was an explosion of objects, beginning with improved tools, painted fetishes, funerals, and personal jewelry, leading, gradually at first, and then precipitously in our own era, to the development of increasingly more subtle and abstract art and music, and the invention of marvelous and magical objects such as televisions, automobiles, computers, neutron bombs, and rocket ships to the moon.

From comparative neurology we know that the function of speech is lateralized and contralaterally related to handedness. The most recently evolved parts of the brain, the cerebral hemispheres are, as their name implies, divided in two. The speech centers are in the left cerebral cortex in right-handed persons and in the right cortex in the fifteen percent or so of left-handed persons. The sensory-motor centers for the coordination of sensation and motor control of the hand are located in the contralateral cortex.

The lateralization of biological functions is a well known evolutionary process involving the duplication of organ systems. The kidneys, lungs, eyes, and ears are laterally duplicated organs with redundant functions. The evolutionary advantage of lateralization is that if one side becomes diseased or damaged the other side can take over with little loss of function. In addition, duplicate eyes and ears provide stereoscopic vision and hearing which improve the ability to locate and manipulate objects in space. The lateralization of the brain for the function of speech involved the internal reorganization, specialization, and hierarchic integration of one half of the pre-existing visual-motor circuitry. One half of the brain continued to be used for sensory-motor coordination, the other was rewired for speech.

The intimate relationship between vision, speech, and the hand suggests that the evolution of speech and of self-consciousness may be correlated with the evolution of artifacts in the archaeological record. As Julian Jaynes noted, words are correlated with things, and the history of words may be related to the history of things such that "each new set of words literally created new perceptions and attentions, and such new perceptions and attentions resulted in important cultural changes which are reflected in the archeological record."[10]

The evolution of language is a complex and controversial subject. There are hundreds of theories and thousands of articles on the subject, and little agreement among the experts.[11] The traditional idea that humans are distinguished from the animals by language has been challenged in recent decades by the discovery that chimpanzees can be taught a sign language of several hundred words. There is a vast difference however, between the chimp's paltry use of words and the rich and diverse products of human language. It remains to be seen whether mother chimps can teach their children to use language and, over undetermined generations, chimp culture and chimp history will evolve.

In any case, language certainly does not begin with the human species. A wide variety of species communicate with vocal calls, gestures, dances, odors, and other biological signals. The genetic code is itself a kind of language, a variable arrangement of signals that cue and regulate different sequences of events. In this sense, language is a biological rather than a specifically human activity. But chimpanzees, dolphins, and bees cannot speak. Only the human animal is neurologically wired for speech and writing—the speech of the hand.

Our hominid ancestors, no doubt, communicated through a variety of calls and gestures, as primates and other creatures do. No one knows, or will ever know, when the first words were spoken. Perhaps the calls and grunts of Ramapithecus were elementary words. Perhaps the Australopithecines, who invented the cutting edge, sat around their campfires at night chatting about the day's events. The sudden appearance of superior tools, fetishes, and funerals about 100,000 years ago, however, suggests that the process had begun to accelerate.

Jaynes has proposed an interesting theory of the origin of language which may help us to imagine a possible pattern of the unfolding of human self-consciousness. The first step in the evolution of language, according to Jaynes, was the development of intentional calls, which are repeated until they change the behavior of the receiver, like teaching a dog to sit by repeating the word "sit" until the dog obeys.

The evolutionary pressure for this change may have been a period of extreme glaciation which produced wide swings in climate and mass migrations of animals together with the Neanderthals who hunted them. Under these circumstances the development of intentional calls could facilitate the hunt and, therefore, the survival of the group. Most likely, the *person* was born in these primeval circumstances. "The person," writes Denis de Rougemont, "is call and answer."[12] Like the child who first appears as a person to the mother when it answers her call, the first humans may have emerged in the call and answer of the Paleolithic hunt.

The first real elements of speech, according to Jaynes, were the modification of the final sounds of intentional calls through changes of pitch and tonation. A nearby tiger, for example, might have been signalled by an excited "Wahee!" while a distant tiger was announced by a more relaxed "Wahoo." In the next step, the modifiers were separated from the calls they modified, creating the first antithetical words, in this case, "near" and "far."

Whenever this event occurred—suddenly in a flash of brilliant invention, or gradually over millions of years—it was a most significant event in human history. In a sense, it was the first event in human history. It was the blooming of a thousand flowers. The development of calls with antithetical meanings was the cutting edge of a process of polarization that split the human organism to its core.

At the level of language, it marks the invention of speech. Anatomically, it represents the beginnings of the internal polarization of the brain as it was being wired for speech. Psychologically it polarized perceptions of the object world into antithetical qualities: near-far, up-down, sky-earth, hot-cold, and eventually, over thousands of years, self-other, past-future, and good-evil.

It is interesting to speculate whether the development of antithetical words and perceptions is correlated with the development of a binary neural circuitry, similar to the on-off sequences of the digital computer, which register in on-off sequences of neuronal activity representations of similarities and differences in the object world. And could the product of this binary linguistic circuitry be the binary logic that Levi-Strauss believes is the common basis of religion and science?[13]

According to Jaynes, the "age of modifiers" lasted until around 40,000 B.C., at which time new and improved tools appear in the archeological record. Jaynes believes this inaugurated the "age of commands," "when modifiers, separated from the calls they modify, now can modify men's actions themselves."[14] Commands suggest the idea of a new form of authority, based partly on the animalistic criteria of sex, age, size, and strength, but perhaps also based on the power of speech. Perhaps the explosion of new tools from this period was sparked by verbal commands, which could mobilize a group to a greater degree of organization and achievement through the transmission from generation to generation of accumulated knowledge and techniques.

The next stage was the "age of nouns" which, according to Jaynes, lasted from 25,000 B.C. to 15,000 B.C. and is correlated with the appearance of cave paintings, barbed spears, pottery, and personal decorations. The invention of nouns and naming must have dramatically increased the magnitude and complexity of the object world, as well as mastery of it. When children first learn to name things they want to name and touch everything in sight. As they search for new objects to name, they simultaneously expand their capacity to speak and their mastery of the object world. Such a process must have been occurring at the threshold of the modern era, when agriculture was invented, some ten thousand years ago.

Jaynes' theory of the origin of language is plausible, fascinating, and richly suggestive. But it is not the only possibility. The timing and sequence of developments may have been different. Jaynes believes that self-consciousness did not appear until after Homer, with the breakdown of the bicameral mind. The growth of self-consciousness from Amos to Ecclesiastes is impressive. But is it not possible that elementary forms of self-consciousness existed tens of thousands of years before? We wonder, did the corpses buried with flowers in the Neanderthal graves have names? Was it Mom or Pop who died, or a beloved child, or a dear hunting companion? And the Cro-Magnon artists who painted caves and wore jewelry, were they aware of themselves as creatures in the midst of creation?

Although the precise diachronic timing of the appearance of the human species, and of speech, is uncertain, the broad outline of the biological sequence of events seems clear. The foundation of human consciousness is the primate system of eye-brain-hand coordination adapted to the location and manipulation of objects. When this system was wired for speech, the human person appeared on earth.

The relationship between the hand, the eye, and the word is fundamental to human consciousness and to the personal ego. The integrity and intelligence of the cerebral cortex is measured by the coordination of these functions in solving problems. Standard intelligence tests are divided into verbal and performance scores which measure separately the problem solving capacities of the word and the hand.[15]

The human mind, culture, and personality are constructed upon the primate eye-brain-hand system and its relationship to objects. Humanity has not advanced very far from its squirrelly ancestors who also liked to handle and collect things. The human love of objects is fueled by the functions of the hand and the eye. Political ideologies which reject the love of objects per se as morally degenerate materialism are doomed to fail because they fail to understand how deeply the relation to objects is rooted in human nature. Even ascetic monks have their beads and their icons.

The development of speech added a new dimension to the organization of action in the object world. Through speech, objects are given social significance. Through regular patterns of daily interaction significant others are woven into one's life, thus becoming part of the sense of self. Psychoanalysts have described the early growth of the ego in terms of the internalization of external objects, including persons.[16] The fictional self consists in large part of internalized others—others who, through relationship, have become part of our sense of self. The loss of a loved, or internalized, object generates feelings of paralytic loss and depression, as if part of the self has been amputated. Conversely, mild depression can sometimes be alleviated by buying or otherwise appropriating a desired object. Psychotherapists blessed with a sense of humor call this "retail therapy." Our social, economic, and political relationships, as well as our sense of self, are bound up with our relationship to the object world.

The development of speech produced not only a new relationship to the object world, but also a new form of consciousness which represents objects, and the relationship between objects, with words, symbols, and concepts. Words bring things to life by animating them with meaning. Gradually, over tens of thousands of years, the act of representing the object world in speech, and the silent rehearsal of speech in thought, came to represent itself to itself as a holographic presence in the metaphorical interior space of mind. And in this process, the human self was born.

CHAPTER TWENTY-TWO

The Numinous Sky and the Personal "I"

> In relation to our position in creation, the universe itself is a ladder by which we can ascent into God.
>
> —Saint Bonaventure, *The Soul's Journey Into God*

Before the first humans became aware of themselves as creatures in the midst of creation, they must have become aware of creation itself. Sometime in prehistory, as the brain was being lateralized and specialized for speech, the early humans became aware for the first time that the day begins with sunrise in the east and ends with sunset in the west, and that the dark of night is followed regularly by the light of dawn. It is difficult to imagine that this was the discovery of a single individual or group. More than likely, these facts simply emerged in consciousness over thousands, perhaps hundreds of thousands of years.

The earliest evidence of human knowledge of facts about the sky comes from the upper Paleolithic Age (c. 30,000 B.C.), from which period corpses have been found interred in the fetal position and facing east.[1] The appearance of burials towards the east suggests that this may be when facts about the sky crystallized into a pattern. Evidence of the preservation of skulls and lower mandibles have been found at archeological sites dating from 400,000 to 300,000 B.C. Burials are known from 70,000 B.C. Burials suggest the belief in survival after death and perhaps, therefore, an awareness of the cycles of birth and death in nature. Burials towards the east suggest an awareness of the cycles of day and night and a linkage between the course of the sun and the fate of the soul.[2] The linkage of the soul and the sky represents the appearance of a new form of specifically human consciousness, different from animal consciousness, but coexisting with it in the human animal.

The archeological evidence of interred corpses facing east suggests that emerging human consciousness was aware of two sets of primary, or archetypical facts: (1) the facts of birth and death; and (2) facts about the sky, the sun, and the moon. These seem like simple facts that every schoolchild knows, but the human infant is not born knowing them. Every human being must sometime learn them for the first time.

My dog, Jamie, "knows" the difference between a live woodchuck that runs or fights, and a dead one which just lies there. But Jamie, like our prehuman ancestors of the dark past, is not aware of death as a fact. She does not know that she is a part of nature, like the woodchuck, the eagle, and the oak, which are born and die in cyclical rhythms. Jamie also "knows" the difference between day and night in that she hunts and plays during the day and sleeps at night (except at full moon). But she does not attend funerals and never trots up to the top of the hill to watch a sunrise or sunset. When my daughter, Lehana, was two years old, she was like Jamie in this respect. When others went to the top of the hill to enjoy the sunset Lehana played with Jamie, bathed in the sun's light but oblivious to its setting. As ontogeny recapitulates phylogeny, the same gradual evolution of conscious mind occurred in the human species and the human individual.

The history of the sky, from the ancient sky gods to modern astronomy, is also a history of human self-consciousness. The sky may seem very remote from human suffering here on earth and a strange place to search for self-knowledge. Yet the sky evokes states of mind and feeling which resonate to the deepest core of the human experience. The history of human consciousness is written in the sky. Through the ages interpretations of the sky have been both mirrors and beacons, reflecting human self-perceptions and guiding human actions. Each age projects its own image onto the sky; and as humanity evolved, its images of itself and the universe also evolved, much as an individual's perspective on life changes with age and experience.

Ancient peoples viewed the sky as a sacred space, alive with gods and spirits whose motives and deeds influenced and authorized events on earth. The ancients expressed their relation to the sky in the personalized metaphors of myth. By contrast, we modern people, flush with the power of science, view the sky as physical space, the locale of weather and fraying ozone layers, of red giants and white dwarfs, of neutron stars, black holes, and cosmic microwave radiation. We express our relation to the sky in the mechanical metaphors of science, as depersonalized matter and energy in a godless cosmos.

On the scale of cosmic time as measured by modern science, humanity is very new to the universe. If the history of the universe is measured in terms of a twenty-four hour clock, the human species is about one second old![3] As much as human interpretations of it have changed, the sky has not changed much from the beginning of human history to the present moment. Simply by stepping outdoors and looking up, we see essentially the same sky that earliest human saw. What has changed is how we perceive and interpret the sky and ourselves. By reflecting on the history of the sky, we can learn about the evolution of the human self.

The Sky Gods

The sky is the embracing background of human life and the eternal witness of human history. It is the archetype of the sacred, the standard of time and magnitude by which all things are measured. Ultimately, the significance of human events is scaled to cosmic events. No wonder then, that the belief in a celestial divinity is virtually universal in all times and places, and that facts about the sky have formed the nucleus of human identity.[4]

In the dawn of human consciousness, the sky gods were manifested as elemental qualities of the sky, such as light, darkness, moisture, and magnitude. Yahweh created the world by separating the light from the darkness. Eliade has suggested that the similarity between the English words "day" and "deity" is a clue to the underlying connection between light and divinity, quintessentially[5] represented by the Aryan sky god Dyaus (Zeus), the grandfather of Indo-European divinities of the light sky.[6]

One of the most popular prayers of the Judeo-Christian world is to a sky god: "Our Father which art in heaven..." The modern Jew, Christian, and Moslem prays to a God who dwells in the sky, as the ancient

Egyptians prayed to the sun god Ra, and the contemporary Australian bushman prays to the sky god Baime. The Hebrew sky god, Yahweh, spoke to Moses from the sky in wind and thunder, and etched the Ten Commandments in stone with a finger of lightning.

The Christian cross symbolizes the intersection of earth and sky. The birth of Christ was signalled in the sky by the star of Bethlehem which guided the three wise men, or Magi, who were astronomers. Christ claimed that he was descended from heaven and that he would return to heaven.[7] After the Crucifixion and Resurrection he ascended to join Father-Sky. "I and my father are one," Christ said,[8] thus establishing the doctrine of the Holy Trinity, the mystical union of Father-Sky and human child.

Everything that happens within the vault of the sky has been worshipped as a hierophany, from sunrises and sunsets, rain and rainbows, thunder and lightning, to the orbital revolutions of the heavenly spheres. Isaac Newton (1642-1727), whose mathematical laws of planetary rotation and attraction transformed medieval concepts of the sky, depicted the Judeo-Christian sky god as a celestial mechanic, inventor and maintainer of the cosmic machine. Albert Einstein, whose theories of relativity and gravitation undermined Newton's God of absolute space and time, viewed his equations for the transformation of energy and matter as "the secrets of the old one."

From their primitive beginnings as elemental manifestations of the sky, the sky gods evolved a complex pattern of relationships with humans on earth. Mircea Eliade describes two interwoven lines of development, each reflecting an inherent celestial quality: first, supreme authority and law; and second, creativity, fecundity, and death.

The supreme authority and sovereignty of the sky gods represents the perception that humans emerge in and from the cosmos, are composed of its elements and governed by its laws. This perception is expressed in the Japanese myth of the cosmic couple, Father Sky and Mother Earth, whose union generates all living things. It is also expressed in the words of the Hebrew sky god Yahweh, when he reminds Adam of his origin and fate: "For dust thou art, and into dust shalt thou return."[9]

The same idea is expressed in the scientific images of the evolution of "the great chain of being." Humans are evolved from single cell organisms, from fish and serpents, from primitive mammals and monkeys. We are like the leaves of a tree that bud in the spring, are nourished by the warm soil and rain of summer, and wither and die in the colorful frost of autumn to fall and merge with the fertile humus of the forest floor. Here, in another form, is the meaning of the riddle of the Sphinx.

The sky gods are sovereigns of the natural order, of the life and death of all beings, of the succession of day and night, and of the rhythms of the seasons. They are also sovereigns of the moral order of obligations and contracts which bind humans to each other, to their rules and their leaders. The celestial and moral sovereignty of the sky gods is symmetrically ascribed to the political or ecclesiastical sovereign. Kings and prelates are often addressed with metaphors borrowed from the sky: Serene Majesty, Highness, Holiness, Radiant Eminence, and so on. Like the celestial sovereign they represent, political sovereigns cast nets of rules, laws, and obligation by which their subjects are bound.[10] The sovereign ruler, like the sovereign sky god, watches and judges his subjects, rewarding their virtues and punishing their disobedience.

The President of the United States is a symbolic representative of the Judeo-Christian sky god, the first amendment to the Constitution notwithstanding. The presidential seal shows an eagle holding arrows or thunderbolts in the left tarsus and an olive branch in the right. The eagle is a messenger between earth and sky, between humans and their sky god, and it carries the sky god's instruments of blessing and punishment: the olive branch symbolizing peace and prosperity, and the arrows of lightning symbolizing suffering and death.

The sovereign sky gods have dominion over the principles of creativity and fecundity; and in degrees of generosity and stinginess they symbolize the dual extremes of human desire and fate: fertility, prosperity, and long life; or barrenness, suffering, and death. We pray to the sky for good fortune and salvation from evil. We lift our glasses to the sky with toasts to good health, long life, and prosperity; and we reflexively jerk our heads towards the sky in moments of joy and anguish, as if to thank our sky god for his blessing, or to curse him for his cruelty. We look to the sky as the divine source of life and death, not merely because of tradition and belief, but because it is our home and we are awed and fascinated by its beauty, magnitude, and permanence.

In many regions of the world a once dominant sky god recedes to the periphery of religious and social life, usurped by more immediate, concrete, and accessible gods.[11] Often, the sky god is displaced by totemic animals or plants which become the nucleus of group or clan identity and organization. Curiously, indigenous sky gods were replaced by the bull around 2400 B.C. across a wide swath of India, North Africa, Europe, and Asia.[12]

The ferocious bellow and charge of the bull symbolizes the thunder and lightning of the sky god, and the bull's legendary sexuality symbolizes rain, the sperm of Father Sky that fertilizes Mother Earth. When Moses descended from Mount Sinai with the stone tablets he was enraged to see his people dancing around a golden calf, Ba'al, God of the fertility of fields and cattle, and archrival of the Hebrew sky god. Moses destroyed the calf and the cult of the bull, thus preserving the special relationship between the Hebrews and their supreme God of the sky, the God of contracts, whose stone tablets became the legal and moral network of Western civilization. If not for Moses, the seal of the President of the United States might well be the bull!

Zodiacs and Horoscopes

From early beginnings as personifications of the natural qualities of the sky, the sky gods evolved into the sovereign divinities of natural, political, and moral law: lord of nature and of contracts; supreme judge of human motives and deeds; omnipresent spirit of the human drama. But the sky gods and their associated mythologies are not purely fictional inventions of a frightened and superstitious human imagination. Myths of the sky developed around a nucleus of facts and arrange and classify these facts into a bricolage that reflects the human sense of self and identity in the cosmos.

Evidence suggests that by 30,000 B.C. the lunar cycle was known. The systems invented to record lunar events gradually evolved into the writing, arithmetic, and calendars of the earliest civilizations.[13] The invention of astronomy is credited to the Babylonians who, by 3000 B.C., had recognized and named several constellations of stars. By early in the first millenium B.C. they knew the apparent annual course of the sun, the phases of the moon, and the periodicity of certain planets. The famous Greek astronomer Ptolemy (c. 200 A.D.) credited the Babylonians with the first successful prediction of an eclipse in 747 B.C.

Based on observations with the naked eye the Babylonians constructed a model of the universe that was also independently discovered by all the great early civilizations of the world in Greece, India, China, and Mexico. Each culture fleshed out the facts with its own distinctive myths, metaphors, and styles. The Babylonian model was a discoid earth sitting on a surrounding ocean and capped by the celestial hemisphere containing the constellations of fixed stars. The earth was the center of the universe and rotating around it were the seven visible spheres: the Moon, Mercury, Venus, the Sun, Mars, Jupiter and Saturn. This model of the universe prevailed until 1543 when Nicholas Copernicus (1473-1543) published a new model of the revolution of the celestial orbs with the sun at the center, thus revolutionizing human identity.

As the ancient astronomers learned new astronomical facts they integrated them into maps of the sky. The Babylonians divided the ecliptic of the sun, the apparent north-south journey of the setting sun through the sky in a year, into compartments, or houses, each of which was identified by a constellation of stars in that part of the night sky. The midpoint of this oscillating journey coincides with the spring and autumn equinoxes, when day and night are of equal length and sunrise and sunset are precisely due east and west respectively. The northernmost point is the summer solstice, when the days are longest in the northern hemisphere; the southernmost point is the winter solstice, when the days are shortest. By dividing the ecliptic first into quarters, then into sixths, eighths, and twelfths, the cyclical path of the sun and constellations replaced the cyclical rhythms of the moon as the basis of the calendar. This circular map of the sky is known as the Zodiac.

The development of the zodiac required a knowledge of arithmetic and the measurement of angles. The ancient astronomers used their newly developed mathematical skills to calculate the physical dimensions of the earth and its relationship to the heavenly bodies. The word geometry means "the measurement of the earth." Eratosthenes (c. 296-194 B.C.), a Greek astronomer based in Alexandria, calculated the circumference and radius of the earth by a process of triangulation. He measured the angle of the sun's rays at noon on the summer solstice in Syene (near Aswan) and in Alexandria. By measuring the distance between the two cities with royal pacers he could calculate the difference of the angle due to the earth's curvature. From this figure he calculated the circumference and radius of the earth.

Using a similar technique of triangulation and a map of the constellations, travelers can identify their precise location on a map of the earth. This is the basic principle of celestial navigation. From its beginnings astronomy was used for practical purposes: for telling the time of day or night, for constructing calendars and setting the timing of planting, harvesting, festivals, and religious rituals, and for navigational guidance for travelers across the oceans and deserts.

As ancient astronomy developed it was continuously embellished with the mythological imagination. The word "zodiac" comes from the Greek *zodiakos* which means "zoo-dial," a "circle of animals," referring to the totemic configurations of the constellations governing the houses of the ecliptic. Ancient maps of the heavens are filled with divine figures and totemic animals: with archers, shepherds, virgins, bears and rams, bulls and crabs, snakes, goats, elephants, birds, and fish.

Against this mythological backdrop of the celestial hemisphere the sun and moon traveled in separate orbital cycles, defining the rhythms of the seasons, the months, the days and nights. Like their Paleolithic ancestors, the civilized ancients recognized the sun as the source of life. They measured time by it, worshipped it as a deity, and described its journey from dawn to dusk and spring to winter in the metaphors of the soul's journey through life.

The Egyptians worshipped a sun god in many forms and names, depending on the time of day and year. The morning sun is Horus, the falcon-faced youth, symbol of beginnings and renewals. The strong noon day sun is the mature, ram-faced Ra. And the setting sun is Osiris, often portrayed as a mummy and symbolizing old age and death. The sun god was depicted as traveling in a boat or as being rolled by scarabs[14] along the body of the sky god, Nut, into the dark underworld of death ruled by Seth, to rise again at dawn as Horus.

The Greek sun god, Helios, traveled across the day sky in a chariot drawn by a team of horses. Plato, who was fascinated by astronomy and astrology, used the myth of the celestial charioteer as a metaphor for the journey of the soul.[15]

Today we know for a scientific fact that the change of seasons is caused by the tilt of the earth's axis and the obliquity of its plane of rotation around the sun. Ancient astronomers also knew that the change of seasons is related to the obliquity of the ecliptic, but their mental images and explanations of this fact were quite different. The key difference is not, as one might assume, that we imagine the earth orbiting the sun while the ancients imagined the sun orbiting the earth. According to the principles of relativity, the facts are explained equally well from either perspective. The striking difference is that modern humans view the universe as a functioning but lifeless machine, while ancient humans viewed it as a living, intelligent organism.

In modern times the transformation of the seasons is conceived as a mechanical process that obeys the laws of physics. In planetariums one can see machine models of a little blue ball revolving obliquely around a luminous globe, illuminating more directly the northern hemisphere in the northern summer and the southern hemisphere in northern winter. The modern image of human identity is changed accordingly. We humans no longer view ourselves as spiritual members of an organic whole. We now view ourselves in the images of Newtonian and Darwinian science as biological machines who populate a godless mechanical cosmos.

Ancient astronomers explained the change of seasons with organic metaphors and models which synchronized[16] celestial and terrestrial events according to the formula, "As above, so below." The zodiac was used as a model of cyclical time through which all things come to pass in their season. The cycle of the seasons, from spring, where the zodiac begins in Aries, through the houses governed by the totemic constellations, to winter and eventually a new spring, is a manifestation of the universal cosmic process in which all things participate in birth, death, and renewal.

The synchronicity of certain celestial and terrestrial events, like the seasons, floods, and eclipses, enabled ancient astronomers to use the zodiac to make predictions. But the zodiac was not purely an instrument constructed of bare facts. It had become overgrown with a tangled web of mythological images and interpretations. The Egyptians began their calendar with the annual, pre-dawn appearance of Sirius (Sothis), the dog star, brightest star in the constellation of Canis Major, which rose at the spring flooding of the Nile, inaugurating the agricultural season. Sirius appeared above the Arabian desert to the east, and like the mythical phoenix was consumed by the flame of the rising sun, only to rise again the next morning, out of her own ashes, so to speak. The annual appearance of Sirius announced the annual appearance of vegetation, and provided the factual basis for the myth of the phoenix which, like the life of Christ, is a metaphor for the birth, death, and regeneration that characterizes the spirit of the cosmos.

Two thousand years ago in Egypt, the harvest began at the evening rising of Spica, brightest star in the constellation of Virgo, the virgin. Virgo is a version of the earth mother, goddess of vegetation and agriculture, who is often depicted holding an ear or sheath of grain, symbol of the harvest.[17] In Greek mythology the great fertile mother is Demeter, whose Latin name is Ceres, from which the word "cereal" is derived. According to legend, Demeter's daughter Persephone was kidnapped by Hades, god of the underworld, who made her his wife. Through the intercession of Demeter, Persephone was permitted to appear on earth once a year at the vernal equinox which, two thousand years ago, coincided with the full moon in Virgo. Plato assigned Demeter to rule the constellation of Virgo, and Demeter was the chief goddess of the Eleusinian mysteries which celebrated the spring reappearance of Persephone from the land of the dead to regenerate the sweet vegetation upon which human life depends.

Because of the precession of the equinoxes, the backwards movement of the zodiac at the rate of approximately one constellation every two thousand years, Sirius no longer rises during the spring flooding of the Nile. Two thousand years ago the vernal equinox, which marked the beginning of the New Year and of the zodiac, coincided with the constellation Aries in the night sky. Two thousand years earlier, it had coincided with the constellation Taurus, the bull. Today it coincides with the constellation Pisces, the fish, symbol of the Christian era. ("Follow me," Christ said to Simon Peter, "and I will make you a fisher of men.")[18] In about 2375 A.D. the sun's position at the vernal equinox will move into the much heralded Age of Aquarius.[19]

The zodiacs of the ancient worlds are no longer correlated with the constellations of the night sky. Celestial and terrestrial events have been thrown out of coordination by the precession of the equinoxes, and the zodiac has become an obsolete antiquity, frozen by centuries of mythological tradition. The zodiac and its tangled web of myths and images seems like poetic fiction with no relation to facts about the sky and earth. But it is as true today as it was in the age of the Olympic gods that when the sun's ecliptic crosses the celestial equator from south to north, Persephone rises again from the dead, along with the phoenix and Christ, to bring new life to earth.

The synchronization of certain heavenly and earthly events, like the seasons and the tides, gave the zodiac impressive predictive powers. Then as now, the power to predict is perceived as magical because it gives humans the possibility of controlling circumstances on which life or prosperity may depend. The zodiac thus came to be perceived as a magical instrument of divination and prophesy.

At first the zodiac was used to make general predictions that affect the group; but since the fate of the group is linked to the fate of its ruler, the zodiac came into use for casting the personal fortunes, or horoscopes of kings. The earliest recorded personal horoscope is from Babylon and is dated 410 B.C.[20] The Greeks, including Pythagoras and Plato, used personal horoscopes widely, as did the Romans and peoples of the Middle East, India, and China. Saint Augustine rejected astrology as superstition, but Saint Thomas Aquinas was its champion. Most of the astronomers of the new science were also astrologers, including Copernicus, Brahe, and Kepler, since science and religion had not yet been fully separated. The astronomical charts of Kepler were used to cast the horoscope of Martin Luther (1483-1546). Today, for many people all over the world, the zodiacal horoscope is the primary instrument of self-knowledge, of character analysis, and of personal guidance through life.

The word "horoscope" comes from the Greek words meaning "to observe the hour," reflecting its original use as a chronometer and calendar. But the personal horoscope derived from the zodiac is based not on the moon and the sun, which are used for telling time, but on the path of the planets, which are not. The cycles of the sun and moon are too regular and predictable to serve as metaphors for the distinctive human personality, which is what makes them useful for the measurement of time. The planets, on the other hand, are well suited as metaphors for the unique human individual. The word "planet" comes from the Greek word meaning "wanderer." Each planet is an individual with its own distinct characteristics, who wanders through the zodiac like the human individual wanders through life: semi-predictably, sometimes rising and setting faithfully, at other times idiosyncratic, changing in apparent velocity and brightness, sometimes appearing to stand still and then changing direction with a disconcerting whimsy.

Over centuries of local attribution and tradition each of the seven heavenly spheres (the five visible planets, the sun, and the moon) became associated with a tutelary deity whose unique hierarchical position, personality, and adventures were associated with particular earthly events and human qualities. Mercury, for example, because it is closest to the sun, was assigned the role of messenger from the gods, and hence, ruler of communication, writing, learning, and trade. The blood-colored Mars was associated with war and conflict. Venus was identified with love. As the planets wander in eccentric orbits through the constellations of the zodiac they form unique patterns of angular relationship: conjunction (0^0), sextile (60^0), square (90^0), trine (120^0), and opposition (180^0). The configuration of these angular relationships at any moment reflects the pattern of vibrations of the heavenly spheres which are supposedly synchronized with events on earth. The personal horoscope is constructed from the pattern of angular relationships of the heavenly spheres at the moment of birth, and is believed to reflect the qualities of the individual soul, and to augur the ebb and flow of its fortunes through life.

While the planetary configurations were (and still are) the basis of the personal astrological horoscope, they were also a great problem for the ancient astronomers. The ancient view of the cosmos placed humanity and earth at the center, and such a system could not explain the planetary orbits without postulating an intricate pattern of epicycles and eccentrics which were constantly being contradicted by astronomical observations. Aristotle's cosmology placed the planets in concentric circles with the epicycles around a spherical earth. Aristotle's system was brought to a culmination by the Greek astronomer Ptolemy (121-161 A.D.), whose *Almagest* became the great bible of astronomy for a thousand years, until 1543, when Nicholas Copernicus, on his deathbed, inaugurated modern astronomy with the publication of his *Revolution of the Celestial Spheres*, in which he classified the earth as one of the six planets that revolve around the sun.

The great virtue of the Copernican system was its mathematical simplicity. By assuming that the planets revolve around the sun most of the Ptolemaic epicycles could be discarded. Nevertheless, Copernicus was afraid to publish his heliocentric theory during his lifetime, and with good reason. It would throw the Catholic mythical-astrological world view out of coordination with astronomy and precipitate a crisis of human identity.

Copernicus had read in Archimedes about Aristarchus of Samos (c. 270 B.C.), whose heliocentric model was suppressed by the Stoics. And Martin Luther had already denounced him as a fool for disbelieving the scriptural view of a cosmos with fixed earth at the center and the sun revolving around it. After all, Joshua had commanded the sun to stand still, not the earth.

Giordano Bruno (1548-1600) used the heliocentric calculations as the basis for a new view of the cosmos, suggesting that humanity could no longer be conceived as the center of the universe. Bruno was burned at the stake by the Catholic Inquisition for his trouble. Johannes Kepler (1571-1630), who learned the Copernican system secretly while studying theology, finally eliminated the need for all epicycles by calculating the mathematical laws of planetary motion. To escape the charge of heresy Kepler denied that his theories described reality or contradicted scripture. He claimed they were only mathematical conveniences. Nevertheless, he was ostracized for his heliocentrism and his mother was tried as a witch by the Inquisition.

The mathematical calculations and telescopic observations of Copernicus, Brahe, Kepler, and Galileo started the avalanche that eventually buried the traditional geocentric astronomy upon which previous western human identity had been based. As a result, astronomy was stripped of its astrological superstructure, and while factual astronomy became the princess of the new science, astrology was relegated to the status of an archaic, pseudo-scientific superstition. As a predictive system astrology is of little value, and its most intelligent supporters minimize its predictive powers. Nevertheless, many intelligent people are attracted to astrology and rely upon it as their primary source of self-knowledge and guidance. This may seem like archaic superstition, but there is some sense in it.

The mythological content of astrology, which has accumulated over thousands of years, richly portrays the human personality in a form which helps to sharpen interpersonal perceptions.[21] All systems of personality are, in effect, interpretations of psychological facts. Any personality theory, whether it be psychoanalysis, the Tibetan Buddhist system of "five families," or astrology, which takes several or more human characteristics or factors, such as courage, perseverance, ambivalence, aggression, love, the ability to communicate, a sense of humor, and so on, and relates them to each other in oppositions and conjunctions, is bound to provide insight into the complex human character. Although astrological predictions are unreliable, everyone can see themselves in the personality configurations that rule the twelve houses of the zodiac.

Astrology is an archaic mythology of the sky that expresses the contradictions and continuities between the human, the natural, and the divine. It is a projection of our sense of our selves onto the sky, and a reading of the sky in search of insight into ourselves. It reveals to us that we human individuals are like the planets, who wander through historical time, swept up in the cycles of natural time, against a backdrop of enduring eternal time.

The Sky and the "I"

Religious myth and scientific theory are both incompetent to convey the overwhelming impact of the majestic sky in contrast to which the drama of the human self here on earth seems an insignificant and transient dream. There is no need to study myths or theories about the sky to realize what Eliade reminds us, "that the sky itself directly reveals a transcendence, a power, and a holiness...simply by being there."[22]

The most spectacular and timeless effect of the sky on the human mind can be experienced by lying on the grass on a clear, moonless night, watching the stars, and noting the brief and subtle moments of transition from the human scene to the heavenly scene and back, from being absorbed in the details of the personal drama of everyday life to being lost in the stars. This transition between the personal "I" and the numinous sky is the dialectic between the infinite and the finite, between the sacred and the profane. In this dialectic the individual experiences concretely the relationship between personal life and existence as a whole.

The experience of the holy is the inner core of religion because it dialectically defines the sense of self. In exoteric religions—Saturday, Sunday, and holiday religions—the experience of the holy is overgrown with a tangled web of mythico-moral beliefs. Rudolph Otto used the term "numinous" to denote the experience of the holy stripped of any rational or moral interpretations.[23]

The experience of the numinous is beyond, or perhaps, more accurately, prior to words, prior to language, prior to reason itself. Efforts to grasp its meaning generate feelings of bewilderment that rational-cognitive interpretations try to define and resolve, dampening the original experience in the process.[24] The numinous quality of the sky can be experienced merely by stepping outdoors and looking up, without judging, interpreting, or commenting on it—just feeling the presence of that something out there that sets us ashudder and aglow. In the words of Saint Augustine: "Ashudder in so far as I am unlike it. Aglow in so far as I am like it."[25]

Rudoph Otto believes that the basic element of the numinous is "creature feeling," which he defines as "the emotion of a creature, submerged and overwhelmed by its own nothingness in contrast to that which is supreme above all creatures."[26] The sky is the archetypical other in contrast to which self experiences itself. This feeling of "selfness," which can be evoked by the sky or any sacred place, object, or symbol, is tinged with anxiety. It is haunted by the sense of being helpless and vulnerable in the face of the *mysterium tremendum*, the vast, awesome mystery of the cosmos.

Abraham expressed this feeling by confessing to being only dust and ashes before the Lord. Job expressed it by wailing that humans cannot hope to contend against God. This feeling of creature-terror is given form by the image of the "Ogre-God," symbol of the gruesome side of life, who tortures, taunts, and mocks his creatures. The Hebrew sky god Yahweh had a cruel and sadistic aspect. When Moses asked, one day, to see God's face, believing he deserved such a special glimpse after serving God faithfully during the exile, the flight from Egypt, and the wanderings through the Sinai desert, Yahweh answered him sharply: "You cannot see may face; no man shall see my face and live." Then, perversely taunting his favorite servant, Yahweh gave Moses the moon, saying, in effect, "You cannot see my face, but you can see my ass."

> I will put thee in a cleft of the rock and will cover thee with My hand while I pass by. And I will take away my hand, and thou shalt see My back; but My face shall not be seen.[27]

The spectral shudder of anxiety in the face of the numinous, which is often experienced as the fear of God, is more than ordinary animal fear. It contains elements of the uncanny, the eerie, and the supernatural, of which animals have no sense and no fear. Rudolph Otto suggests that this creature-feeling of terror and awe at the numinous "emerging in the mind of primeval man, forms the starting point of the entire religious development in history." We would add that this creature-feeling is also the starting point of the human sense of self. The sense of self is evoked in contrast to the sense of the numinous.

If in the instant before the personal "I" becomes lost in it, the sky evokes a creature-feeling, an awareness of self as a creature in the midst of creation, then looking away from the sky towards others in everyday social life has the opposite effect. Social and personal life are characterized by the denial of creature existence and the infusion of the world with "supernatural" projections of self.

Cosmic anxiety implies the development of a mental capacity which is unique and different from any animal predisposition. If religion begins with a sense of mystery, when humans were first haunted by existence, then at the same time, these humans must also have been spooked by a sense of self, set off in contrast to existence by being the observer of it.

A sense of the uncanny implies a sense of the canny. A sense of the presence of a mysterious *wholly other* implies a sense of the presence of a *familiar something sensing the otherness*. The beginning of religion likely coincides with the beginning of human self-consciousness, at the moment when the human animal became aware of its existence as a creature in the midst of creation.

Cosmic anxiety is only one pole of creature consciousness, the negative pole, at which the helplessness and vulnerability of the creature are experienced as a terror of personal annihilation. At the positive pole is the glow of fascination and attraction for the numinous, an acceptance of vulnerability to it, a desire to renounce the self and merge with the numinous in joy.

Both poles of creature-consciousness are grounded in the awareness of self in relation to the numinous. But while the negative pole loves the self and seeks its preservation and enhancement, the positive pole loves the numinous and depreciates the self by comparison. The great seal of mysticism is the realization of the subordination of self to the numinous and the primacy of the numinous over the self.

In the mystical traditions the numinous is portrayed as the plenitude of being, the pure mother of all things, the perfection of virtue and wisdom. The personal "I" is portrayed as the locus of illusion, imperfection, and sin. Rudolph Otto phrases it this way: "Mysticism continues to its extreme point this contrasting of the numinous object as the 'wholly other,' with ordinary experience."[28]

> For one of the chiefest and most general features of mysticism is just this *self-depreciation* (so plainly parallel to the case of Abraham) the estimation of the self, of the personal "I" as something not perfectly or essentially real, or even as a mere nullity....And on the other hand, mysticism leads to a valuation of the transcendent object of its reference as that which through plenitude of being stands supreme and absolute, so that the finite self contrasted with it becomes conscious even in its nullity that 'I am naught, Thou art all.'[29]

CHAPTER TWENTY-THREE

The Polarization of Paradise: The Myth of Eden

> The individual has in his own lifetime to follow the road that humanity has trod before him.
>
> —Erich Von Neuman, *The Origins and History of Consciousness.*

Although Charles Darwin's theory of evolution is supported by a strong foundation of scientific evidence many religious people reject it as contrary to scripture. Interpreted literally, the Bible teaches that God created the first humans fully formed, in a special divine act of creation. Darwin's theory of evolution teaches that humans are evolved from animals, adding insult to the injury already done to the Christian world view by the Copernican and Newtonian sciences.

The scientific facts of evolution do, indeed, contradict literal interpretations of creation in the Old Testament. But it is like the contradiction between apples and oranges: they are different, yet both are fruit. The facts of evolution and the myths of creation are contradictory, yet both are true: one factually, the other metaphorically.

Creation myths are metaphors for the facts of evolution. Myths of the creation of the world are metaphors for the evolution of consciousness. "The genesis of the world" writes Mircea Eliade, "serves as the model for the formation of a man."[1] Compare Eliade's thought to Saint Bonaventure's idea quoted in the epigram at the beginning of the previous chapter: "In relation to our position in creation, the universe itself is a ladder by which we can ascent into God." The similarity of perception in a medieval philosopher and a modern historian of religion is a reflection of the fact that the question of personal identity—"Who am I?"—is simultaneously a question about the origin of self, the origin of consciousness, the origin of humanity, and the origin of the world.

Carl Jung regarded religious myths as archetypes, or primordial images of the stages in the evolution of human consciousness. Erich Neumann, a follower of Jung, compares the evolution of consciousness to Haeckle's controversial biogenetic law: "Ontogeny recapitulates phylogeny," or, in plain language, the development of the human individual repeats the stages of the development of the human species. According to Neumann:

> In the course of its ontogenetic development, the individual ego consciousness has to pass through the same archetypical stages which determined the evolution of consciousness in the life of humanity. The individual has in his own lifetime to follow the road that humanity has trod before him.[2]

The idea that creation myths serve as models for the formation of a person is expressed in psychoanalysis as the link between neurosis and history.[3] Like Rousseau and Kant before him, Freud believed that the problems of the individual must be understood in the context of the evolution of the race, and he sought the origin of neurosis in the history of civilization.

Freud dated the origin of neurosis to the mythical moment when the primal horde, wracked by the guilt of patricide, established society, religion, and morality in order to repress the destructive effects of the sexual and aggressive drives.[4] When conscience was set against instinct, society was set against the individual, and the individual was set against himself.[5] "The doctrine of the universal neurosis of mankind," writes Norman O. Brown, "is the psychoanalytical analogue of the theological doctrine of original sin."[6]

The Evolution of Human Self-Consciousness

The emergence of human self-consciousness from unreflective animal consciousness is often represented in myth as the emergence of light from darkness.[7] In the Old Testament myth of creation God created the world by separating the light from the darkness: "And God said, Let there be light: and there was light."[8] The origins of the world, and of human consciousness, are thus aptly represented in the metaphors of the sky, the hand, and the eye, as the making of light. In other creation stories the world begins with a word or a thought, depicting the beginnings of human consciousness in speech.

The emergence of light from darkness symbolizes the emergence of something out of nothing. In terms of the evolution of self, it represents the emergence of someone out of no one. In the antithetical symbolism of the ego, nothingness, or non-ego, is interpreted to be a featureless void which, nevertheless, is perfect in its wholeness and plenitude.

In the antithetical symbolism of the ego, nothingness is also perceived as having the dual powers of fecundity and annihilation. The numinous void is both *origin* and *return, mother* and *death,* God the *savior* and God the *ogre.* As the *Urgrund,* or "ground of being," the primordial emptiness is also symbolized by the circle, the sphere, the cosmic egg, and by the heavenly serpent, Uroboros, who feeds on its own tail, weds itself, and reproduces the world in an eternal cosmic cycle of self-sufficient regeneration. In this primitive, pre-emergent stage, the ego does not exist to itself as the duality of observer and observed. There is only the relatively undifferentiated unity of *all* and *nothingness.* The ego is still submerged in the unconscious, a mere potentiality in the unpolarized brain and unself-conscious mentality of the primeval hominid.

The mythical coming of the light represents the dawn of self-consciousness, when the first humans became aware of the cycles of day and night, and of themselves as creatures in the midst of creation. The appearance of light is the appearance of the consciousness of other and, hence, of the consciousness of self. The polarization of the cosmos into light and darkness symbolizes the polarization of paradise, the emergence of antithetical speech, perceptions, and thought. The concept of God as Urgrund, as the undifferentiated creative principle of the world, is a metaphor for the pre-polarized state of human consciousness. "Yahweh," writes Carl Jung, "is a God-concept that contains the opposites in a still undivided state."[9]

In many cultures the first stages of the creation of the world from the undifferentiated void are depicted as a hierogamy, a sacred marriage of the world parents who symbolize divine polarities. In Greek, Egyptian, and Japanese mythology, the cosmic couple are Father Sky and Mother Earth, whose androgynous embrace symbolizes the interpenetrating coexistence of opposites and brings forth the thousand things of the world. In Chinese religion, the primitive polarized principles are *yang* and *yin* set in tantric embrace within the infinite circle of the *tao*.

These mythical images are metaphors for the polarization of paradise, the evolutionary process involving the polarization, or lateralization of the brain for speech. The first elements of speech created an entirely new moment in evolution, the birth of a new form of consciousness, based on a binary logic, capable of distinguishing similarities and differences in the object world. The appearance of this mode of consciousness is represented in myth by the creation of light and the division of opposites.

The vocalization and perception of antithetical qualities advanced the hominid eye-brain-hand system to a new level of intelligence, capable of manipulating, classifying, and manufacturing new tools and objects to solve the problems of survival. This intelligence also added new dimensions to the perception of reality: the dimensions of personal ego, moral action, and historical time, each created by the respective antithetical perceptions of self-other, good-evil, and past-future. In the antithetical categories of polarized consciousness, the origin of humanity is perceived as an ambivalent event. For on the one hand it represents the birth of a new and powerful intelligence. On the other hand, it represents the death of innocence, the fall from paradise into the abyss of history and the awareness of death.

The Myth of Eden

The myth of Eden is a metaphor for the transformation of animal to human consciousness. Eden, or Paradise, represents the pre-polarized state of consciousness, when pre-humans lived among the animals, communicating with them without speech. The expulsion, or Fall, represents the polarization of paradise, when the brain becomes lateralized for speech, inaugurating self, morality, and history.

The myth of Eden is a compound metaphor, a bricolage derived from different periods and cultures. The serpent, who moults its skin and seems to emerge from its corpse reborn, is an ancient symbol of death and regeneration, of nothingness and the oscillation of opposites, who tempts Eve to taste of duality. The tree is the *axis mundi*, the axis of the world, the sacred staff which stretches from earth to heaven, like Jack's beanstalk, pointing the way for humans to follow. Adam and Eve are the mythical first humans, the world parents, whose expulsion from Paradise marks the beginning of the human species.

In the Biblical myth of Genesis, Adam and Eve are expelled from Paradise and become fully human as the result of their sin, *original sin*, which is the universal neurosis of humanity. In the Bible, Adam's sin is depicted as a particular act: disobeying God and eating the forbidden fruit. But original sin cannot be a particular act which humans can avoid or evade. Original sin must be inherent in human nature, a product of evolution. The Danish philosopher Søren Kierkegaard saw this:

> To explain Adam's sin is therefore to explain original sin, and no explanation is of any avail which explains original sin and does not explain Adam. The deepest reason for this is to be discovered in the essential characteristic of human existence, that man is an individual and as such is at once himself and the whole race, in such wise that the whole race has part in the individual, and the individual has part in the whole race....Adam is the first man; he is at once himself and the race....Therefore what explains Adam explains the race and vice versa.[10]

Kierkegaard was a Dane, an individualist, and a rebel who rejected the traditional Pauline Christian doctrine of original sin as the awakening of concupiscence, or sexual desire. Kierkegaard loved freedom and regarded the capacity to choose as the critical difference between humans and animals. He interpreted original sin as a psychological quality which entered the mind of Adam before sexual desire did.

When God forbad Adam to eat the fruit of the tree of the knowledge of good and evil, the prohibition dialectically awakened in Adam the consciousness of the possibility of choice. Prohibition means choice. Prohibition makes no sense except in the context of choice, of the possibility of the prohibition being violated. Like all humans, Adam experienced the possibility of freedom with dread. Kierkegaard regards dread as "the characteristic ambiguity of psychology." "Dread," he writes, "is a sympathetic antipathy and an antipathetic sympathy."[11] Dread, in other words, is the play between desire and aversion—the experience of desiring what we fear and fearing what we desire.

Dread is the polarization of consciousness manifested as the awareness of positive and negative in every possibility. The first commandment is the negation which creates the possibility of freedom. When God commanded Adam: "No! Of that tree thou shalt not eat." Adam became aware of the possibility: "Yes! Of that tree I want to eat." Like the child who becomes self-conscious at the moment it is paralyzed by parental prohibition, Adam was shocked into humanity by a divine, cosmic "No!" The taboo marks the beginning of choice and morality. The freedom to choose is haunted by the possibility of the wrong choice. Freedom is haunted by guilt just as "Yes!" is haunted by "No!" The possibility of freedom haunted by guilt means the end of innocence. "Every human action is contradictory," said Mao Zedong, unconsciously echoing the ancient Hebrew perception that evil is the price of free choice.

In the Biblical myth of Genesis, the serpent tempts Eve to eat the forbidden fruit by promising her that she will not die, as God warned. On the contrary, the serpent vowed, "Your eyes shall be opened, and ye shall be as gods, knowing good and evil."[12]

The serpent is a symbol of death and rebirth—of duality. Facing the serpent, Eve faced the fact of death and the dual possibilities of good and evil. The fact of death is probably one of the earliest facts known to humans. The sudden appearance of burials in the Middle Paleolithic period suggests that the Neanderthals were aware of the fact of death. Burials with the corpse facing east and covered with flowers suggests the desire for rebirth, perhaps for immortality. The temptation of Eve by the serpent is a metaphor for the nascent awareness of death and the dialectical development of the desire for eternal life.

The fear of death and the desire to be God are the fundamental characteristics of the human ego. The desire to be God is a universal human Happiness Project. "The best way to conceive of the fundamental project of human reality," wrote Jean Paul Sartre, "is to say that man is the being whose project is to be God....To be man means to reach toward being God. Or if you prefer, man is fundamentally the desire to be God."[13] This idea is not new with Sartre. Plato thought that "all men do all things, and the better they are the more they do them, in hope of the glorious fame of immortal virtue; for they desire the immortal."[14] Dante echoed Plato with the cry, "How man makes himself eternal!"[15]

The desire to be God is a reaction against the fear of death. "The last act is tragic," Blaise Pascal lamented. "However happy all the rest of the play is, at the last a little earth is thrown upon our head, and that is the end forever."[16] The fear of death is generated by the nascent ego's perception of itself as transient and insignificant in relation to the cosmos. The fear of death is the ego's fear of its own dissolution, of the disappearance of someone into no one. The dialectical desire of the ego is to be God, to be immortal and invulnerable, to live happily forever. It is the symbolic extension of life's vital impulse to survive and prevail. Constantly threatened by the specter of its own evaporation, the ego struggles to assert itself, to make itself durable by attaching to durable objects, to survive death through fame and immortalization, to draw its portrait in the Rock of Ages.

The desire to be God is not a philosopher's fantasy, indulged in idle moments. It is a metaphor for the Happiness Projects of the individual and the species. "Desire reaches beyond itself," wrote Sartre, meaning that our concrete personal desires express our deepest longings in relation to life as a whole. Our personal wishes, aspirations, and ambitions, no matter how trivial, can be strategies for transcending the fear of death.

Self-knowledge requires an awareness of the ego's fear of dissolution and its desire to be God, or to live forever through serial reincarnations. The personality of the human individual and the human species are expressions of these vital strivings, as Ernest Becker wrote:

> What we call man's personality or his life style is really a series of techniques that he has developed, and these techniques have one major end in view—the denial of the fact that he has no control over death or over the meaning of his life. If you expose this denial by undermining or exposing his techniques, you undermine his whole personality—which is the same thing.[17]

As soon as Adam and Eve tasted the forbidden fruit their eyes were opened and they became as gods, knowing good and evil. The eyes are a metaphor for consciousness. Opening the eyes and seeing the light symbolize the transformation of consciousness from animal to human. The instrument of this transformation was the forbidden fruit. In this sense, the mythical apple of Eden was a psychedelic substance (psychedelic = mind manifesting) like LSD, but with an opposite effect.[18]

The apple was a fruit forbidden by God because it creates the ego. LSD is a fruit forbidden by society because it dissolves the ego. Eating it opens the doors of the perception of paradise (or hell) and results in the expulsion from society.[19] The fruit of the tree of the knowledge of good and evil generates the linguistic net of antithetical meanings, the knowledge of self and other, of good and evil, and of history and death. To eat it is to be expelled from Paradise. The expulsion from Paradise is a metaphor for the evolution of antithetical speech, for the emergence of duality from the ineffable tao. It is expressed poetically in the Chinese *Tao Te Ching*, the *Book of the Way of Life:*

> The Tao described in words is not the real Tao.
> Words cannot describe it.
> Nameless it is the source of creation;

> Named it is the mother of all things.
> Whenever the most beautiful is perceived ugliness arises,
> Whenever good is perceived, evil exists, its natural opposite.
> Thus perception involves opposites;
> Reality and fantasy are opposing thoughts.
> Difficult and simple oppose in degree;
> Long and short oppose in distance;
> High and low oppose in height;
> Shrill and deep oppose in tone;
> Before and after oppose in sequence.[20]

As soon as Adam and Eve ate the psychedelic apple they became ashamed. "And the eyes of them both were opened, and they knew that they were naked; and they sewed fig leaves together, and made themselves aprons."[21] Shame is the dialectical product of pride. It appears where pride fails. If pride is the desire to be God, then shame is the antithetical exposure of the mortal animal body. We become ashamed when our social performance breaks down, when words and actions stumble, momentarily stripping away the social self to reveal a flawed creature. Pride is the denial of finite creatureliness. Shame is the exposure of it.

Covering the genitals with fig leaves symbolizes the repression of the animal body. It represents the Oedipal transition of the species, the rite of passage from the animal to the human, analogous to the passage from infancy to social maturity.[22] The repression of the body is the equivalent of a pledge of allegiance to symbol, self, and society. Every society establishes a system of morality requiring the repression and control of the body through which it gains control over the mind. Prohibitions against incest, masturbation, sexual perversions, suicide, cannibalism, and the use of certain mind-altering substances serve the deeper function of establishing the power of the social group over the individual.

Today we think of incest narrowly, as a tragedy of the nuclear family. In primitive societies, however, where families are extended into clans and tribes, rules governing incest determine who can marry who and, thus, form the basis of social organization. The prohibition of suicide denies the individual control over death. Control of sex and drugs establishes society's dominion over the body. By establishing its authority over pleasure and death society establishes itself, in the eyes of the individual, as God.

The expulsion from Paradise is the Fall into history. It introduces a moral element into evolution, not as a particular sin, but as the capacity to choose. Original sin is the evolution of choice as antithetical paths of action. The capacity for choice, in turn, is derived from the evolution of antithetical language and antithetical perceptions of the object world.

Good and evil are abstractions of right and wrong actions, of *Yes!* and *No!*, issued as verbal commands. The regulation of behavior by verbal command required a more rapid and flexible form of learning than that provided by the genetic code or the reflex arc. It required the capacity to store, retrieve, and modify information almost instantaneously. It required, in other words, the development of memory.

Through memory verbal commands and moral rules remain accessible and effective long after they are received. Through memory the past comes into consciousness. From the memory of the past the future is dialectically created, as memories are aligned in sequences of before and after, drawn from the visual-spatial sequences of "in front of" and "behind." The future is a memory to come. The memory of the past and the imagination of the future are the Fall into historical time.

Analogue and Digital (Dualistic) Mind

The evolution of memory required a massive increase in the volume and complexity of the cortical information storage system. This was accomplished with astonishing rapidity over the past thirty- to seventy-thousand years by the inward convolution of the cerebral cortex and the vigorous growth of the frontal lobes.[23] At the same time, the primate eye-brain-hand coordination system became lateralized for speech. The development of speech and memory dramatically increased the intelligence of humans over the apes.

From the viewpoint of evolution, intelligence is an instrument of adaptation to the problems of life. The new binary logic of the human brain increased the ability to learn from failures as well as successes, to develop new tools and techniques for hunting and gathering and, eventually, to domesticate animals and plants. As an evolutionary tool intelligence enables the human to grasp and manipulate facts in a way analogous to how the primate hand grasps and manipulates objects. This ability to know and apply facts has enabled the human species to survive, adapt, and prevail over a wide range of global and historical conditions.

There is an ironic underside of intelligence, however. The binary logic of the human intellect has also created the dualistic consciousness of self and other, of good and evil, and of past and future. The other side of the coin of intelligence is self-consciousness, neurosis, and madness. Neurosis and madness are manifestations of intelligence gone wild.

The development of speech and intelligence implies the development of discursive mind. Through the incessant inner dialogue of discursive mind, self constantly strives to overcome its existential bewilderment, calculating how to escape from evil and death and find the path to eternal happiness. This discursive, inner narrative is *avidya*, ignorance, one of the three poisons, and the primary cause of the suffering we humans inflict on ourselves and others. One of the functions of Buddhist *shamatha*, or tranqulity meditation, is to quiet and stabilize discursive mind, thus creating the possibility of sanity.

The lateralization of the brain for speech created a new form of specifically human consciousness which coexists with animal consciousness. Eden and the Fall represent two contrasting forms of consciousness. Eden represents animal consciousness. The Fall represents the evolution of specifically human consciousness.

The difference between the human and animal mind can be visualized by comparing them to computers. The human mind is comparable to a digital computer and the animal mind is comparable to an analogue computer:

> Analogue Computer : Animal Mind
> Digital Computer : Human Mind

The difference between analogical and digital thinking can be illustrated by a thought experiment or visualization. Imagine yourself in a garden filled with spring flowers. The warm breeze is perfumed by a sweet fragrance. The earth smells like fine, aged compost. Birds chirp happily as they find their morning breakfast. The latticework of green stems on which the flowers float sways in the breeze. The morning sun is hot.

> Morning sun
> Warms my back:
> Dawn Zazen[24]

Then, as we are enjoying our lovely garden, thoughts appear as commentary. "What a lovely morning. How beautiful the flowers are. I am so happy. I want to live here forever. But, damn! I owe $6000 in back taxes on my property. I must somehow find the money to pay it or I could lose my house, my land, and my lovely garden. How terrible that would be!"

The smells, sights, sounds, and feelings of the garden are analogue thinking. The commentary, worry, and images of transcendence and failure are digital thinking. The difference between analogue and digital thinking can be grasped by comparing analogue and digital computers. Analogue computers are physically contiguous with the states they represent. Thermometers, speedometers, and pressure gauges are analogue computers. The thermometer is physically immersed in the solid, liquid, or gas whose temperature it measures. The speedometer is directly linked to the rotating wheel whose velocity is being calibrated: the faster the wheel spins, the higher the velocity reading.

Sense consciousness is analogue thinking. The sense organs are physically altered by the objects or states they sense. The retina of the eye responds to the light patterns emitted by the visualized object. The ear resonates with the vibrations of the sound it hears. The nose sniffs molecules which evaporated from the object it smells. Touch, pressure, and heat impinge physically on the skin.

While analogue thinking is contiguous with the world it represents, digital thinking separates the representation from what it represents. There is no intrinsic connection between the symbol and its referent. For example, the word processor I am writing on digitalizes my thoughts by converting each letter of the alphabet into a sequence of binary on-off signals. An eight bit computer can register any of 256 (2^8) combinations of eight binary sequences. For example, if *on* is "+" and *off* is "-", then:

A = ——————————
B = +-————————
C = -+————————
D = ++————————

and so on.

There is no intrinsic relationship between the on-off sequences and the letters of the alphabet. "A" could also be ++ ++ ++ ++ ++ ++ ++ ++, or any other of the possible combinations of eight binary digits. Strings of these binary digits can form words, just as letters form words, and long strings and trees of binary digits can represent sentences, ideas, even subtle philosophical points.

Analogue representations are signs. Digital representations are symbols. The difference is that there is an intrinsic connection between a sign and what it stands for. For example, smoke is a sign of fire. Symptoms of illness are signs: fever is a sign of infection; abdominal pain may be a sign of appendicitis, and so on. In each case, the sign is a physical manifestation of what it represents.

There is no intrinsic connection between a symbol and its referent. A symbol is defined as something that stands for something else. Symbols are things—physical objects, sounds, scripts, electronic signals—which are interesting not in themselves, but for what they represent. Digital thinking substitutes symbols for things themselves. Since there is no intrinsic connection between a symbol and its referent, anything in the universe may be used as a symbol of anything else.

Language is a product of digital thinking. It substitutes symbols for things. For example, the word "tree" is *baum* in German or *arbol* in Spanish. There is an experiential and logical gap between a word and a thing. By substituting symbols for things, language creates the means to think of something not present, to conjure images of trees while standing in a treeless desert. The ability to think of something not present is a milestone in the evolution of intelligence. Human symbolic thinking is unique in the animal kingdom. It makes possible the construction of a historically new universe of imaginary things, beings, events, and states which are the content and constant preoccupation of dualistic mind.

Another characteristic of digital thinking is that it is dialectical, or antithetical. It is the dynamic interplay of opposites. The value or meaning of a binary digit resides not in the individual components of the binary pair, but in the relationship between them. The digit "+" has a different value depending whether it is paired with "+" or "-", and also depending upon whether "-" comes before or after it. The binary digits "+-" and "-+" have the same components but antithetical meanings. Binary digits are the template of dualistic mind. Dualistic mind operates through a dialectic or dynamic antithesis in which objects, actions, and events are knowable not in themselves, but only in relation to other objects, actions, and events.

Primitive words and concepts have antithetical meanings.[25] They signify clearly contrasting opposites as binary pairs: so-called antithetical words such as near/far, hot/cold, up/down, right/left, good/bad, etc. Each member of the binary pair gets its meaning from the other. Right has no meaning without left. Up means nothing without down. Good has no meaning without evil.

Antithetical words reflect the mind's tendency to appreciate qualities by contrast. For example, hot/cold represents an antithetical pair, each pole of which is identified and perceived in relation to the other. If we place our hand in water heated to 110 degrees Fahrenheit, the water will feel warm compared to water at 50 degrees, but it will feel cool relative to water at 170 degrees.

By the same logic, we could not experience happiness if we did not also experience pain, suffering, and unhappiness. How would we recognize it? Happiness would be like the air we breathe. We never think of air until it smells bad or we are suffocating. Then we can think of nothing but air. The same is true for happiness. We would take happiness for granted and never notice it unless we could contrast it with unhappiness.

Consider a list of primitive binary words. A brief analysis will show that they are arbitrarily arranged. There is no intrinsic connection between left, dark, female, and death. The list below reflects prevailing patriarchical and Caucasian values. Nevertheless, note how the two columns aggregate into a pattern from which perspective the world seems polarized.

left	right
dark	light
down	up
earth	sky
female	male
death	life
other	self
past	future
evil	good
black	white

Digital thinking polarizes the mind and gives it a dialectical quality. Dialectic is the interplay of opposites. Carl Jung called it "enantiodrama," the drama or dance of opposites. The basic concepts or structures of dualistic mind are composed of antithetical pairs, each of which has meaning only in relation to its opposite: self/other, life/death, past/future, good/evil, and so on. Out of the dynamic of this enantiodrama mind creates the fictional entities of self, society, death, historical time, and value.

Dualistic mind operates through a dynamic antithesis or dialectical process in which objects, actions, and events are knowable not in themselves, but only in relation to other objects, actions, and events. In this sense digital or dualistic mind is capable of perceiving only relative truths, truths which are discernable only in relationship to antithetical reference points. Self can be known only in relation to other. Death is known only by the living. The future gets its meaning from the past. Good is known only by contrast to evil, and so on.

A few examples may illustrate how the sense of self emerges together with the capacity for antithetical thinking. Consider the word "before." It refers to an event which once was present but now is past. A birthday party commemorates an event which happened before and now exists only as a memory. However, the word "before" implies a point in time which comes "after." Memories of the past imply a present in which the remembering occurs. In this sense, memories imply the "existence" of a future.

From the viewpoint of the past, the present is the future. By imagining oneself in the past, looking forward to the present, one gets a perspective on time in which the present is seen as future. Projecting this image further, it is possible to imagine a time when the present would be past. Thus is the future created out of memory. From the point of view of the future, now has already happened. Like memories of the past from which it is antithetically generated, the future exists only in our minds.

Consider the idea of death. As far as we know, animals are not aware of death. Humans are aware of death because we can remember people who have died. Only digital mind can contrast being alive and being dead. When grandmother was alive she was very tender and loving. But when she died, her name and memory evoke the idea of death.

The idea of persons who once existed but now have vanished into nothingness gives rise to the idea of death. But what is death? We can see and examine dead bodies. We can anticipate and experience dying. But can we experience death? Does death exist? Or is it only a terrifying, disembodied fiction, an idea in the digital minds of the living drawn from our knowledge of dead bodies and the certainty of our future fate?

Language gives things an "existence" separate from any actual, physical existence. The Old Testament story of God giving Adam the power to name the animals expresses a deep insight into digital mind. Naming an idea, like "death," gives it an illusory existence. Naming the locus of dualistic mind "John" or "Mary" gives it an illusory existence. Digital thinking and language give us the ability to create imaginary dimensions of existence which become our mansions—the structures we live in. Self is the illusory mansion of dualistic mind. Dualistic or digital mind lives in a self-created world of symbols, and mistakes those symbols as having substantial reality, as if the word "tree" actually has bark and leaves and could be chopped down and burned to warm us in the winter. Thus is self born as the personal "I"—antithesis of the numinous sky and the archetypical other.

Digital thinking is a significant advance in the biological evolution of intelligence. Humans have risen above all the other animals by literally putting two and two together. On the other hand, digital mind also has a dark side. It can deny what exists and reify fictions. Buddhists call this dark side *avidya*—ignorance.

Digital mind enables us to think logically and to communicate with each other. These basic neuro-psychological skills are the foundation of science and society. On the other hand, digital mind can run off on its own, creating pure symbols with no objective referents, generating purely imaginary objects, personae, events, and dramas—illusions, delusions, phantasms, ghosts, and fictions.

The same basic mental function which brings us modern medicine, engineering, and electronics also brings us superstitions, false beliefs, madness, and specifically human violence. It is as if the validity of logic and the knowledge conveyed by words carry with them as a shadow an alienation from deeper truths, an obfuscation—as through a glass darkly—of a reality which is revealed only by suspending rational, discursive thought and transcending the illusion of a substantial self.

The Self-Created Self

The story of human evolution, as it is framed by modern science, explains perfectly well the evolution of a fictional self which mistakenly takes itself as substantial and real. In the context of evolution the human ego, or self, evolved when the primate eye-brain-hand system was wired for speech. The binary logic of speech generated a new form of consciousness, digital or dualistic consciousness, which experiences life in the antithetical dimensions of past/future (historical time), good/evil (values and evaluated actions), and self/other (society.) The living continuity and coherence of these antithetical dimensions is represented by digital consciousness to itself through the false imputation of a substantial interior presence, a self, which is identified with the life force and the fetishized life-territory.

In an act of reflexive self-creation, the signifying agent signifies itself as a person[26] who dwells in its own metaphorical inner space. It identifies and perceives itself as the center of its being and perceives its territory of objects and meanings as projections of itself. Its mission is to protect itself and its territory, to satisfy and enjoy itself, to expand, to prosper, and to be happy. This mission is constantly threatened, however, by impermanence, emptiness, and contradictions which flow kaleidoscopically through historical time, bounded by the biological events of birth and death, beyond which lies the unknown.

The interior presence, or holographic "I," desires long life and happiness, but is haunted by the presentiment of suffering and death. In its stubborn attachments to fixed reference points, in its relentless pursuit of permanence, substance, and happiness, the illusory self generates the misery it imposes on itself and others. The most precious insight that Buddhism has to offer the West is that only by deep meditation on the paradoxes of self can the human individual and the human species rescue itself from itself.

Transforming Suffering

CHAPTER TWENTY-FOUR

Meditation on Happiness

We began this meditation on happiness by observing that the fundamental tragedy of life is that everyone wants to be happy, yet everyone suffers and dies. What have we learned that might help us to transcend this tragic condition? Perhaps only this: that one of the deepest, most fundamental human desires *is* to transcend this condition—to find happiness in the shadow of sorrow and death—and that this search for happiness is the basic motivation of our thoughts and actions and, hence, profoundly shapes our emotions, our character, and our culture.

The Search for Happiness through Religion

Over the course of human history people have experimented with many paths they hoped would lead to the transcendence of suffering and death and the achievement of lasting happiness. The original, basic, and most enduring of these paths is religion. Varied and diverse as human religions are, they share a fundamental similarity. They all propose the same basic formula for the pursuit of happiness and the escape from suffering and death, namely, a view of existence and a code of moral conduct consistent with that view. One of the most fundamental tenets of religion is that happiness is achieved by bringing mind and conduct into harmony with god, which means, in effect, into harmony with existence.

For example, in the Christian tradition existence is viewed as a manifestation of the will of God, the creator. This implies that the laws governing natural phenomena are an expression of the will of God, who made them so. Happiness, thus, is achieved by union with God by means of bringing mind and conduct into harmony with existence, or "natural law." The faithful Christian who seeks eternal happiness is enjoined to view the world according to "the word of God" and the words of the authentic prophets of God, and to conform conduct to the prescribed code of rituals and ethics which flow from these teachings.

The message is basically the same in the Buddhist tradition, although it is conveyed in different language, metaphors, and images. Buddhists, as we have seen, do not believe in a creator god. In this sense, Buddhism may be considered an atheistic religion. In the Buddhist view, existence is an eternal flow of phenomena which are impermanent and lacking true substance. Existence is emptiness masquerading as form. In Christianity, God is the ultimate nature of all phenomena; in Buddhism emptiness is the nature of all phenomena. In this sense, God and emptiness are roughly analogous concepts.

In the Buddist view, suffering and unhappiness are caused by the failure to perceive the true nature of existence as empty and, instead, perceiving it as permanent and substantial. This includes falsely perceiving self as a solid, enduring substance, thus reifying and deifying it. This error of view generates the false idea that happiness can be achieved through the selfish satisfaction of desires. The false path to happiness, the path to unhappiness and suffering, is the search for self-satisfaction. The true path to happiness, from the Buddhist point of view, requires the realization of emptiness, including the emptiness of self. This realization helps dissolve the solidified self and the false idea that selfish satisfaction is the path to happiness, and replaces it with a clear insight into the nature of self, which opens the path to acceptance, inner calm, equanimity, virtue, and compassion.

It is thus evident that, in both the Buddhist and the Christian traditions happiness is achieved through the alignment of self with the true nature of existence, whether perceived as God or as emptiness, and the conformation of conduct with the moral codes which flow from this view. Both traditions teach that, to the degree that we see the world through the idiosyncratic lenses of our own selfish desires and fears, and to the degree that we pursue happiness through the satisfaction of our own selfish strivings, we are sinners who will be punished, by God or by the laws of karma, with unhappiness, suffering and death.

The profound, enduring, but forgotten insight of the religious view is that happiness can be found only through taming the self. One can succeed at all one's Happiness Projects—secular success, wealth, reputation, marriage and family, material riches, and all the pleasures that go with them—and still not be happy. We want more. We want the difficult, the improbable, and the impossible. Our desires are insatiable. We are addicted to *desire* itself. And these selfish strivings are the common root of the suffering we impose on ourselves and others. The only solution, the only way to transcend this self-imposed tragedy, is to undertake a self-motivated transformation, a program of self-training and self-discipline, which brings mind and conduct into harmony with the realities of human life and the facts of existence.

For humans who lived in primitive communities and, perhaps, for the pious modern human, the religious view and path pervade every aspect of life from the most mundane details of the daily routine, to the milestones of birth, maturity, marriage, and death. This is what is meant by the term "holistic," an archaic condition which "new age" people are trying to recreate. Holistic has the dual meaning of "whole" and "holy." By contrast, the typical contemporary secular individual has lost this holistic, integrated view and path of life and, unknowingly, suffers deeply from this loss.

With the historical decline of religion modern peoples have increasingly come to rely primarily on science and politics to provide the path to happiness in this life. In this century science and the state have replaced god as the ultimate authority. The modern human's view of the world is primarily derived from science. Instead of looking to religion for guidance to life, modern people now look to science and the scientific expert. In yesteryears, the shaman, the priest, and the pastor were the experts on personal suffering. Today, we look to the psychiatrist, the psychologist, and the social worker who, if they are qualified, are viewed primarily as scientists and, thus, are unable to frankly embrace religious insights and prescriptions. Yesterday, explanations of human suffering were personal and moral. Today they are impersonal and scientific.

The problem, as we have seen, is that the scientific view of the world is an insufficient guide for the subject's journey through life. As I have attempted to show, science, by its own rules of procedure, disassociates itself from religion and ethics. The scientific view of existence is de-animated, de-spiritualized, and de-mythologized. It describes matter and energy not in the language of story, myth, and metaphor but in mathematical formulae from which no ethical principles or guidance for life can be deduced.

The modern human who relies solely on science for guidance to life is, thus, in the tragic but self-created dilemma of adhering to a view of the world which is explicitly, by its own tenets, not valid as guidance for life. Today, our ethical sensibilities are divorced from a holistic or integrated view of the world, and are, thus, both confused and rigid. In the modern world ethics are either mindlessly absolute or relative and situational, either leaving no room for "normal" human greed, lust, avarice, and aggression, or rationalizing and justifying them.

Today, many modern peoples also look to their government, as they once looked to their gods, for the source of both nourishment and punishment, the former represented by the olive branch in the American eagle's right talon, and the latter by the sheath of arrows in the left. When people are unhappy they cry, "Our government has failed us!" First, we mourned the death of God.[1] Now we mourn the failure of government.

The Search for Happiness through Science and Politics

The French Revolution and the European Enlightenment, as we have noted, mark the transfer of jurisdiction over the problems of happiness and suffering from religion to science and democracy. The rise of science led to the development of new technology which, in turn, led to new industry. Those with inherited wealth and/or the initiative to commercialize the new science became the kings and barons of the new capitalist class. Democracy theoretically provides for the equal distribution of political power, but it is silent on the problem of the unequal distribution of wealth. With time, the gap widened between the relatively small wealthy, capitalist class and the masses of the poor. By the middle of the nineteenth century it had become clear to some that democracy and science had not led to the greatest happiness for the greatest number. On the contrary, it had perpetuated and even aggravated the problem of the unequal distribution of suffering.

The unequal distribution of wealth and, hence, of happiness and suffering, generated class conflict. The severe poverty and suffering of the lower classes generated feelings of envy, jealousy, and resentment towards the upper classes. And the upper classes, who lived in great wealth, power, and privilege, were contemptuous and afraid of the lower classes and, thus, defensively aggressive towards them. In this historical context a radical vision emerged of a new synthesis of politics and science which would end the unequal distribution of wealth. This new vision, associated with the name of Karl Marx, has been called "scientific socialism" because it is a marriage of science and politics. Before Marx, science was used by the few to make their fortune by exploiting the labor of the masses while the state remained *laissez faire*, hands off. Karl Marx's innovation was to bend science to the service of the state in a heroic effort to eliminate class divisions, exploitation, and conflict and recreate the paradise of community lost with a new, communist society of economic equals.

In its early years in the West, as in Russia today, laissez faire capitalism led to the exploitation of labor, class conflict, gross economic inequality, and a high crime rate. The subsequent Marxist-Communist reaction against this sorry state of unequal suffering eventually led to totalitarianism, tyranny, and the suppression of initiative and creativity. Until recently, the world has seemed to be hopelessly polarized between the two ideologies of capitalism and communism. The two political systems are polar opposites, projections of dualistic mind. They represent antithetical and mutually contradictory solutions to the problem of human happiness. One favors free enterprise and economic competition and the other favors a highly regulated and controlled economy. Yet, each is seen by its adherents as the best path to happiness on earth. As opposites, they have contradictory virtues and flaws. Capitalism stimulates initiative and enterprise, but the freedom which is its necessary precondition leads to social variance, deviance, and disorder. Communism promotes an orderly society, but at the cost of stifling initiative and creativity.

History is witness to the fact that capitalism and communism each contain within themselves the flaws which lead to their own demise. The freedom which is necessary for capitalism to flourish eventually leads to social experimentation, deviance, and crime. Dissatisfaction with the unequal distribution of happiness under capitalism eventually leads to revolution towards a more regulated, closed society and, at the extreme, to a totalitarian police state. Closed societies, on the other hand, dialectically generate rebellion and counterrevolution in the name of freedom.

Each political system has tried to eliminate its flaws by swinging towards the opposite pole, trying to copy the virtues of the other while avoiding its own flaws. The West, particularly the United States, has attempted to control its inner turmoil, deviance, and disorder by increasing the power of the state. The communist world has already stagnated and collapsed under the oppressive weight of its own state tyranny and has opened itself to free enterprise in order to stimulate economic initiative and consumer satisfaction. As the Communist Soviet Union failed and fell into its opposite form of an open society, with all its inherent disorder, the United States, suffering from intolerable internal disorder, has increasingly taken the form of its former totalitarian adversary.

Over the past seventy years, especially during the era of the cold war, the Soviet Union and the United States have represented the two polar ideological extremes. The global dialectic between capitalism and communism has led to the growing realization that both political systems have failed in their pure forms. As pure ideologies they have no possibility of fulfillment. They are doomed to a continual dialectical struggle against each other.

The historical dialectic between capitalism and communism has now become more subtle. Recently, governments around the world have begun to define and control the limits of their political oscillations. This dampened dialectic involves finding a balance between state regulation and control on the one hand, and personal and economic freedom on the other. It consists of political shifts between conservatives (who lean towards the pole of capitalism) and liberals (who lean towards the pole of socialism) and back, as each swing becomes excessive in its trajectory. This political dialectic reflects the psychological fact that both freedom and order, in balance, are necessary conditions of the happy life. Rather than seeking one extreme or the other, the intelligent approach seems to be pragmatic problem solving, a "piecemeal social engineering" which takes into account the fact that social policies often lean too far in one direction or the other and constantly need to be revised and reversed to the proper degree and with proper timing. The intelligent politics of the future will, hopefully, involve a balancing of antithetical forces rather than conflict between them.

At the turn of the millenium, it should be evident that politics is an incomplete and, therefore, unsatisfactory solution to the problem of human happiness. Politics is necessary for people to live together peaceably in society, but the power of politics to promote human happiness is limited. It cannot offer a coherent view of existence, without which people are cosmically disoriented and alienated from the ground and source of existence. Politics can only offer a fetishized or narrow view of life.[2] Government can spend and redistribute money. It can build roads and bureaucracies. It can wage wars. It can regulate individual and corporate behavior by making laws and forcing people to obey them under the threat of fines, imprisonment, or death. But government cannot help people to find inner peace and happiness. The rule of law is vital to human freedom; but, by itself, law is insufficient for the guidance of life. Law is necessarily more limited in scope than ethics. A society in which all ethical precepts were laws enforced by the state would be oppressive. On the other hand, a free society ruled by law whose citizens do not also voluntarily follow a code of ethical conduct would lose its moral fibre and, eventually, fall into either anarchy or totalitarianism.

Recently, an awareness has dawned in American political life that something is missing from politics, namely, religion and religious ethics. Many people believe that some significant modern social problems such as high crime rates, delinquency, drug abuse, teen pregnancy, spousal abuse, pornography, and sexually transmitted diseases are the result of the decline of religious values. This view, as it is currently expressed, has merit but is also flawed. The problem is that religion cannot be revived by politics and government. The current campaign to revive religious values through such means as tougher criminal and social sanctions against drug abuse, homosexuality, sexual promiscuity, and abortion, or constitutional amendments to prohibit flag burning and permit prayer in public schools, will merely expand the power of the state without providing the cosmology, the mythic view, the meticulous morality, or the esthetic richness of old-time religion.

While those who advocate the revival of religion through politics may be sincere and well motivated, the explanations they offer for the breakdown of society are deficient and the solutions they advocate are largely symbolic and ineffective. It is naive to blame the moral degeneration of the United States on liberals, or the media, or the libertinism of Hollywood, the hippies, and radicals of the sixties. From the historical point of view, the primary causal factor responsible for the decline of religion, community, and therefore of "family values," is the rise of science and scientific technology, which began around four hundred years ago. The knowledge and techniques, or view and path, of science are more powerful and, therefore, more appealing to people than religion. Religions which opposed science lost their appeal and remained static, while science satisfied human needs and stimulated the evolution of human consciousness and society.

The initial impact of science was to undermine the traditional religious world-view upon which ecclesiastical authority is based. As the scientific view of the world replaced the religious view the authority of religion declined. As the authority of religion declined traditional moral codes lost credibility and appeal. As the moral fibre of Western culture disintegrated society broke down.

Science has undermined religion not only by contradicting the traditional religious cosmology, but also in the more powerful and mundane sense, by giving us the knowledge and techniques to produce tangible goods that give us pleasure, which religion cannot. For these reasons fundamentalist Christianity rejects the Darwinian theory of evolution, and fundamentalist Islam rejects modernity, which is the product of science and technology. They believe that the enemy of their religion is science and scientific technology. It may be closer to the truth, however, to suggest that religions are hostile towards science and technology because they are unable or unwilling to integrate scientific knowledge into their religious world-view, and because people love the fruits of technology.

The Search for Happiness through Consumer Goods

The decline of traditional religion and the rise of politics and science as the new hoped-for means to happiness has produced a new human condition: a secular, market society driven by the profit motive and a culture of consumers who believe that happiness can be won by buying and consuming goods. Religions promise an intangible future happiness after death. Who can collect on that? Science and technology deliver tangible goods we can enjoy in life, goods we desire, goods we think will make us happy. Most people love nice things—beautiful homes and furniture, sleek and powerful cars, state of the art audio and video, the latest computer, designer clothing, and rich food and drink. Science helps us to make and possess these things. The replacement of religion by science and politics has created a culture of consumers who believe that buying and owning goods is the best path to happiness. Marx called this the "fetishization of commodities." In our capitalist society this slogan is expressed in the corporate motto: "Better living through chemistry." And it is subtly if cynically echoed in the famous yuppie T-shirt logo, "Whoever dies with the most toys wins."

Consumerism is a condition of rampant, unregulated desires stimulated by the ubiquitous quasi-mythic images of product advertising which urge and seduce us into believing that happiness can be achieved through buying and consuming goods. The "secular religion of consumerism" leads only to an endless cycle of working for money, spending and buying, accumulating debt, and working to pay it off. Thus is generated the daily grind and rat race. In such a culture, desire is out of control. There are an endless variety of consumer goods to buy and satisfactions are transient. The purchase of a new toy—a car, or a TV, or a new outfit—is associated with a fleeting feeling of satisfaction, soon followed by the arising of a new desire, a new Happiness Project, and a new series of obstacles, frustrations, and problems. The Tibetans have a saying which they quote with an ironic smile: "If you have a camel, your troubles are as big as a camel."

The advent of consumerism is associated with an increased level of personal and emotional suffering. Consumerism is too narrow a view and path of life to bring much happiness. It is a poor replacement for traditional religion. It lacks a cosmology and provides only a vestigial system of relativistic ethics. Nevertheless, people love to shop. I have heard many people say that when they feel down, they shop. They call it "retail therapy," unaware that they are talking about their religion, or rather what has replaced their old, now vestigial religion, consumerism. Not too long ago churches with their gothic arches and heaven-seeking steeples occupied the center of towns. Now the center of towns are occupied by shopping malls, banks, insurance companies, and corporate office buildings.

But retail therapy will not solve the problems of a cold marriage, a delinquent child, or a sick parent. It does not compensate for a life spent in servitude to making money in order to pay off debts from past purchases so one can buy more. It does not solve the problems of sickness and death, which haunt us even as we drive our new car out of the dealer's lot. Consumerism leads only to the generation of new desires, more work for more money to buy and consume more toys. It is enough to drive one to drink. No joke intended!

In my view, the spiritual emptiness of consumerism, which comes with an exclusive reliance on science and politics as guidance for life, stimulates the desire to escape secular life altogether, into the therapeutic delirium of alcohol or drugs. The scientific experts seem to be confused and uncertain about why people use drugs. They are the victims of their own deceptive rhetoric. They assume that, if a drug is illegal, it must be bad, without any value whatsoever, and so they cannot understand why people use them. They believe people use drugs because they are addictive, or because of peer pressure, or because of some dark, mysterious, self-destructive motives. Our efforts to deal with our drug problem are obstructed by our inability to understand its causes. It is another case of suffering caused by ignorance.

The reasons people use drugs are typical self-secrets, knowledge we hide from ourselves. The reasons are obvious but so difficult to accept that we refuse to see them. The simple, basic reason people use psychoactive drugs is because they feel bad and they want to feel good. They feel bad because life is difficult. They feel bad because they do not have a view of the world which explains or rationalizes their pain. They feel bad because their desires are endless and out of control. They suffer, therefore, from their own frustration, aggression, and depression.

As a rule, people who use drugs lack an effective religion which can console them and inspire them to courage and compassion. The society which condemns them also creates the conditions from which they want to escape. People use drugs as a palliative, to escape from suffering. Most of the illegal, so-called "recreational" drugs that people self-administer serve roughly the same functions as the drugs psychiatrists administer as medicines to relieve depression and anxiety. People who tend to be down and depressed take uppers. People who are anxious, agitated, and insomniac take downers. At the present time there are two forms of treatment for depression—one legal and one illegal. A large number of depressed people consult psychiatrists and are legally prescribed Prozac or some other antidepressant. Another large number medicate their depression themselves with illegal substances like cocaine, speed, and marijuana. Prozac, cocaine, and speed, no matter how psychiatrists try to differentiate them, have in common a mood elevating effect on the psyche. People abuse alcohol and drugs because they seek the pleasure of relief and forgetfulness from the drudgery, pain, and emptiness of commercial-secular life.

Our so-called drug problem is one of the prices we have paid for the rise of science, the decline of religion, and the evolution of a culture of consumerism.

The breakdown of religion *is* the breakdown of society. When religion breaks down, people lose their connection to earth and sky, to their origins and destiny and, therefore, to themselves and others. The breakdown of religion is the breakdown of society because social relationships are primarily moral. The breakdown of morality in relationships necessarily leads to animosity, resentments, conflict, fragmentation, and ultimately to social disintegration.

Emile Durkheim observed in his classic study of suicide that the breakdown of traditional religious authority leads to a condition he called "anomie," the absence of norms.[3] One of the functions of religion is the establishment of norms, rules, ethics, guides for life. When these norms break down, the limitations on desire are weakened. The intensification of desire which accompanies the decline of religious morality naturally leads to an increase in personal suffering and its *sequela*, such as suicide.

Modern societies are experiencing an epidemic of suicide, especially among the young and the elderly. As in the case of drug abuse, the scientific experts do not understand suicide very well, and for the same reasons. We do not like to face the truth about ourselves. The truth is that if the purpose of life is to be happy, and happiness does not seem possible, then life will not seem worth living. People commit suicide when they lose the hope for future happiness—when all their Happiness Projects fail.

Although many people disapprove, it is understandable when old people with fatal illnesses want to die. It is more difficult to understand why healthy young people would want to die. The reason is that they suffer from failed Happiness Projects and the confusion, purposelessness, anxiety, and depression that follow. They counted on success in school, in a future career, or in a particular relationship as the key to their happiness. They commit suicide because their high hopes are dashed and they feel helpless to reconstruct them. This is consistent with the fact that the primary symptoms of depression and suicide are feelings of hopelessness and helplessness.

Thus, we glimpse how the decline of traditional religion and religious morality leads to a condition of social anomie which, combined with a reliance on science, politics, and the ethos of consumerism, permits desire to run rampant in a culture of narcissism. This, in turn, causes an increase in personal frustration which leads to aggression, crime, despondency, drug abuse, and many of the forms of personal and emotional suffering we call mental illness.

The Search for Happiness through Psychotherapy

One of the historical responses to the new, intense forms of personal suffering associated with modern life has been the development of a new social institution—psychotherapy. The mission of psychotherapy is to help relieve mental and emotional suffering and to provide some guidance towards happiness. In this sense, psychotherapy has inherited one of the functions of religion. For this reason Otto Rank called psychotherapy "the grandchild of religion."[4]

Psychotherapy is very popular in the West, and for good reason. It has been helpful to many people. It is a technique, developed over the past hundred years, to help the suffering subject become more self-aware so it can live a more intelligent, disciplined, and happy life. It is curious, therefore, that there is no agreement about how or why psychotherapy works. And while psychotherapy can be very helpful, it also has its limitations and dangers.

The success of psychotherapy is apparently independent of the theoretical orientation of the therapist. Psychotherapy is likely to be helpful if the therapist is perceived by the patient as supportive and empathetic no matter whether the therapist is a psychoanalyst, a cognitive therapist, a Gestalt therapist, a behaviorist, or merely a nondescript counselor. Therapy is also more likely to succeed if the therapist is experienced, mature, tactful, and communicates effectively. Most observers would also agree that a successful outcome depends upon the motivation, effort, openness, and psychological sensitivity of the patient.

In my view, psychotherapy consists, essentially, of a relationship between two people, one called a helper the other a sufferer. Actually, both are sufferers, and the therapist is often personally helped by what is learned from therapy. Hopefully, however, the therapist is more mature and wiser than the patient. The two engage in conversations which focus on the thoughts, feelings, actions, and life problems of the sufferer. The aim is to help reduce or eliminate the patient's pain and to help him or her find some way to an increased measure of happiness. In one form or another, psychotherapy is guidance for life. It works in many of the ways that religion works.

Some psychotherapy works simply by providing support and affirmation, as a priest might do for a penitent. It can be very helpful for people in emotional pain to know that someone is sympathetic, someone is on their side. When we are in pain we lose confidence in ourselves and we may fall into agonizing self-doubt and self-hatred. It can be a great relief to hear someone say, "I understand how you feel. I support you. I may not agree with everything you do. But I am your friend."

Sometimes the sufferer is helped by experiencing the therapist as role model. Many people grow up with no idea of what it means to be a competent, compassionate human being. The therapist may be the first reasonable adult they have ever talked to. Merely sitting and talking regularly to an intelligent, kind person can be inspiring and transforming. This is why religious people want to be in the presence of a "master." The master's very mode of being rubs off. Nothing needs to be said, which is why Meher Baba was respected by many as a teacher although he did not utter a word in decades. One can feel the presence of a master and move with it, like one can feel the rhythm of music and dance.

When I first sought a teacher, Ngodup Burkhar, translator for Kenpho Karthar Rinpoche, urged me to see Rinpoche, "just to experience his presence," which, indeed, was extraordinary. I later learned the Vajrayana practice of *guru yoga* which is a kind of role modeling through visualization in which the guru is perceived as having the qualities of an enlightened being. By relating to and identifying with these qualities the practitioner may be able to achieve a greater degree of positive self-transformation. The therapist may not be a master, but some people can benefit merely by sitting and talking with an experienced therapist.

At other times, therapy may offer the opportunity for confession and reflection. An old religious aphorism teaches that "confession is good for the soul." Why? Because confession brings the fresh air of honesty to the self-created fog of self-deception in which we all live. Confession requires two virtues which are prerequisites to a happy life: courage and honesty. Confession first requires the courage to face one's self. Second, it requires the honesty to admit truths one may not want to see. We are all in the situation of the alcoholic in denial. To become sober the alcoholic must admit, "I am an alcoholic." Similarly, to grow, mature, and be happy it is helpful to be able to admit through confession: "I lust!" "I covet!" "I hate!" "I want more of this and more of that for myself!"

The necessary second part of confession, without which it may be only a meaningless, deception-enhancing ritual, is introspection and reflection. If I confess my greed but do not reflect on it, I will have merely made myself more comfortable with it, no matter what trail of suffering it leaves in my life and the life of those around me. On the other hand, if I reflect upon the consequences of my greed and its impact on my life, I may choose to relate to it differently, if only for the sake of my own happiness. One of the keys to successful psychotherapy is the patient's own developing awareness of and self-reflection on his or her thoughts, feelings, and actions. In Buddhism this reasoned reflection is called analytic meditation. It means thinking about things—not in the ordinary way of pointless, rambling, discursive thought, but with the aim of improving the clarity of awareness and of thinking logically about one's experiences.

When therapy goes deeper it transforms the sufferer's thoughts, feelings, and actions more radically. In religious terms, we would say that a thorough therapy will recast the sufferer's view and path. This results in an alteration of character, a kind of growth and maturation, which transform the manner and style of working with the challenges and problems of life.

The "depth psychologies," whose stated goal is to understand and transform the human self at its core, aim to reveal this core to itself by making the unconscious conscious. Thus they share with Buddhism the goal of ever increasing awareness. In psychotherapy, as in Buddhism, this expanding consciousness necessarily includes an increased acknowledgment of one's desires, aversions, and narcissistic attachment to self. To be happy one must relax the resistance to examining these three poisons and become more aware of how they shape one's actions in the world and, through the laws of karma, determine the quality of one's life.

This is a difficult process. It too requires courage and honesty. We humans wear so many masks and disguises and hide so many secrets from ourselves. Sometimes the fear and resistance to seeing are too strong. The patient comes to therapy, but does not want to inquire within. At such a moment the experienced Buddhist psychotherapist may rely on his or her own Dharma practice and sit quietly, attentively, and authentically, practicing patience in the presence of the patient. If the therapist is truly authentic and not merely hiding behind a therapeutic or meditative technique, a patient therapist can be very reassuring and help the patient to relax and open to an honest self-examination.[5] Sometimes, when people relax deeply, they discover something authentic within themselves, especially when relaxation is accompanied by confession and reflection.

One of the most daunting problems with psychotherapy is that, while it functions as spiritual guidance for the subject in the journey through life, it is usually viewed as a form of medical treatment for mental illness. This crippling perception is the official view of the American Psychiatric Association and the health insurance industry. Most people who go to psychotherapy must be given a psychiatric diagnosis in order to receive insurance reimbursement for some of the cost. The professional identity of the psychiatrist hinges on psychotherapy being defined as a medical rather than as a spiritual enterprise. If psychotherapy were perceived as a religious or moral activity, psychiatrists would be seen as priests rather than as medical doctors, and health insurance companies would not pay for it. There is, thus, tremendous social pressure to see psychotherapy as medical. This means that whatever wisdom the therapist can impart to the patient must be smuggled in, disguised as officially sanctioned medical treatment. And it must be smuggled quickly, in order to meet the managed care criteria of brief psychotherapy.

The socially mandated deception which defines psychotherapy as medical creates great confusion amongst therapists, their patients, and society as a whole. There is a public pretense that psychotherapy is a medical-scientific enterprise and that therapists are scientists—of a sort. To be licensed as a psychotherapist one must have an advanced medical, master's, or doctoral degree from an approved institution. This implies that one's knowledge is scientific and reputable, rather than religious, no matter how wise.

Most psychotherapists pretend (often on TV talk shows) to be scientific experts or, at least, to base their knowledge and opinions on scientific research. Most therapists would also say that they are not supposed to take positions on moral issues, make moral judgments, or to transmit moral values to their patients. Indeed, if they view themselves as scientists, they are prevented from doing this by the self-imposed limitations of their own philosophy and methodology.

Paradoxically, psychotherapists deal with nothing other than moral issues, even if they fail to recognize them as such. And they cannot help but transmit to the patient something about their moral values, no matter how hard they try to appear "neutral" or "objective." Psychotherapists are regarded by most people, and consulted by many, as experts on all kinds of moral and social problems, from drug abuse, child abuse, and spousal abuse, to divorce, custody disputes, delinquency, crime, and sexual misconduct. Often, people accused of crime or other forms of misconduct are required by courts or employers to submit to psychotherapy, the more scientific the better, presumably in order to "cure" the offender's moral flaws.

The medical disguise of psychotherapy is confusing to medical and non-medical psychotherapists alike. Psychiatrists are increasingly trained in psychopharmacology and neurology rather than in psychotherapy. They tend to ignore the moral and spiritual dimensions of their patient's problems and sufferings. As a result, many psychiatrists do not understand their patients as subjects and are not competent psychotherapists. Most psychologists and social workers, on the other hand, are intimidated by and yield to the dominant ideology of the medical model, and view a wide variety of mental and emotional sufferings as diseases, on which psychiatrists are experts, and which often must be treated with psychiatric drugs. This creates uncertainty and confusion in the mind of the non-medical therapist about whether the patient's symptoms are caused by external factors, such as past psychological traumas or "biochemical imbalances," or whether they are the result of the patient's own desires, fears, thoughts, actions, and ignorance. As a result of this almost ubiquitous confusion, many people do not receive competent therapy.

Society is also confused by the medical model of psychotherapy. Society usually appeals to the scientist for expert knowledge about the world and human problems in the world. Accordingly, people look to science to understand mental suffering. The scientist, however, gives causes as explanations. Scientific studies of crime, like scientific studies of mental illness, invariably conclude that external factors such as poverty, illiteracy, unemployment, child abuse, drug abuse, and so forth are responsible for the problem.

The view that social factors, rather than individual people, are responsible for crime, has been associated with the liberal point of view. In reaction against this conservatives, particularly of the religious right, ridicule liberals and insist that individuals are responsible for their actions. They often hypocritically falter, however, on psychiatric issues such as alcoholism and addiction, where they adopt the prevailing medical model. The confusion and conflict of views on the issue of personal responsibility creates confusion in society as a whole about whether individuals are responsible for their actions or not. From the scientific (or "clinical") point of view, which is the officially accepted view, free choice is an illusion. Human behavior is caused rather than chosen. It follows from this that no one is responsible for their actions. From the religious point of view, however, free choice is God-given, and the rational human being is responsible for his and her actions.

To the degree that psychotherapists believe they are treating mental illnesses scientifically, they must view patients as not personally responsible for their suffering. The idea that a sufferer is even partially responsible for his or her own suffering is often viewed with suspicion today, especially in psychiatric circles. In fact, it is specifically contradicted by the prevailing view of mental and emotional suffering, the medical model of mental illness. The medical model states that certain forms of suffering, such as anxiety, depression, bulimia, and addiction, are not the responsibility of the sufferer. On the contrary, these negative emotions and disruptive behaviors are thought to be caused by factors external to the personal agent such as organic brain pathology or oppressive social circumstances. The idea that a person diagnosed with mental illness may, in some sense, be responsible for their suffering is criticized as "blaming the victim."

The problem, however, is that in order for therapy to work the therapist must teach the patient to increasingly take responsibility for his or her thoughts, feelings, and actions. Drug treatment programs typically define alcoholism and addiction as diseases and then, paradoxically, design a treatment program to induce the patient to take responsibility for their addiction. The confusion about whether suffering is caused by external factors or is the result of the sufferer's own moral actions leads to confusion between not *having* responsibility for one's suffering, as is the case in most physical illnesses, and not *taking* responsibility, as is the case of alcoholism, addiction, criminality, and many so-called mental illnesses.

Although psychotherapy may properly be described as the grandchild of religion, and even though it displays many of the qualities of a religion—particularly dogmatism and a revulsion for heresy—it is not an adequate replacement for religion. There is no single psychotherapeutic world-view which synthesizes objective knowledge with guidance through life as well as functioning religions do. Psychotherapy is fragmented into a multiplicity of dogmatic orthodoxies, splinter groups, and heresies. Like the five blind men who each palpate a different part of the elephant—the trunk, the tusks, the legs, the body, and the tail—and see it as five different creatures, psychotherapists tend to see the problem of suffering from their own narrow point of view. To most psychiatrists mental suffering is mental illness and has a biological cause. To most cognitive psychologists the problem is wrong view. To behavioral psychologists the problem is wrong conditioning. To interpersonal therapists the problem is primarily bad relationships. To the psychoanalyst the problem is bad parenting.

In spite of its flaws, psychotherapy can help people to find some degree of relief from their self-imposed suffering and deal more intelligently and effectively with the problems of life. Psychotherapy can help people to solve specific life problems, and it can help them learn how to solve life problems for themselves. Sometimes, good, brief therapy helps a person to find an opening, to grow, to learn new ways of seeing and relating to other people and situations. Psychotherapy can be the first step on a journey of introspection and self-reflection. It can be the first step towards seeking happiness within, through a transformation of one's view of and actions in the world. In this sense, I think of psychotherapy as "pre-Dharmic."

The Search for Happiness Within: The Four Thoughts

Many people have come to the realization that they cannot find happiness through their religion, through the good graces of their government, through buying and consuming goods, or through psychotherapy. Many people have also discovered that they are not fulfilled by their careers or their relationships. No matter how successful they are they may feel something vital is missing from their lives. They may realize that they must find happiness within themselves, but they have no idea how to do it. They think it means bravely but grimly bearing their suffering alone. With these people in mind, it may be helpful to conclude with a brief glimpse of the Buddhist path to happiness within.

The Tibetan word for Buddhist is *nang-pa,*which means "insider" or "one who goes within." Going within means paying attention to one's mind and the workings of the mind. The secrets of happiness we hide from ourselves lie within our own minds. The mind is also the key to the pain and suffering we inflict on ourselves and those around us. The inner path to happiness requires paying attention to mind and cultivating mind. The Tibetan practice of *lo jong* literally means taming and training the mind.[6]

One of the first teachings I received from Khenpo Karthar Rinpoche is called The Four Thoughts That Turn the Mind Within, or The Four Thoughts That Turn the Mind Towards Religion. They are also known as the "four ordinary preliminaries" of Vajrayana tantric practice.[7] Reflection on these thoughts is a potent method for becoming aware of the esoteric truths we hide from ourselves; in other words, for learning the secrets of the inner path to happiness.

The Four Thoughts are: precious human birth, impermanence, karma, and the inherent unsatisfactoriness of secular life. The meaning of the fourth thought is that enduring happiness cannot be found in the outer, social world through success, wealth, fame, nor even through good relationships. No matter how wonderful they may seem by conventional social standards, each of these activities is inherently unsatisfactory because dualistic mind is inherently flawed. Dualistic mind projects *samsara* onto every aspect of the secular world, and we relate to the secular world through the desires, aversions, and self-clinging of dualistic mind. To say that secular life is inherently unsatisfactory is equivalent to saying that dualistic mind is inherently the cause and locus of our suffering. Therefore, the teachings logically continue, to find lasting happiness it is necessary to look within and tame and train one's own mind.

Taken together, the Four Thoughts provide an integrated view of the sufferer's dilemma and the way out. The teaching on precious human birth is based on the belief in rebirth and the view that human birth is difficult to achieve. From this point of view, many lifetimes of virtuous action are required to achieve a human rebirth, during which one may be reborn in lower realms of life before the laws of karma reward virtue with a precious human birth. One need not believe in rebirth to appreciate this teaching, however. It can be interpreted simply to mean that human life is precious, whether rebirth exists or not.

The teaching on impermanence includes the awareness of death. We are all certain to die—time, place, and manner of death unknown. This makes life all the more precious. The teaching on karma reminds us that we all seek happiness, and that the keys to the kingdom of happiness lie in our own hands or, rather, in our own intentions and actions. Since life is precious and short, it is necessary to begin now to purify ourselves, our deeds, and our way of being in the world if we hope to achieve happiness in this world, or the next. Turning one's attention within, towards one's own mind in the search for happiness, is the "first principle aspect of the path." It is one of the first commitments on the spiritual journey.

The Three Principle Aspects of the Path

Buddist teachings are often summarized in terms of the "three principle aspects of the path": renunciation, compassion, and the wisdom realizing emptiness. They correspond roughly to the main tasks of the Hinayana, the Mahayana, and the Vajrayana teachings, although all three principles are contained in all three paths. The first step on the path of renunciation is to begin searching for happiness within; the first step because it implies the gradual renouncing of the world as the source, locus, and cause of our happiness (and unhappiness). Renouncing the world does not mean rejecting the world. One can learn to live in it and with it, skillfully and positively, experiencing it and enjoying it, without taking it too seriously in any ultimate sense. Renouncing the world does not mean that one must live as a monk. A monks's renunciation vows are more extreme than a married, working person's need to be. Renunciation is a path of gradually diminishing grasping. It is a voluntary relinquishing of one's stubbornly held selfish desires and aversions, not out of a sense of guilt, or a sense of duty, but from the direct, authentic, personal knowledge of the futility of seeking happiness through them. Turning the mind within, which is the path of renunciation, implies making a commitment to becoming familiar with the workings of one's own mind through meditation.

Renunciation is the hallmark of the Hinayana path. Basically, in a down-to-earth sense, it means taking care of oneself and not being a nuisance or burden to others. It means getting one's own house in order. This requires effort, perseverance, discipline, and patience—four of the six *paramitas* or transcending virtues. These virtues are necessary to help us transcend the temptations of the samsaric world and focus on the path of inward reflection and examination which reveals the secrets of happiness.

Getting one's house in order means bring some order and discipline to one's mind. Our minds are the mansions in which we live. Ordinary, dualistic mind is disorderly. It is constantly agitated by hypermentation. We are constantly thinking in a stream of free association, but with so little awareness that if we were asked what we are thinking about we would have a hard time giving a coherent answer. Yet our stream of consciousness constantly provokes negative emotions such as anxiety, anger, and depression. If we think an angry thought we will feel angry. If we think a depressing thought we will feel depressed. An old Buddhist maxim says: "Person with busy mind is bound to suffer."

There is a basic form of Buddhist meditation, called *shamatha* in Sanskrit, which is an antidote to the rambling hypermentation of dualistic mind; it is a stabilizing meditation or tranquility meditation. In Tibetan it is called *shi ne*, which literally means "dwelling in peace." It involves, in effect, training the mind to pay attention to the present moment.

When we are lost in hypermentation, we are usually thinking about the past or the future. We may be blissed out by the fantasy of some wished-for pleasure, or freaked out by the nightmare of a dreaded problem. Turbulent, discursive, dualistic mind prevents us from seeing clearly because it constantly obstructs the awareness of the present moment, and the present moment is always where life occurs. Our thoughts are the veil through which we see the present, as through a glass darkly. If we are unaware of the present we blind ourselves to the facts of life, and live instead in the wishful-fearful projections of dualistic mind.

Shamatha focuses the mind on the present moment, through breath awareness or some similar technique of mindfulness. Focusing on the present quiets the mind. This is because dualistic mind lives in secular time. It can remember the past and anticipate the future. It can imagine pleasures and pains that have not yet happened, may never have happened, or may never happen. The ego is lost in historical time. Compared to the turbulent surf of samsara, a present-centered mind is quiet, serene, undisturbed, and clear, like the still waters of a deep mountain lake.

Quieting the mind has its own euphoriant effect. It is like the relief one feels after leaving the cacaphony of city traffic for the quiet of a country meadow or a still forest pool. If one practices shamatha only for the feeling of inner peace and quiet, one will have received a great insight into the secrets of happiness. But shamatha has another function. A quiet, still mind can see the truths of existence more clearly than a mind confused by unceasing and frantic hypermentation. Chogyam Trungpa Rinpoche described this function of shamatha using the metaphor of the lamp on the miner's cap to represent our awareness. Ordinary mind is like a lamp which is constantly moving without focusing on anything in particular and, thus, is unaware of the true nature of the surroundings. Meditative mind is like a miner's lamp which is steady and penetrating, revealing clearly and distinctly every feature of the world around us.

When the mind is quiet, steady, and clear, it can turn its attention on itself. This process of becoming familiar with our minds is called *vipashyana* meditation, also known as insight or analytic meditation. Since our knowledge of the world and ourselves is gained through mind, the analysis of mind reveals previously hidden knowledge about the nature of the phenomenal world, including ourselves. Through vipashyana we can become familiar with the operations of our mind—our desires, aversions, and selfishness—as well as the facts of existence—suffering, impermanence, and emptiness.

The second principle aspect of the path is compassion, the hallmark quality of the Mahayana path. The secret of this teaching is that happiness is not possible without compassion. We think of compassion as for the benefit of others and, indeed, it is. But compassion also undermines narcissism, which is one of the primary causes of the pain we inflict on ourselves. Analytic meditation can give us insight into our narcissistic motivations and strivings, and help us to see how they create our own troubles and pain. Once we have seen this clearly, it is a matter of acting intelligently, in one's own self-interest, to tame the selfish beast within and turn one's power and skill to helping others do the same. It is like pulling one's hand from the flame once we realize it burns.

Developing compassion is one of the most difficult aspects of the path. On first reflection, compassion seems contrary to the life instinct which, in humans, is sublimated into selfishness. The basic biological principles of life are self-protective and self-enhancing. It is, therefore, counter-intuitive to altruistically surrender the selfish impulse and replace it with a concern for others. The first obstacle to the development of compassion, therefore, is self-clinging.

The second obstacle to the development of compassion is going to the opposite extreme of giving oneself away. The path of wisdom is a path of balance. Extreme virtue, to the point of caricature, is often an ego game, a materialistic or greedy attitude disguised as spirituality. Chogyam Trungpa Rinpoche called this "spiritual materialism," ego clinging in the guise of ego transcendence.[8] "How wonderful I am for being so spiritual, giving, and compassionate," is the call of the novice.

The dialectics of compassion are revealed in the practice of generosity, another of the six transcending virtues. Generosity is not merely a matter of giving away money or precious objects. Generosity is giving of oneself. It is lovingly giving oneself to others. In Buddhist psychology the virtue of generosity has two potential flaws. One, obviously, is stinginess, which is a form of self-clinging. The other flaw is giving away too much. Giving out of guilt, or out of shame, or out of pride is not generosity. Giving in order to get something back is not generosity; it is a form of contrived selfishness which disguises itself as compassion.

Khenpo Karthar Rinpoche explained it this way: In paraphrase, he said, "People want to see me and talk with me all the time. If I met with everyone I would have no time to eat or rest. I would die in a few weeks and then I would be no good to anyone. So I limit the time I can give for interviews." This extraordinarily compassionate man was teaching that saying yes to everyone is not compassion. It is a form of servitude, probably born in guilt. Compassion permits saying no. Compassion is predicated on the first pinciple aspect of the path, which teaches us to take care of ourselves, for our sake as well as for others. In its deeper meaning, therefore, developing compassion involves finding a balance between what we need for our own physical and spiritual well-being and what we are able to give others. Compassion is a balance between being an individual and being in relationship with others.

The third principle aspect of the path is developing the wisdom that realizes the emptiness of all phenomena, including the emptiness of self. This special wisdom, or insight, is gained through vipashyana and other advanced meditations such as Mahamudra and Dzog Chen. Vipashyana means "special or superior insight." The fruit of vipashyana is the wisdom which realizes emptiness. This is the wisdom of the sixth paramita, the sixth transcending virtue. It is the full development of the capacity to see and is, thus, the antidote to *avidya*, the ignorance which is at the root of our self-imposed troubles and unhappiness.

The wisdom which realizes emptiness is in proper harmony with the facts of existence. As we noted earlier, this is a prerequisite for enduring happiness. The realization of emptiness provides a coherent cosmology of the world which can serve as a solid foundation for the guidance of life. If phenomena are impermanent and empty of true substance, if self is impermanent and lacking substance or soul, then we must train our minds to accept the fact, rather than to deny and repress it. We must beware (be aware) of ego's attempts to find solid, enduring reference points in order to identify, protect, preserve, and expand itself. For this is the cause of much of the suffering we impose on ourselves and others.

The first principle aspect of the path, renunciation, teaches us to take care of ourselves, at least so we are not a burden on others. It is training in self-discipline and self-reliance. The second principle aspect of the path, compassion, permits us to overcome our crippling narcissism and actually connect with other people at the heart, which means with empathy for their Happiness Projects. This is the secret of loving relationships. The third principle aspect of the path is the wisdom realizing emptiness. It is the wisdom which sees existence as a dance without a dancer. When the spiritual journey into our own minds leads us to this wisdom, there is nothing more to do than laugh and join the dance.

Notes

Chapter 1. The Secrets of Happiness

1. Mohandas K. Gandhi, *An Autobiography: The Story of My Experiments with Truth* (Boston: Beacon Press, 1957), xiii.

2. The Buddha, quoted in Piyadassi Thera, *The Buddha's Ancient Path* (London: Rider, 1964), 27.

3. Exod. 33:20.

4. Chogyam Trungpa Rinpoche, *Illusion's Game: The Life and Teaching of Naropa* (Boston: Shambala, 1994), 100.

5. Piyadassi Thera, *Ancient Path,* 24.

6. Alan Watts, *Psychotherapy East and West* (New York: Random House, 1961), 3-4.

7. Ronald Leifer, "The Common Ground of Buddhism and Psychotherapy," presented at the First Karma Kagyu Conference on Buddhism and Psychotherapy at International House, New York City, 1986.

8. The common boundary between psychotherapy, medicine, and religion has often degenerated into a conflict about whether psychotherapy is a medical or a moral enterprise. I have written widely on this subject as has my friend and teacher Dr. Thomas Szasz. See Ronald Leifer, *In the Name of Mental Health: The Social Functions of Psychiatry* (New York: Science House, 1969); and Thomas S. Szasz, *The Myth of Mental Illness* (New York: Hoeber-Harper, 1961).

9. Norman O. Brown, *Life Against Death: The Psychoanalytic Meaning of History* (New York: Random House Vintage Books, 1959), 4.

10. Thomas Moore, *Care of the Soul: A Guide For Cultivating Depth and Sacredness in Everyday Life* (New York: Harper Collins, 1992). This book presents a Jungian approach to awareness of the shadow as a means of discovering esoteric wisdom.

11. Ernest Becker, *The Denial of Death* (New York: The Free Press, 1973).

12. Becker's concept of the Oedipal Transition will be discussed more fully in Chapter 15, "The Evolution of Desire into the Happiness Project."

13. Buddhist refuge vows involve a commitment to open oneself to the Buddha, the Dharma, and the *sangha* or religious community.

Chapter 2. The Reconciliation of Science and Religion

1. Isaiah 3: 10,11

2. Auguste Comte, *The Positive Philosophy of Auguste Comte* (New York: Appleton, 1853).

3. Bertrand Russell quoted in William Barrett, *The Illusion of Technique*, vol. 3 (Garden City, NY: Anchor Press, 1978), 3.

4. Karl Popper, *The Logic of Scientific Discovery* (New York: Science Editions, 1961).

5. Daniel Dennett, "Towards a Cognitive Theory of Consciousness," in *Brainstorms* (Cambridge: MIT Press, 1978) . See also Francisco J. Varela, Evan Thompson, and Eleanor Rosch, *The Embodied Mind* (Cambridge: MIT Press, 1993).

6. Thomas S. Szasz, *The Meaning of Mind: Language, Morality and Neuroscience* (Westport, CT: Praeger, 1996).

7. Barrett, *Illusion of Technique*, 33.

8. Albert Einstein, *Out of My Later Years* (New York: Philosophical Library, 1950), 30.

9. For a complete discussion of antithetical mind see Chapter 23, "The Polarization of Paradise."

10. Gilbert Ryle, *The Concept of Mind* (New York: Barnes and Noble, 1949), 8.

11. Mircea Eliade, *Myths, Dreams, Mysteries: The Encounter Between Contemporary Faiths and Archaic Realities* (New York: Harper and Row, 1960), 156.

Chapter 3. The Case History of a Typical Sufferer

1. *Samsara* is a Sanskrit word which refers to the cycle of births and deaths, i.e., the cycle of changes which we experience in ordinary secular life.

2. I have written about this extensively. See Ronald Leifer, "Psychotherapy, Scientific Method and Ethics," in *American Journal of Psychotherapy*, vol. 20, no. 2 (April 1966), 295-304; and, *In the Name of Mental Health: The Social Functions of Psychiatry* (New York: Science House, 1969).

3. See chapters 18, 19, and 20.

4. Peter Kramer, *Listening to Prozac* (New York: Viking Press, 1993).

5. I have discussed this question in detail in numerous writings over the years. For a summary see Ronald Leifer, "Psychiatry, Language and Freedom," in *Metamedicine*, vol. 3 (1982), 397-416.

6. Anaclitic depression occurs when infants or children are deprived of proper mothering.

7. This point of view is developed in my essay, "The Deconstruction of Self: Commentary on 'The Man Who Mistook His Wife for a Hat: And Other Clinical Tales' by Oliver Sacks," in *The World and I* (June 1986); reprinted in *Journal of Contemplative Psychotherapy* 4 (1984), 153-177.

8. George Engel, an internist and psychiatrist at the University of Rochester Medical Center where I interned, held a similar view of the three foundations of understanding, which he called "the bio-psycho-social model."

9. This is why I believe that the medical model of psychiatry contributes to the general store of ignorance and repression. I have written about this exhaustively: See Leifer, *In the Name of Mental Health*; Ronald Leifer, "The Medical Model as Ideology," *International Journal of Psychiatry* 9 (1970); Ronald Leifer, "The Medical Model as the Ideology of the Therapeutic State, "*Journal of Mind and Behavior* 2 no. 3-4 (Summer 1990), 247-258, reprinted in *Amalie,* 15 no. 1 (February 1993).

10. Sigmund Freud, *Civilization and Its Discontents* (Garden City, NY: Doubleday Anchor, 1958), 16.

11. Ngondro (*sngon 'gro*) is a Tibetan word which means "to go before" or "preliminary." The ngondro teachings and practices are preliminaries to the study and practice of tantra and other advanced practices.

Chapter 4. View, Path, Fruition

1. H.H. The Fourteenth Dalai Lama, *The Bodhgaya Interviews*, José Ignacio Cabezón, ed. (Ithaca: Snow Lion, 1988).

2. For a contrast between "relative" truth and "absolute" truth see Tai Situ Rinpoche, *Relative World, Ultimate Mind* (Boston: Shambala, 1992).

3. Lati Rinbochay, *Mind in Tibetan Buddhism,* trans., ed. and intro. by Elizabeth Napper (Ithaca: Snow Lion, 1980).

4. Leifer, "Common Ground."

5. Alan Wallace, *Journey From Solitude* (Ithaca: Snow Lion, 1989). Wallace advocates reliance on faith for insight, although it is not clear what he means by faith. Nevertheless, this book is an excellent introduction to the Lam Rim, or Gradual Path of Enlightenment, and to Atisha's Seven Points of Mind Training.

6. John Dewey, *Human Nature and Conduct: An Introduction to Social Psychology.* (New York: H. Holt and Co., 1927).

7. Western cognitive psychotherapy is based on the same logic, namely, that a wrong view of life or a life situation will lead to neurosis and pain for oneself and others.

8. Tai Situ Rinpoche, *Way to Go: Sowing the Seed of Buddha,* Ken Holmes, ed. (Scotland: Kagyu Samye Ling, 1991).

9. Saint Bonaventure used this metaphor of a journey towards God, or Jacob's ladder. Saint Bonaventure, *The Soul's Journey Into God,* Ewart Cousins, ed. and trans. (New York: Paulist Press, 1978).

10. Jamgon Kongtrul Rinpoche, personal communication.

Chapter 5. Who Is Buddha and What Did He Teach?

1. Popper, *Scientific Discovery.* Popper's suggestion that a scientific fact must, in principle, be falsifiable by observation, has been generally accepted as a *sine qua non* of any scientific fact.

2. The significance of the purity of conception (Jesus) and birth (Buddha) is that the life stories of Buddha and Jesus are metaphors, or myth, of the mind's journey through life, rather than literal biographies. The denial of the body is a way of giving primacy to mind.

3. Khenpo Karthar Rinpoche, "The Four Noble Truths: The Early Life of the Buddha Shakyamuni," *Densal,* 6, no. 2 (Spring, 1985).

4. Edward J. Thomas, *The Life of Buddha as Legend and History* (London: Routledge & Kegan Paul, 1969).

5. Sigmund Freud, *The Future of an Illusion* (Garden City: Doubleday Anchor, 1964).

6. Piyadassi Thera, *The Buddha's Ancient Path,* 40.

7. Sir M. Monier-Williams, *Buddhism: In Its Connection with Brahmanism and Hinduism and in Its Contrast with Christianity* (Varanasi, India: Chowkamba Sanskrit Series, 1964).

8. H.H. the Dalai Lama, *The Opening of the Wisdom Eye* (Wheaton, IL: The Theosophical Publishing House, 1966).

Chapter 6. The First Noble Truth

1. Kramer, *Prozac.*

2. Sigmund Freud, *The Problem of Anxiety* (New York: W.W. Norton, 1963).

3. Anna Freud, *The Ego and the Mechanisms of Defense* (New York: International Universities Press, 1946).

4. Becker, *Denial of Death.*

5. Becker was familiar with Buddhism. His first book was a critique of Zen for requiring the submission of the disciple to the master. Becker saw this as repeating the error of the European dark ages, when the Catholic Church controlled the minds, thoughts, and writings of the intellectuals of that era. See Ernest Becker, *Zen: A Rational Critique* (New York: W.W. Norton, 1961).

6. Heraclitus quoted in Walter Kaufmann, *Philosophic Classics: Thales to St. Thomas* (Englewood Cliffs, NJ: Prentice-Hall, 1961), 19.

7. Rainer Maria Rilke, "Duino Elegy # 9," in *The Selected Poetry of Rainer Maria Rilke,* Stephen Mitchell, ed. and trans. (New York: Random House Vintage Books, 1982).

8. *The Ithaca Journal,* January 13, 1987.

9. Otto Rank, *Beyond Psychology* (New York: Dover, 1958).

10. Percy Bysshe Shelley, "Ozymandias" in *Complete Poetical Works*, Newell F. Ford, ed. (Boston: Houghton-Mifflin, 1975), 366.

11. Interesting to note, the word "planet" also means "wanderer." The idiosyncratic wanderings of the planets under the old Ptolemaic system reminded astrologers of the uniqueness and unpredictability of the human individual. So the planets, in astrology, became identified with individual personalities and characteristics. Thus, in two cultures, the human individual is seen as a "wanderer," like the planets, an energy in perpetual samsaric flux.

12. This is the title of John Dewey's epistemology. See John Dewey, *Knowing and the Known* (Boston: Beacon Press, 1949). Dewey's theory of knowledge, better than most philosophers', captures the concept of dualistic or relative mind, which is shared by both Buddhists and quantum physicists.

13. The Buddha, "The Heart Sutra," in *Buddhist Wisdom Books: The Diamond Sutra; The Heart Sutra*, Edward Conze, trans. (New York: Harper and Row, 1958), 81.

14. In chaos theory, which is a mathematical theory of change, chaos is defined as the absence of fixed, stable reference points.

15. See Agehananda Bharati, *The Light at the Center: The Context and Pretext of Modern Mysticism* (Santa Barbara: Ross-Erikson, 1976).

Chapter 7. The Second Noble Truth

1. *Random House Dictionary of the English Language*, Unabridged Edition, 1966.

2. Plato, "Symposium" in *The Philosophy of Plato*, Irwin Edman, ed., Benjamin Jowett, trans. (New York: The Modern Library, 1956), 365.

3. Piyadassi Thera, *Ancient Path*, 41.

4. Gen. 3:16-19.

5. See: Brown, *Life Against Death*; Becker, *Denial of Death;* and Ernest Becker, *Escape from Evil* (New York: The Free Press, 1975).

6. The Buddha, in *Middle Length Discourses of the Buddha: A New Translation of the Majjima Nikaya*, Bhikku Nanamoli and Bhikku Bodhi, trans. (Boston: Wisdom Publications, 1995), 181.

7. See below, chapter 15, "The Evolution of Desire."

Chapter 8. Self and Identity or Basic Bewilderment

1. The term "bricolage" is borrowed from Lévi-Strauss, who viewed the primitive theorist as a "bricoleur," an artist who creates images of self and the world by using bits of experience from here and there. See Claude Lévi-Strauss, *Tristes Tropiques* (New York: Atheneum, 1964).

2. Jamgon Kongtrul Rinpoche at the Westchester Hospital Division of New York Hospital, Cornell University Medical School Department of Psychiatry, unpublished videotape.

3. Jordan Scher, ed., *Theories of the Mind* (New York: The Free Press, 1962).

4. René Descartes, "Meditations on First Philosophy," in *The Philosophical Works of Descartes*, Elizabeth S. Haldane and G. R. T. Ross, eds. (Dover Publications, 1931), 149.

5. To my knowledge, Chogyam Trungpa Rinpoche was the first to use the term "basic bewilderment," although it refers to a state of fundamental confusion which has been traditionally recognized and discussed in Buddhist psychology.

6. Andrei Voznesensky, "Who are We?" in *Antiworlds* (New York: Basic Books, 1966), 46.

Chapter 9. Neurosis

1. Gregory Zilboorg and George W. Henry, *A History of Medical Psychology* (New York: W. W. Norton, 1941).

2. Luigi Galvani in *Treasury of World Science* (New York: Philosophical Library, 1962), 359-364.

3. The Tibetan religio-medical concept of "winds" is analogous to the European concept of humors as well as of energy.

4. Sohan Lal Sharma, unpublished manuscript. The same can be said for modern physicians, informed by psychiatrists. I believe the present belief that a wide variety of "mental illnesses" have physical causes is as unfounded as the eighteenth century belief that neurosis had a physico-neurological basis. But this is another story, not directly relevant to the subject of this book.

5. The First Psychiatric Revolution refers to the liberation of confined psychiatric patients from public mental hospitals by Pinel and others. The Second Psychiatric Revolution was the invention of psychoanalysis by Freud. The Third Psychiatric Revolution is biological psychiatry which, as we have seen from this short history, is not a revolution at all, but a continuation and repetition of the belief, based on faith in science, that mental suffering is caused by neuro-chemical imbalances.

6. Albert Deutsch, *The Mentally Ill in America: A History of Their Care and Treatment from Colonial Times*, 2nd rev. ed. (New York: International Universities Press, 1937). See also Leifer, *In the Name of Mental Health.*

7. This is the move that Jeffrey Moussaieff Masson called *The Assault on Truth: Freud's Suppression of the Seduction Theory* (New York: Farrar, Straus and Giroux, 1984). See chapters 18 and 19 for a fuller discussion of this subject.

8. For a fuller discussion see Leifer, *In the Name of Mental Health*, and Szasz, *Myth of Mental Illness.*

9. Ibid.

10. Trogawa Rinpoche, "Mental Health," *Journal of Contemplative Psychotherapy* 6, 11-25.

Chapter 10. Suffering as a Motive of Mental Life

1. Becker, *Denial of Death.*

2. Leifer, *In the Name of Mental Health.*

3. Ibid.

4. Thomas Szasz, *Ceremonial Chemistry: The Ritual Persecution of Drugs, Addicts and Pushers* (Garden City, NY: Anchor Press, 1974).

Chapter 11. Suffering in Western Religion

1. Gen. 3:16-19.

2. Julian Janes, *The Origins of Consciousness in the Breakdown of Bicameral Mind* (Boston: Houghton-Mifflin, 1976).

3. Isa. 3:10, 11.

4. John Bowker, *Suffering in the Religions of the World* (Cambridge: Cambridge University Press, 1970), 9.

5. For a modern version of this question see Harold S. Kushner, *When Bad Things Happen to Good People* (New York: Avon Books, 1981).

6. Job 1:1.

7. Job 1:22.

8. Horace Kallen, *The Book of Job as a Greek Tragedy* (New York: Hill and Wang, 1959).

9. Bowker, *Suffering*, 22-24.

10. Job 14:1-12.

11. Job 7:16-17.

12. Job 9:2, 3.

13. Job 38:4-7.

14. Kallen, *Book of Job*, 43.

Chapter 12. Oedipus Rex: Tragic Hero of the West

1. Sophocles, *Oedipus the King*, Stephen Berg and Diskin Clay, trans. (New York: Oxford University Press, 1978), 78.

2. Ibid., 123.

3. Such a view is expressed by Chogyam Trungpa Rinpoche. See *Illusion's Game: The Life and Teaching of Naropa* (Boston: Shambala, 1994).

4. Ernest Becker, *The Birth and Death of Meaning* (New York: The Free Press, 1971).

5. See chapter 15 for a fuller discussion of the evolution of lust and aggression.

Chapter 13. Jesus

1. Matt. 5:17; 26:56.

2. Bowker, *Suffering*, 45.

3. Paul 9:20

4. 1 Chron. 21:1; Job 1:6; and Zech. 3:1. See Bowker, *Suffering*, 51.

5. Bowker, *Suffering*, 82.

6. John 12:27

7. Matt. 27:46

8. Mark 2:17; also Matt. 9:13 and Luke 5:32.

9. Matt. 5:43-45.

10. Bowker, *Suffering*, 7.

11. John 10:7, 9, 11. See also St. Bonaventure, *Soul's Journey*, 55.

12. Exod. 20:13.

13. Rom. 13:9

14. Matt. 5:21-6.

15. Luke 6:45

16. Monier-Williams, *Buddhism*, 548.

17. Matt. 6:27-8.

18. Matt. 6:34.

19. Col. 1:24.

20. This is the archetypical theme portrayed in folktales, legends, and cinema of the triumph of the cross over the evil vampire, devil, and beast.

21. Augustine, *The City of God* (New York: Modern Library, 1950), iv, 28.

22. Richard St. Victor, "The Twelve Patriarchs," in *Richard of St. Victor* (New York: Paulist Press, 1979).

23. St. Bonaventure, *Soul's Journey*.

24. Ibid., 108-9.

25. William Manchester, *A World Lit Only By Fire* (Boston: Little Brown, 1992).

26. Benjamin Nelson, "Self Image and Systems of Spiritual Direction in the History of European Civilization," in *The Quest for Self-Control: Classical Philosophies and Scientific Research*, S. Kalusner, ed. (New York: The Free Press, 1965); John T. McNeill, *A History of the Cure of Souls* (New York: Harper and Row, 1951).

27. The modern psychiatrist, too, is considered to have the responsibility to identify mentally ill people and, by persuasion and coercion, to "help" them to accept the fact that they are ill (confess), and to "reform" them through therapy.

28. Russell Hope Robbins, *The Encyclopedia of Witchcraft and Demonology* (New York: Bonanza Books, 1981), s.v. *Malleus Malificarum.*

29. Rank, *Beyond Psychology.*

Chapter 14. Suffering and Politics

1. Ernest Becker, *The Structure of Evil: An Essay on the Unification of the Science of Man* (New York: Braziller, 1968), 305.

2. The Enlightenment ideal of an encyclopedic synthesis of science in the service of humanity was brought to a culmination in the work of Auguste Comte (1790-1857). The similarity of the hope for salvation through religion and through science was tersely expressed by T. H. Huxley who described Comtism as Catholicism without Christianity. See Lewis S. Feuer, *Marx and Engels: Basic Writings on Politics and Philosophy* (Garden City, NY: Doubleday, 1959), 449.

3. Stanley Diamond, "The Search for the Primitive," in *Man's Image in Medicine and Anthropology*, Iago Goldston, ed. (New York: International Universities Press, 1963). See also Stanley Diamond, *In Search of the Primitive: A Critique of Civilization* (New York: E.P. Dutton, 1974).

4. Jean Jacques Rousseau, *Discourse on the Origin of Inequality*, in *Great Books of the Western World*, vol. 38, Robert Maynard Hutchins, ed. (Chicago: Encyclopedia Britannica, 1952), 329.

5. Ernst Cassirer, *Rousseau, Kant, Goethe* (Princeton: Princeton University Press, 1945).

6. Ibid., 21.

7. Jean Jacques Rousseau, *Confessions* (Baltimore: Penguin Books, 1953).

8. Rousseau, *Discourse*, 342.

9. Diamond, *Primitive.*

10. Bowker, *Suffering*, 137.

11. Lewis S. Feuer, *Marx and Engels: Basic Writings on Politics and Philosophy* (Garden City, NY: Doubleday, 1959).

12. Ibid., 263.

13. Ibid., 168.

14. Ibid., 263.

15. Karl Marx, *Thesis on Feuerbach*, quoted in Feuer, *Marx and Engels*, 244.

16. Feuer, *Marx and Engels*, 263.

17. Ibid., 43.

18. Marx, *Feuerbach*, 245.

19. The writings of Tom Szasz, myself, and others critical of coercive psychiatric interventions, such as involuntary treatment and hospitalization, recognize this tyranny of the helper.

20. See above, chapter 6.

21. Piyadassi Thera, *Buddha's Ancient Path*, 60.

22. Quoted in Bowker, *Suffering*, 94.

Chapter 15. The Evolution of Desire into the Happiness Project

1. Brown, *Life Against Death*, 83.

2. See chapter 23, "The Polarization of Paradise."

3. Becker, *Birth and Death of Meaning*.

4. Ernest Becker calls this project "The Oedipal Project." See *The Birth and Death of Meaning*.

5. Becker, *The Denial of Death*.

6. Emile Durkheim, *The Elementary Forms of Religious Life* (New York: The Free Press, 1965).

7. The best example is the coalition of psychiatry and the state, where the state grants psychiatrists the power to label people as mentally ill, which then justifies the state depriving that individual of freedom. See Thomas Szasz, *Law, Liberty and Psychiatry: An Inquiry Into the Social Uses of Mental Health Practices* (New York: MacMillan, 1963); and Leifer, *In the Name of Mental Health*.

8. Gen. 2:16-17.

9. Freud, *Civilization and Its Discontents*, 34.

10. Sigmund Freud, *Totem and Taboo* (New York: Random House Vintage Books, 1913).

11. Freud's theories were about men, particularly men of his culture and class. Freud himself admitted he knew little about female psychology.

12. Becker, *Birth and Death of Meaning*.

13. This cryptic neologism will be explained in chapters 21-23.

Chapter 16. Religion and Law: Desire as Sin and Crime

1. The Buddha in *A Buddhist Bible*, Dwight Goddard, ed. (Boston: Beacon Press), 31.

2. Ibid., 4.

3. Ibid., 8.

4. Ibid.

5. Piyadassi Thera, *Ancient Path*, 60.

6. Isaiah 3:10,11

7. Wild Beast Test. Rex v. Arnold, 16 How. Tr. 695, 1724. See Thomas Maeder, *Crime and Madness: The Origins and Evolution of the Insanity Defense* (New York: Harper and Row, 1985).

8. Daniel McNaghton's Case. 10 Clark and Finnelly 200, 8 Eng. Rep. R. 718 1843.

9. See Ronald Leifer, "Psychiatric Expert Testimony and Criminal Responsibility," *American Psychologist* 19, no. 11 (November 1964): 825-830; Ronald Leifer, "The Concept of Criminal Responsibility," *ETC: A Review of General Semantics* 24, no. 2 (1967): 177-190; and Leifer, *In the Name of Mental Health.*

Chapter 17. Desire: The Basis of Ethics and Morality

1. Plato, "Philebus," in *Great Books of the Western World*, vol. 7, 610.

2. Richard Taylor, *Reflective Wisdom: Richard Taylor on Issues That Matter*, John Donnelly, ed. (Buffalo: Prometheus Books, 1989) .

3. Ethyl M. Albert, Theodore C. Denise, and Sheldon P. Peterfreund, *Great Traditions in Ethics* (New York: American Book Co., 1953), 11.

4. Plato, "Symposium," in *Great Books of the Western World*, vol. 7, 162.

5. Lama Gendun Rinpoche, "Free and Easy: A Spontaneous Vajra Song," in Nyoshul Khenpo and Lama Surya Das, *Natural Great Perfection* (Ithaca: Snow Lion, 1995).

6. Augustine, *The Confessions of St. Augustine* (New York: Pocket Books, 1956), 134-5.

7. Ibid., 30.

8. Ibid., 140.

9. Ibid., 147.

10. Ibid., 31.

11. Ibid., 192.

12. Ibid., 190.

13. Ibid., 197.

14. Ibid., 85.

15. Ibid., 198-9.

16. Acts 9:1

17. Gal. 5:19-21.

18. Rom. 8:1-13.

19. Thomas Hobbes, *Leviathan* (New York: Dutton, 1950).

20. Benedict Spinoza, "Ethics," in *Great Books of the Western World*, vol. 31, 416.

21. Ibid., 416.

22. Immanuel Kant, "Fundamental Principles of the Metaphysic of Morals," in *Great Books of the Western World*, vol. 42.

23. Arthur Schopenhauer, "The World as Will," in *The Philosophy of Schopenhauer*, Irwin Edman, ed. (New York: The Modern Library, 1928), 249.

24. Ibid., 252-4.

25. Ibid., 50.

26. Ibid., 310.

Chapter 18. Psychotherapy: The Psychology of Hidden Wishes

1. Rank, *Beyond Psychology*; Watts, *Psychotherapy*; Szasz, *Ceremonial Chemistry.*

2. The medical model is a conceptual paradigm or template by which mental and emotional states are viewed as mechanical causes and effects, like medicine views bodily events. The medical model is basically a non-moral mechanism. See Szasz, *Myth of Mental Illness*; Leifer, *In the Name of Mental Health*; Leifer, "The Medical Model as the Ideology of the Therapeutic State"; and Leifer, "Psychiatry, Language and Freedom."

3. Freud said, "No one, needless to say, who shares a delusion ever recognizes it as such." See Freud, *Civilization*, 32.

4. "*Doch noch ein mal*," "still one more time." In his Pulitzer Prize winning book, *The Denial of Death*, Ernest Becker entitled one chapter, "Freud: Noch Ein Mal," "Freud: One More Time."

5. Jacques Lacan, *Four Fundamental Concepts of Psychoanalysis* (New York: Norton, 1978).

6. Sigmund Freud, *An Autobiographical Study* (New York: W.W. Norton, 1935), 13.

7. Ernest Jones, *The Life and Work of Sigmund Freud: The Formative Years and the Great Discoveries 1856-1900*, vol. I, (New York: Basic Books, 1953).

8. Freud used cocaine frequently for a time called "The Cocaine Period." He drank it as a tea, presumably to relieve the pain and dyspepsia associated with his long-standing cancer of the jaw caused by his addiction to tobacco. See Jones, *Freud.*

9. Jones, *Freud.*

10. Frank Sulloway, *Sigmund Freud: Biologist of the Mind* (New York: Basic Books, 1979); See also Robert Holt, "A Review of some of Freud's Biological Assumptions and Their Influence on His Theories," in *Psychoanalysis and Current Biological Thought*, Norman S. Greenfield and William C. Lewis, eds. (Madison, WI: University of Wisconsin Press, 1965).

11. Sigmund Freud and Joseph Breuer, *Studies in Hysteria* (Boston: Beacon Press, 1937).

12. Sigmund Freud, "Some Points in a Comparative Study of Organic and Hysterical Paralysis," in *The Collected Papers of Sigmund Freud*, vol. I, Ernest Jones, ed. (London: Hogarth Press, 1956).

13. Charcot held a chair in neuropathology at the Salpetriere, a Parisian mental hospital for aged women and others. Hysteria was commonly seen here, it was believed, because of the high population of neurotic women. The term "hysteria" is Greek for "wandering womb," the Greek explanation of the syndrome. See Zilboorg and Henry, *History of Medical Psychology*.

14. Freud, *Organic and Hysterical Paralysis.*

15. Freud, *Autobiographical Study*, 53.

16. Sigmund Freud, in *Abstracts of the Standard Edition of the Complete Psychological Works of Sigmund Freud* (New York: International Universities Press, 1973), 10.

17. See Szasz, *Myth of Mental Illness* for a fully developed argument of this thesis.

18. Freud, *Autobiographical Study*, 53-55.

19. Freud and Breuer, *Sudies in Hysteria*, 114.

2. Ibid., 133.

21. Ibid.

Chapter 19. Neurosis: The Dialectic of Desire

1. Freud and Breuer, *Studies in Hysteria*, 98-9.

2. Ibid., 100.

3. Ibid., 101.

4. Ibid., 102.

5. Ibid., 111.

6. Ibid., 103.

7. Ibid., 60.

8. Hans Reichenbach, *The Rise of Scientific Philosophy* (Berkeley: University of California Press, 1951). See also others of the Vienna Circle.

9. Freud and Breuer, *Studies in Hysteria*, 117.

10. Ibid.

11. Freud, *Autobiographical Study*, 53.

12. Ibid., 54.

13. Szasz, *Myth of Mental Illness*, 80.

Chapter 20. Desire and the Discontent of Civilization

1. Sigmund Freud, *The Interpretation of Dreams*, James Strachey, trans. (New York: Basic Books, 1956).

2. Sigmund Freud, *Beyond the Pleasure Principle: A Study of the Death Instinct in Human Behavior* (New York: Bantam Books, 1963).

3. See chapter 7.

4. Freud, *Civilization*.

5. Ibid., 11.

6. *"Wer Wissenschaft and Kunst besitzt, hat auch Religion; Wer jene beide nicht besitzt, der habe Religion!"* Ibid., 23.

7. Ibid.

8. Freud, *Civilization*, 25.

9. Ibid., 26.

10. Ibid., 26-27.

11. Ibid.

12. Ibid., 96.

13. Becker, *Denial of Death.*

14. Ibid., 2-3.

Chapter 21. The Evolution of Self: The First Humans

1. See chapter 8.

2. Nietzsche, Friedrich, *The Genealogy of Morals*, trans. Francis Golffing (New York: Doubleday, 1956).

3. To make this sign, hold the palm up facing outward as if in a sign of peace. Then appose the index finger and thumb to make a circle.

4. Lewis Mumford, *The Myth of the Machine* (New York: Harcourt, Brace, Janovich, 1967), 5.

5. Jaynes, *Bicameral Mind.*

6. Eccles. 1:2

7. Jaynes, *Bicameral Mind*, 295ff.

8. Michel Foucault, *The Order of Things: An Archeology of the Human Sciences* (New York: Pantheon Books, 1970), 386-7.

9. From the Buddhist perspective, this is a question about the evolution of the body—the material base of mind.

10. Jaynes, *Bicameral Mind*, 132.

11. John E. Pfeiffer, *The Emergence of Man* (New York: Harper and Row, 1978), ch. 19.

12. Denis De Rougemont, quoted in D.T. Suzuki, Erich Fromm and Richard De Martino, *Zen Buddhism and Psychoanalysis* (New York: Grove Press, 1963), 27.

13. Lévi-Strauss, *Tristes Tropiques.*

14. Jaynes, *Bicameral Mind*, 133.

15. The neural coordination of the word and the hand is poorly understood. In right-handed persons the speech and hand centers are in the left cerebral cortex, suggesting close coordination. However, they seem also to be able to interfere with each other. A case has been reported of an autistic child who could draw like da Vinci or Picasso in the judgment of eminent art critics. Autistic children do not learn to speak normally, as if they are improperly wired for speech. When this autistic girl was given speech therapy her artistic abilities deteriorated and her drawings became no better than an average child her age. It is as if the word confused the hand, or as if the logic of language saps the genius of art. Everyone

has experienced the interference of motor tasks by speech or thought. The athlete loses concentration by talking or thinking while trying to hit a ball. Tying a necktie and explaining how to tie it are different tasks which may embrassingly interfere with each other. The exception is singing. The right brain seems to be wired for speech if the words are set to music.

16. W. Ronald D. Fairbairn, *Psychoanalytic Studies of the Personality* (London: Tavistock and Routledge and Kegan Paul, 1952); and W. Ronald D. Fairbairn, "Synopsis of an Object-Relations Theory of the Personality," *The International Journal of Psychoanalysis* 44, 224-225.

Chapter 22. The Numinous Sky and the Personal "I"

1. Mircea Eliade, *A History of Religious Ideas* (Chicago: University of Chicago Press, 1978).

2. Ibid., 8-11.

3. Carl Sagan, *The Dragons of Eden* (New York: Random House,1977).

4. Mircea Eliade, *Patterns in Comparative Religion* (New York: New American Library, 1974).

5. "Quintessence" was the fifth essence of the Greeks, along with earth, air, fire, and water. The Greeks believed the stars were composed of this essence.

6. Eliade, *Patterns.*

7. John 3:13.

8. John 10:30.

9. Gen. 4:19

10. Eliade, *Patterns.*

11. Ibid.

12. Ibid.

13. Ibid.

14. The scarab or dung beetle is an ancient object of veneration for the practical reason that it converts manure into usable nitrogen fertilizer. The scarab is thus a catalyst for the transformation of the waste products of life into new life. The cattle eat the grass and the scarab transforms manure into fertilizer for new grass. In mythical form, the scarab pushes the sun through its cycles of light and darkness.

15. Plato, "Phaedrus," in *The Philosophy of Plato*, Irwin Edman, ed. (New York: The Modern Library, 1956), 286.

16. The mystical concept of synchronicity, which conceives of the universe as an integrated, organic whole, is the basis of astrology and of the *I Ching*. In this ancient form of sortilege, or divination by lot, six pairs of binary digits (heads/tails, long/short, on/off) are thrown like dice to give one of sixty-four possible hexagrams. The hexagram that appears on a particular throw is believed to be

synchronized with divine and natural forces as they become manifest in the being of the player. See C. G. Jung, "Synchronicity: An Acausal Connecting Principle," in *Collected Works*, Bollingen Series, vol. 8 (Princeton: Princeton University Press, 1966).

17. The Virgin Mary, mother of Christ, is an evolved form of Demeter, the earth mother. Mary's harvest was Jesus, who died and was resurrected as the savior of humanity on Easter morn, in the first days of spring.

18. Matt. 4:19

19. Rupert Gleadow, *The Origin of the Zodiac* (New York: Atheneum, 1969), 55.

20. Ibid., 209.

21. For an excellent example of astrology as literature see John Jocelyn, *Meditations on the Signs of the Zodiac* (Rudolf Steiner Publications, 1970).

22. Eliade, *Patterns*, 38-39.

23. Rudoph Otto, *The Idea of the Holy* (New York: Oxford University Press, 1958), 7.

24. Ibid., 26.

25. Augustine, *Confessions*, 9; Otto, *Idea of the Holy*, 28.

26. Otto, *Idea of the Holy*, 10.

27. Exod. 33:22-3.

28. Otto, *Idea of the Holy*, 29.

29. Ibid., 21.

Chapter 23. The Polarization of Paradise: The Myth of Eden

1. Eliade, *Myths, Dreams, Mysteries*, 197.

2. Erich Neumann, *The Origins and History of Consciousness* (New York: Pantheon Books, 1954), xvi.

3. Brown, *Life Against Death*, 12.

4. Sigmund Freud, *Totem and Taboo: Resemblances Between the Psychic Lives of Savages and Neurotics* (New York: Random House Vintage Books, 1946); Sigmund Freud, *Moses and Monotheism* (New York: Vintage Books, 1967).

5. Brown, *Life Against Death*, 3.

6. Ibid., 6.

7. Ernst Cassirer, *The Philosophy of Symbolic Forms* (New Haven: Yale University Press, 1953), 94.

8. Gen. 1:3.

9. Jung, *Collected Works*, vol. 9, 11.

10. Kierkegaard, *Concept of Dread*, 26-27.

11. Ibid., 38.

12. Gen. 3:5.

13. Jean Paul Sartre, *Existentialism and Human Emotions* (New York: Philosophical Library, 1957), 63.

14. Plato, *The Symposium*, 166.

15. Dante, *The Inferno*, Charles Singleton, trans., Bollingen Series LXXX (Princeton: Princeton University Press, 1970), Canto XV:85, 159.

16. Blaise Pascal, *Pensées*, in *Great Books of the Western World*, vol. 33., 211.

17. Ernest Becker, in Ron Leifer, "The Legacy of Ernest Becker," *Kairos* 2, 8-21.

18. John M. Allegro, *The Sacred Mushroom and the Cross: Fertility Cults and the Origins of Judaism and Christianity* (Garden City, NY: Doubleday, 1970).

19. Aldous Huxley, *The Doors of Perception* (New York: Harper and Row, 1963).

20. Frank J. MacHovec, trans., *The Book of Tao* (Mount Vernon, NY: The Peter Pauper Press, 1963), 1, 33.

21. Gen. 3:7

22. Becker, *The Denial of Death*, 34-7.

23. In animals, the frontal lobes are the neural centers of olfaction. It has been remarked that humans gained memory and intelligence at the sacrifice of smell. Nevertheless, the memory of smell is the most acute of all sensory memories.

24. *Mountain Record*, Zen Mountain Monastery (Fall, 1987).

25. Sigmund Freud, "The Antithetical Sense of Primal Words," in *Collected Papers*, vol 4 (London: Hogarth Press, 1910), 184-191.

26. The word "person" is derived from the Greek *per sona*, "the sound coming through," i.e. the sound coming through the mask in Greek drama.

Chapter 24. Meditation on Happiness

1. Gabriel Vahanian, *The Death of God: The Culture of Our Post-Christian Era* (New York: George Braziller, 1957).

2. For a full discussion of fetishization see Becker, *Denial of Death.*

3. Emile Durkheim, *Suicide* (Glencoe, IL: The Free Press, 1951).

4. Rank, *Beyond Psychology.*

5. This possibility is becoming increasingly rare in an era of managed care.

6. Chogyam Trungpa Rinpoche, *Training the Mind: Cultivating Loving-Kindness*, Judith L. Lief, ed. (Boston: Shambala Press, 1993); Dilgo Khyentse Rinpoche, *Enlightened Courage: An Explanation of Atisha's Seven Point Mind Training* (Ithaca: Snow Lion, 1993).

7. Jamgon Kongtrul Rinpoche, *The Torch of Certainty*, Judith Hanson, trans. (Boulder: Shambala, 1977).

8. Chogyam Trungpa Rinpoche, *Cutting Through Spiritual Materialism*, John Baker and Marvin Casper, eds. (Boulder: Shambala, 1973).

Bibliography

Albert, Ethyl M., Theodore C. Denise, and Sheldon P. Peterfreund. *Great Traditions in Ethics*. New York: American Book Co., 1953.

Allegro, John M. *The Sacred Mushroom and the Cross: Fertility Cults and the Origins of Judaism and Christianity*. Garden City, NY: Doubleday, 1970.

Augustine. *The City of God*. New York: Modern Library, 1950.

———. *The Confessions of St. Augustine*. New York: Pocket Books, 1956.

Barrett, William. *The Illusion of Technique*. Vol. 3. Garden City, NY: Anchor Press, 1978.

Becker, Ernest. *The Birth and Death of Meaning*. New York: The Free Press, 1971.

———. *The Denial of Death*. New York: The Free Press, 1973.

———. *Escape from Evil*. New York: The Free Press, 1975.

———. *The Structure of Evil*. New York: Braziller, 1968.

———. *Zen: A Rational Critique*. New York: W.W. Norton, 1961.

Bharati, Agehananda.*The Light at the Center: The Context and Pretext of Modern Mysticism*. Santa Barbara: Ross-Erikson, 1976.

Saint Bonaventure. *The Soul's Journey into God*. Translated and edited by Ewart Cousins. New York: Paulist Press, 1978.

Bowker, John. *Suffering in the Religions of the World*. Cambridge: Cambridge University Press, 1970.

Brown, Norman O. *Life Against Death: The Psychoanalytic Meaning of History*. New York: Random House Vintage Books, 1959.

Cassirer, Ernst. *The Philosophy of Symbolic Forms*. New Haven: Yale University Press, 1953.

———. *Rousseau, Kant, Goethe*. Princeton: Princeton University Press, 1945.

Chogyam Trungpa Rinpoche. *Cutting Through Spiritual Materialism*. Edited by John Baker and Marvin Casper. Boulder: Shambala, 1973.

———. *Illusion's Game: The Life and Teaching of Naropa*. Boston: Shambala, 1994.

———. *Training the Mind: Cultivating Loving-Kindness*. Edited by Judith L. Lief. Boston: Shambala, 1993.

Comte, Auguste. *The Positive Philosophy of Auguste Comte*. New York: Appleton, 1953.

Conze, Edward, trans. *Buddhist Wisdom Books: The Diamond Sutra and The Heart Sutra*. New York: Harper and Row, 1958.

H.H. the Fourteenth Dalai Lama. *The Bodhgaya Interviews*. Edited by José Ignacio Cabezón. Ithaca: Snow Lion, 1988.

———. *The Opening of the Wisdom Eye*. Wheaton, IL: The Theosophical Publishing House, 1966.

Dante. *The Inferno*. Translated by Charles Singleton. Bollingen Series LXXX. Princeton: Princeton University Press, 1970.

Dennett, Daniel. "Towards a Cognitive Theory of Consciousness." In *Brainstorms*. Cambridge: MIT Press, 1978 .

Descartes, René. *The Philosophical Works of Descartes*. Edited by Elizabeth S. Haldane and G. R. T. Ross. Dover Publications, 1931.

Deutsch, Albert. *The Mentally Ill in America: A History of Their Care and Treatment from Colonial Times*. New York: International Universities Press, 1937.

Dewey, John. *Human Nature and Conduct: An Introduction to Social Psychology*. New York: H. Holt and Co., 1927.

———. *Knowing and the Known*. Boston: Beacon Press, 1949.

Diamond, Stanley. *In Search of the Primitive: A Critique of Civilization*. New York: E.P. Dutton, 1974.

———. "The Search for the Primitive." In *Man's Image in Medicine and Anthropology*. Edited by Iago Goldston. New York: International Universities Press, 1963.

Dilgo Khyentse Rinpoche. *Enlightened Courage: An Explanation of Atisha's Seven Point Mind Training*. Ithaca: Snow Lion, 1993.

Durkheim, Emile. *The Elementary Forms of Religious Life*. New York: The Free Press, 1965.

———. *Suicide*. Glencoe, IL: The Free Press, 1951.

Einstein, Albert. *Out of My Later Years*. New York: Philosophical Library, 1950.

Eliade, Mircea. *A History of Religious Ideas*. Chicago: University of Chicago Press, 1978.

———. *Myths, Dreams, Mysteries: The Encounter Between Contemporary Faiths and Archaic Realities*. New York: Harper and Row, 1960.

———. *Patterns in Comparative Religion*. New York: New American Library, 1974.

Fairbairn, W. Ronald D. *Psychoanalytic Studies of the Personality*. London: Tavistock and Routledge and Kegan Paul, 1952.

———. "Synopsis of an Object-Relations Theory of the Personality." *The International Journal of Psychoanalysis* 44: 224-225.

Feuer, Lewis S. *Marx and Engels: Basic Writings on Politics and Philosophy*. Garden City, NY: Doubleday, 1959.

Foucault, Michel. *The Order of Things: An Archeology of the Human Sciences*. New York: Pantheon Books, 1970.

Freud, Anna. *The Ego and the Mechanisms of Defense*. New York: International Universities Press, 1946.

Freud, Sigmund. *Abstracts of the Standard Edition of the Complete Psychological Works of Sigmund Freud*. New York: International Universities Press, 1973.

———. "The Antithetical Sense of Primal Words." In *Collected Papers*. Vol. 4. London: Hogarth Press, 1910.

———. *An Autobiographical Study*. New York: W.W. Norton, 1935.

———. *Beyond the Pleasure Principle: A Study of the Death Instinct in Human Behavior*. New York: Bantam Books, 1963.

———. *Civilization and Its Discontents*. Garden City, NY: Doubleday Anchor, 1958.

———. *The Future of an Illusion*. Garden City, NY: Doubleday Anchor, 1964.

———. *The Interpretation of Dreams*. Translated by James Strachey. New York: Basic Books, 1956.

———. *Moses and Monotheism*. New York: Vintage Books, 1967.

———. *The Problem of Anxiety*. New York: W.W. Norton, 1963.

———. "Some Points in a Comparative Study of Organic and Hysterical Paralysis." In *The Collected Papers of Sigmund Freud*. Vol. I. Edited by Ernest Jones. London: Hogarth Press, 1956.

———. *Totem and Taboo*. New York: Random House Vintage Books, 1946.

Freud, Sigmund, and Joseph Breuer. *Studies in Hysteria*. Boston: Beacon Press, 1937.

Galvani, Luigi. *Treasury of World Science*. New York: Philosophical Library, 1962.

Gandhi, Mohandas K. *An Autobiography: The Story of My Experiments with Truth*. Boston: Beacon Press, 1957.

Gleadow, Rupert. *The Origin of the Zodiac*. New York: Atheneum, 1969.

Goddard, Dwight, ed. *A Buddhist Bible*. Boston: Beacon Press, 1966.

Holt, Robert. "A Review of Some of Freud's Biological Assumptions and Their Influence on His Theories." In *Psychoanalysis and Current Biological Thought*. Edited by Norman S. Greenfield and William C. Lewis. Madison: University of Wisconsin Press, 1965.

Huxley, Aldous. *The Doors of Perception*. New York: Harper and Row, 1963.

Jamgon Kongtrul Rinpoche. *The Torch of Certainty*. Translated by Judith Hanson. Boulder: Shambala, 1977.

Jaynes, Julian. *The Origins of Consciousness in the Breakdown of Bicameral Mind*. Boston: Houghton-Mifflin, 1976.

Jocelyn, John. *Meditations on the Signs of the Zodiac*. Rudolf Steiner Publications, 1970.

Jones, Ernest. *The Life and Work of Sigmund Freud: The Formative Years and the Great Discoveries 1856-1900*. Vol. I. New York: Basic Books, 1953.

Jung, C. G. "Synchronicity: An Acausal Connecting Principle." In *Collected Works*. Bollingen Series VIII. Princeton: Princeton University Press, 1960.

Kallen, Horace. *The Book of Job as a Greek Tragedy*. New York: Hill and Wang, 1959.

Kant, Immanuel. "Fundamental Principles of the Metaphysic of Morals." In *Philosophic Classics: Thales to St. Thomas*. Edited by Walter Kaufmann. Englewood Cliffs: Prentice-Hall, 1961.

Khenpo Karthar Rinpoche. "The Four Noble Truths: The Early Life of the Buddha Shakyamuni." *Densal* 6, no. 2 (Spring 1985).

Kramer, Peter. *Listening to Prozac*. New York: Viking Press, 1993.

Kushner, Harold S. *When Bad Things Happen to Good People*. New York: Avon Books, 1981.

Lacan, Jacques. *Four Fundamental Concepts of Psychoanalysis*. New York: Norton, 1978.

Lati Rinbochay. *Mind in Tibetan Buddhism*. Translated, edited and introduced by Elizabeth Napper. Ithaca: Snow Lion, 1980.

Leifer, Ronald. "The Common Ground of Buddhism and Psychotherapy." Presented at the *First Karma Kagyu Conference on Buddhism and Psychotherapy* at International House, New York City, 1986.

———. "The Concept of Criminal Responsibility." *ETC: A Review of General Semantics* 24, no. 2 (1967): 177-190.

———. "The Deconstruction of Self: Commentary on 'The Man Who Mistook His Wife for a Hat: And Other Clinical Tales' by Oliver Sacks." *The World and I* (June 1986). Reprinted in *Journal of Contemplative Psychotherapy* 4 (1984): 153-177.

———. *In the Name of Mental Health: The Social Functions of Psychiatry*. New York: Science House, 1969.

———. "The Legacy of Ernest Becker." *Kairos* 2: 8-21.

———. "The Medical Model as Ideology." *International Journal of Psychiatry* 9 (1970).

———. "The Medical Model as the Ideology of the Therapeutic State." *Journal of Mind and Behavior* 2, nos. 3-4 (Summer 1990): 247-258. Reprinted in *Amalie* 15, no. 1 (February 1993).

———. "Psychiatric Expert Testimony and Criminal Responsibility." *American Psychologist* 19, no. 11 (November 1964): 825-830.

———. "Psychiatry, Language and Freedom." *Metamedicine* 3 (1982): 397-416.

———. "Psychotherapy, Scientific Method and Ethics." *American Journal of Psychotherapy* 20, no. 2 (April 1966): 295-304.

Lévi-Strauss, Claude. *Tristes Tropiques*. New York: Atheneum, 1964.

MacHovec, Frank J., trans. *The Book of Tao*. Mount Vernon, NY: The Peter Pauper Press, 1963.

Maeder, Thomas. *Crime and Madness: The Origins and Evolution of the Insanity Defense*. New York: Harper and Row, 1985.

Manchester, William. *A World Lit Only By Fire*. Boston: Little Brown, 1992.

Masson, Jeffrey Moussaieff. *The Assault on Truth: Freud's Suppression of the Seduction Theory*. New York: Farrar, Straus and Giroux, 1984.

McNeill, John T. *A History of the Cure of Souls*. New York: Harper and Row, 1951.

Monier-Williams, Sir M. *Buddhism: In Its Connection with Brahmanism and Hinduism and in Its Contrast with Christianity*. Varanasi: Chowkamba Sanskrit Series, 1964.

Moore, Thomas. *Care of the Soul: A Guide For Cultivating Depth and Sacredness in Everyday Life*. New York: Harper Collins, 1992.

Mumford, Lewis. *The Myth of the Machine*. New York: Harcourt, Brace, Janovich, 1967.

Bhikku Nanamoli, and Bhikku Bodhi, trans. *Middle Length Discourses of the Buddha: A New Translation of the Majjima Nikaya*. Boston: Wisdom Publications, 1995.

Nelson, Benjamin. "Self Image and Systems of Spiritual Direction in the History of European Civilization." In *The Quest for Self-Control: Classical Philosophies and Scientific Research*. Edited by S. Kalusner. New York: The Free Press, 1965.

Neumann, Erich. *The Origins and History of Consciousness*. New York: Pantheon Books, 1954.

Nietzsche, Friedrich. *The Genealogy of Morals*. Translated by Francis Golffing. New York: Doubleday, 1956.

Nyoshul Khenpo, and Lama Surya Das. *Natural Great Perfection*. Ithaca: Snow Lion, 1995.

Otto, Rudoph. *The Idea of the Holy*. New York: Oxford University Press, 1958.

Pascal, Blaise. "Pensées." In *Great Books of the Western World*. Vol. 33. Edited by Robert Maynard Hutchins. Chicago: Encyclopedia Britannica, 1952.

Pfeiffer, John E. *The Emergence of Man*. New York: Harper and Row, 1978.

Piyadassi Thera. *The Buddha's Ancient Path*. London: Rider, 1964.

Plato. "Phaedrus." In *The Philosophy of Plato*. Edited by Irwin Edman. New York: The Modern Library, 1956.

———. "Philebus." In *Great Books of the Western World*. Vol. 7. Edited by Robert Maynard Hutchins. Chicago: Encyclopedia Britannica, 1952.

———. *The Philosophy of Plato*. Edited by Irwin Edman. Translated by Benjamin Jowett. New York: The Modern Library, 1956.

———. "Symposium." In *Great Books of the Western World*. Vol. 7. Edited by Robert Maynard Hutchins. Chicago: Encyclopedia Britannica, 1952.

Popper, Karl. *The Logic of Scientific Discovery*. New York: Science Editions, 1961.

Rank, Otto. *Beyond Psychology*. New York: Dover, 1958.

Reichenbach, Hans. *The Rise of Scientific Philosophy*. Berkeley: University of California Press, 1951.

Rilke, Rainer Maria. *The Selected Poetry of Rainer Maria Rilke*. Edited and translated by Stephen Mitchell. New York: Random House Vintage Books, 1982.

Robbins, Russell Hope. *The Encyclopedia of Witchcraft and Demonology*. New York: Bonanza Books, 1981.

Rousseau, Jean Jacques. *Confessions*. Baltimore: Penguin Books, 1953.

———. *Discourse on the Origin of Inequality*. In *Great Books of the Western World*. Vol. 38. Edited by Robert Maynard Hutchins. Chicago: Encyclopedia Britannica, 1952.

Ryle, Gilbert. *The Concept of Mind*. New York: Barnes and Noble, 1949.

Sagan, Carl. *The Dragons of Eden*. New York: Random House, 1977.

Saint Victor, Richard. *Richard of St. Victor*. New York: Paulist Press, 1979.

Sartre, Jean Paul. *Existentialism and Human Emotions*. New York: Philosophical Library, 1957.

Scher, Jordan, ed. *Theories of the Mind*. New York: The Free Press, 1962.

Schopenhauer, Arthur. *The Philosophy of Schopenhauer*. Edited by Irwin Edman. New York: The Modern Library, 1928.

Shelley, Percy Bysshe. *Complete Poetical Works*. Edited by Newell F. Ford. Boston: Houghton-Mifflin, 1975.

Sophocles. *Oedipus the King*. Translated by Stephen Berg and Diskin Clay. New York: Oxford University Press, 1978.

Spinoza, Benedict. "Ethics." In *Great Books of the Western World*. Vol. 31. Edited by Robert Maynard Hutchins. Chicago: Encyclopedia Britannica, 1952.

Sulloway, Frank. *Sigmund Freud: Biologist of the Mind*. New York: Basic Books, 1979.

Suzuki, D.T., Erich Fromm, and Richard De Martino. *Zen Buddhism and Psychoanalysis*. New York: Grove Press, 1963.

Szasz, Thomas S. *Ceremonial Chemistry: The Ritual Persecution of Drugs, Addicts and Pushers*. Garden City, NY: Anchor Press, 1974.

———. *Law, Liberty and Psychiatry: An Inquiry Into the Social Uses of Mental Health Practices*. New York: MacMillan, 1963.

———. *The Myth of Mental Illness*. New York: Harper, 1961.

Tai Situ Rinpoche. *Relative World, Ultimate Mind*. Boston: Shambala, 1992.

Taylor, Richard. *Reflective Wisdom: Richard Taylor on Issues That Matter*. Edited by John Donnelly. Buffalo: Prometheus Books, 1989.

Thomas, Edward J. *The Life of Buddha as Legend and History*. London: Routledge and Kegan Paul, 1969.

Trogawa Rinpoche. "Mental Health." *Journal of Contemplative Psychotherapy* 6: 11-25.

Vahanian, Gabriel. *The Death of God: The Culture of Our Post-Christian Era*. New York: George Braziller, 1957.

Varela, Francisco J., Evan Thompson, and Eleanor Rosch. *The Embodied Mind*. Cambridge: MIT Press, 1993.

Voznesensky, Andrei. *Antiworlds*. New York: Basic Books, 1966.

Wallace, B. Alan. *A Passage from Solitude*. Ithaca: Snow Lion, 1992.

Watts, Alan. *Psychotherapy East and West*. New York: Random House, 1961.

Zilboorg, Gregory, and George W. Henry. *A History of Medical Psychology*. New York: W. W. Norton, 1941.